June

To Dad - with love,

Carolyn
+
John

EYE ON THE WORLD

EYE ON THE WORLD

Walter Cronkite

COWLES BOOK COMPANY, INC., NEW YORK

ACKNOWLEDGMENTS

Casey Stengel, the eminent banker and former baseball manager, is reported to have said after one of his New York Yankee teams won a World Series, "I couldn't have done it without my players." This book is largely the product of what I believe to be the best team of journalists in the world—the correspondents and reporters of CBS News.

Here, then, are the men who covered the persons and events making up this work:

CAN THE WORLD BE SAVED?—Associate producer Ron Bonn shaped and wrote many of the CBS Evening News special reports on the environment. Others directly quoted in interviews or reports include White House Correspondent Dan Rather and Terry Drinkwater, Bill Plante, Phil Jones, Bill Stout, Charles Kuralt, Morton Dean, Foster Davis, and Ed Rabel.

THE CEASELESS FIRE—The awful complexities and all-too-real dangers of the Middle East were illuminated by such correspondents as Bob Allison, John Sheehan, Larry Pomeroy, Don Webster, Bert Quint, Ike Pappas, Winston Burdett, Morley Safer, and Marvin Kalb.

A BEGINNING, A MIDDLE, AN END (?)—Continuing coverage of the continuing tragedies of the Indochina war, at home and abroad, was offered by Diplomatic Correspondent Marvin Kalb and by Correspondents Bob Schieffer, Bruce Dunning, John Laurence, Bill McLaughlin, Gary Shepard, Richard Threlkeld, Bert Quint, Bernard Kalb, and Morley Safer.

THE STATE OF THE NATION—A GENERATION GAP—WOMEN OF THE WORLD, UNITE!—Contributors dealing with what pertains and what portends for the United States included Correspondents Barry Serafin, Morley Safer, Bruce Morton, Bob Schieffer, Daniel Schorr, George Herman, Dan Rather, David Culhane, Mike Stanley, Ike Pappas, Morton Dean, John Laurence, and Gary Shepard.

SUCH INTERESTING PEOPLE—The famous, the infamous, and the unknown were examined by Chief Foreign Correspondent Charles Collingwood, Bob Allison, David Schoumacher, Daniel Schorr, Congressional Correspondent Roger Mudd, David Culhane, Charles Kuralt, and Murray Fromson.

And through it all, of course, the wise commentary of Eric Sevareid.

This book would not have been possible without the research and writing of a longtime CBS Evening News colleague, John Mosedale, and the editing of our CBS Evening News editor, John Merriman. My gratitude for their diligent and distinguished work is boundless.

I am also indebted to Gladys J. Carr, Senior Editor of Cowles Book Company, and Mrs. Frances Guenette, CBS News Photo Researcher.

CONTENTS

PHOTO CREDITS

CAN THE WORLD BE SAVED?

(p. 2) Bruce Davidson/Magnum; (p. 37) Bruce Davidson/Magnum; (p. 39) Burk Uzzle/Magnum; (p. 40) Bruce Davidson/Magnum; (p. 41) Bettye Lane; (p. 42) Burk Uzzle/Magnum; (p. 43) Bruce Davidson/Magnum; (p. 44) Bettye Lane; (p. 44) World Wide Photos; (p. 45) United Press International; (p. 45) United Press International; (p. 46) Rex Gary Schmidt/U.S. Dept. of the Interior, Bureau of Sport Fisheries and Wildlife; (p. 47) United Press International; (p. 47) United Press International; (p. 48) U.S. Dept. of the Interior, Bureau of Sport Fisheries and Wildlife; (p. 49) United Press International; (p. 49) United Press International; (p. 50) Burk Uzzle/Magnum; (p. 51) Luther C. Goldman. U.S. Dept. of the Interior, Bureau of Sport Fisheries and Wildlife.

THE CEASELESS FIRE

(p. 54) Cornell Capa/Magnum; (p. 76) Bruno Barbey/Magnum; (p. 77) Bruno Barbey/Magnum; (p. 77) Bruno Barbey/Magnum; (p. 78) United Press International; (p. 78) Micha Bar-am/Magnum; (p. 79) United Press International; (p. 80) United Press International; (p. 81) Bruno Barbey/Magnum; (p. 81) Bruno Barbey/Magnum; (p. 82) Wide World Photos; (p. 83) Wide World Photos; (p. 83) United Press International; (p. 83) Sam Mazmanian/United Press International; (p. 84) Bruno Barbey/Magnum; (p. 84) Bruno Barbey/Magnum; (p. 85) Bruno Barbey/Magnum; (p. 86) Bruno Barbey/Magnum; (p. 87) United Press International.

A BEGINNING, A MIDDLE, AN END(?)

(p. 90) Philip Jones Griffiths/Magnum; (p. 133) Philip Jones Griffiths/Magnum; (p. 134) Wide World Photos; (p. 135) Wide World Photos; (p. 136) Philip Jones Griffiths/Magnum; (p. 137) Philip Jones Griffiths/Magnum; (p. 138) Wide World Photos; (p. 138) Wide World Photos; (p. 139) Wide World Photos; (p. 140) Philip Jones Griffiths/Magnum; (p. 141) Wide World Photos; (p. 141) Wide World Photos; (p. 142) Wide World Photos; (p. 142) Wide World Photos; (p. 143) Wide World Photos; (p. 144) Wide World Photos; (p. 144) Philip Jones Griffiths/Magnum; (p. 145) Philip Jones Griffiths/Magnum; (p. 146) CBS News; (p. 147) Philip Jones Griffiths/Magnum.

THE STATE OF THE NATION

(p. 150) Bonnie Freer; (p. 181) Wide World Photos; (p. 181) Associated Press; (p. 182) Wide World Photos; (p. 182) Wide World Photos; (p. 183) Leonard Freed/Magnum; (p. 184) Howard Brodie; (p. 185) Howard Brodie; (p. 185) Howard Brodie; (p. 186) Howard Brodie; (p. 186) Howard Brodie; (p. 187) Howard Brodie; (p. 188) Howard Brodie; (p. 189) Howard Brodie; (p. 190) Howard Brodie;

(p. 191) Gene Daniels/Black Star; (p. 192) Wide World Photos; (p. 193) Dorothea Lange/Magnum; (p. 194) Wide World Photos; (p. 194) Wide World Photos; (p. 195) Dorothea Lange/Magnum; (p. 196) United Press International; (p. 197) Wide World Photos; (pp. 198-99) Leonard Freed/Magnum; (p. 200) Wide World Photos; (p. 200) Wide World Photos; (p. 201) Wide World Photos; (p. 202) Burk Uzzle/Magnum; (p. 203) Wayne Miller/Magnum.

A GENERATION GAP

(p. 206) Tim Manning/Morristown Daily Record through Wide World Photos; (p. 222) Burt Glinn/Magnum; (p. 223) Roger Malloch/Magnum; (p. 224) Charles Harbutt/Magnum; (p. 225) Dennis Stock/Magnum; (p. 226) Charles Harbutt/Magnum; (p. 227) Roger Malloch/Magnum; (p. 227) Roger Malloch/Magnum; (p. 228) Leonard Freed/Magnum; (p. 229) Leonard Freed/Magnum; (p. 230) Leonard Freed/Magnum; (p. 230) Marilyn Silverstone/Magnum; (p. 231) Wayne Miller/Magnum; (p. 232) Leonard Freed/Magnum; (p. 233) Leonard Freed/Magnum; (p. 234) Roger Malloch/Magnum; (p. 235) Charles Harbutt/Magnum; (p. 236) Wide World Photos; (p. 237) Wide World Photos; (p. 237) Wide World Photos; (p. 238) John Filo/Valley Daily News, Tarentum, Pa.; (p. 239) John Filo/Valley Daily News, Tarentum, Pa.; (p. 239) Douglas Moore/Kent State University News Service; (p. 240) United Press International; (p. 241) Bonnie Freer; (p. 242) Charles Harbutt/Magnum; (p. 243) Roger Malloch/Magnum; (p. 244) Leonard Freed/Magnum; (p. 245) Charles Harbutt/Magnum; (p. 246) Roger Malloch/Magnum; (p. 247) Bonnie Freer.

WOMEN OF THE WORLD, UNITE!

(p. 250) United Press International; (p. 259) Leonard Freed/Magnum; (p. 260) Bettye Lane; (p. 261) Burt Glinn/Magnum; (p. 262) Bonnie Freer; (p. 263) Bettye Lane; (p. 264) Bettye Lane; (p. 264) United Press International; (p. 265) Bettye Lane; (p. 266) United Press International; (p. 267) Burt Glinn/Magnum; (p. 268) United Press International; (p. 268) Leonard Freed/Magnum; (p. 269) Leonard Freed/Magnum; (p. 270) Leonard Freed/Magnum; (p. 271) Library of Congress Photo via United Press International.

SUCH INTERESTING PEOPLE

(p. 274) Dominique Berretty/Magnum; (p. 296) Marc Riboud/Magnum; (p. 297) Erich Lessing/Magnum; (p. 298) Henri Cartier-Bresson/Magnum; (p. 299) Henri Cartier-Bresson/Magnum; (p. 300) Bruno Barbey/Magnum; (p. 300) Bruno Barbey/Magnum; (p. 301) René Burri/Magnum; (p. 302) Elliot Erwitt/Magnum; (p. 303) Wide World Photos; (p. 303) Fred Ward/Black Star.

Introduction

Tolstoy saw history as a series of events in remorseless sweep past men who were only incidentals. This view has long been disputed and the events of the decade of the seventies only add further questions.

That history repeats itself seems to me simplistic. Back-to-back centuries do not compare; neither do decades; neither do years. There is, of course, no particular reason to think in terms of ten-year periods. It is only a matter of historical convenience. But, taking advantage of that convenience, we have attempted, as any newsman must, to report events markedly significant beyond the moment, and to relate stories to each other, for we live in a time when almost all stories are related: Cambodia is as much a part of Kent State as Kent State is part of the state of the nation.

Richard Nixon is not John Kennedy and Nixon's America as the seventies take shape is not the America of John Kennedy as the 1960s proceeded. The old decade ended in an American malaise that touched much of the world; the new decade opened with a restlessness that disturbed it. Man leaped toward the stars in the 1960s; in the new decade, he came to realize he was groping toward them through his own muck.

It's been observed that the story of mankind is the story of silken slippers descending the stairs as wooden shoes ascend them. The superpowers of the 1970s were coming to realize as had other superpowers of earlier eras that colonization is at best only temporarily advantageous and, over the long run, unviable. The peasant proved obdurate under the wings of great bombers.

The living peoples of the earth are getting younger all the time. Youth is remarkably impatient with ancient wrongs and just as likely to confuse that impatience with wisdom.

All these fears form a dangerously combustible mixture. But if it is difficult to look ahead with hope, it is futile, based on what we have seen, to see the future in despair. More than most years, 1970 seemed a time when, in Yeats's phrase, "things fall apart; the center cannot hold." The old power blocs splintered; free world elections showed new patterns or no patterns at all; youth picked and chose among the teachings of its elders; everywhere—from American labor unions to Mideastern dynasties—the establishment was under challenge.

The extent of that challenge and the response to it will be the continuing story of the 1970s.

What we've attempted to do here is

offer a kind of overview of the opening of the decade of the seventies in terms of the men and events likely to shake our lives and shape our futures. This is a highly selective choice of happenings whose effects are most likely, it seems to me, to remain with us. The discerning critic—is there any other kind?—will find favorites missing. Trend-spotters are rarely infallible and, fallible, I may have overlooked a trend or two.

This book is a combination of two media —utilizing the immediacy of on-the-scene reporting with the opportunity for reflection offered by the permanence of print.

Any book attempting to springboard from news events into the future faces the danger of finding no water in the pool. Events do not stop happening. Thus, the mercury first discovered early in 1970 in Lake Erie perch turned up later in the year in tuna wrested from the ocean deeps. When you read these pages, it may be in your beefsteak. The noise pollution problem posed by the SST was stalled by Congress at the end of 1970; it may take wing again even as you open this book.

Similarly, we found it advisable to avoid stories dangling as this book went to press—the unsolved murder of union leader Joseph Yablonski, the courts-martial of various My Lai defendants. And there seemed little point including here, important though they are, stories of labyrinthine complexity to which we could offer no particular dimension—the bankruptcy of Penn Central Railroad, as an instance.

So what we have set down in these pages is likely to remain important or in some other way memorable a decade hence. The incisiveness of these reports seems to me striking, the "instant analysis" under recent attack holds up, and the quality of prose spoken by men often literally under the gun is nothing short of first-rate.

There is a great difference between prose meant to be read and the spoken word. The spoken words printed here, it seems to me, often leap from the page. In attempting this merger of media, then, we're trying something I don't think has been attempted before, in addition to running the risk always swirling in the clouded crystal ball.

I think the results are worth it. I hope you agree.

—Walter Cronkite

Can the World Be Saved?

that is not doomsday rhetoric.
it is, rather, the central question of our epoch.
in his proper concern over the fate posed by nuclear war, Western
man cogitates on the mushroom cloud blotting out the poet's prophecy:
"this is the way the world ends, not with a bang but a whimper."
the whimper, it has been suggested, of the last man, the last woman,
choking for a final gasp of air, a final gulp of poisoned water.
the whimper, perhaps, of the last child born
to a world collapsed by too many humans.

As scientists gather in Buenos Aires to study ways of fighting that city's air pollution, pines along the Appian Way are reported dying from the exhaust of passing automobiles, and Tokyo sees the sun for the first time in almost a week, during which some nine thousand residents are reported stricken by a thick, pervasive industrial smog. A Moscow newspaper charges that industrial pollutants are destroying the Ural River, which courses fifteen hundred miles through the Soviet Union before emptying into the Caspian Sea. Without tough measures, it is predicted, in ten years the Ural will be a dead body of water. And so on, and on—to the point of grim humor: In Madrid, Spain, the municipal "Fountain of Youth" is officially declared polluted.

Every year American power plants pour more than 800 million tons of carbon dioxide into the skies. Some scientists suspect that carbon dioxide can turn the planet into a kind of greenhouse, sealing in heat so that temperatures gradually rise until the polar icecaps melt and a new deluge covers the lands of the earth.

At the same time, we are pouring out ground-up solids, dust, at the rate of almost 10 million tons a year. Some meteorologists fear that dust is already filtering out too much sunlight, so that the world's temperature already has started down toward a new ice age.

And that pattern repeats: a science so far behind technology that it can't predict which of two opposite catastrophes will occur.

But society, obsessed with short-term gains and gross national products, continues on course, assuming, like Mr. Micawber, that something will turn up. The United States alone pours more than 22 million tons of sulfur dioxide into the atmosphere, where it combines to form sulfuric acid. The United States alone adds 100 million tons of deadly carbon monoxide to the air we breathe. The United States alone, by the best current estimate, annually throws away 2.5 billion tons of pollution into the water, land, and sky.

The authoritative voices of scientists—not professional gloom seekers but men used to examining the problem objectively—offer no reassurance to the "I'll worry about that tomorrow" school.

Lamont Cole, a Cornell University zoologist:

> I would be very surprised if there is not a worldwide food crisis within the next ten to fifteen years. But the sad thing here is that we could make the earth uninhabitable and not realize it for twenty-five or thirty years. We could have released some chemical that could poison the marine vital, plankton, which would mean that we would eventually start running out of oxygen, or we could be doing so much genetic damage to the human population that a few generations hence the offspring won't be viable, and in neither case would we know that we'd done this until long after it was too late to turn back. . . . It could already have happened.

3

Athelstan Spilhaus, president of the American Association for the Advancement of Science:

> I think one of the great errors that's made is in having a man who's in charge of air pollution, a man who's in charge of water pollution, a man who's in charge of solid wastes. The solid waste man will burn his stuff, put a horrible smoke into the air, and say, well, that's not my business, that's the air pollution guy's business. And then the air pollution fellow will wash out the stuff in a chimney and discharge it into a river, and that's not his business, that's the water pollution man's business.

Rene Dubos, bacteriologist and professor at Rockefeller University:

> If we continue destroying the natural environment, which is really part of human life, we will thereby destroy any chance that we can continue to express those qualities that have made human civilization. We will survive as animals, but not as human beings that have created civilization out of the splendor of the earth.

George Wald, Nobel Prize winner and Higgins professor of biology at Harvard University:

> There is no other place in the solar system for us, and I think we must be aware of that and not be fooled into thinking anything else. And, as I think my friend Lewis Mumford said so well, there's nothing in the remainder of the solar system as precious as one acre of the earth. We'd better take good care of that acre.

And above it all, the specter of overpopulation. In Doctor Wald's words, "We're not being asked to start controlling the population; we're being told. We have to. The whole human enterprise, the whole human race, is threatened as never before."

Confronted, then, with the facts, the continuing question has been the sort of effort man would make to start sweeping up, after a kind of rowdy party over the centuries, during which thoughts of paying the piper were largely left to nature nuts, as ecologists were called not so long ago.

It is not a matter, however, of clipping along, chipping away at the old pollution problem. Apart from the obvious invitations to political infighting, criticisms by some environmentalists, opposition from special interest groups, the issue is sometimes that of the U.S. government against the U.S. government. As far back as February 4, 1970, the President said the federal government "is one of the nation's worst polluters" and ordered federal facilities to stop fouling the air and water. Russell Train, chairman of the Council on Environmental Quality, explained to reporters the problem and the directives for those involved:

"They are required to install the necessary procedures, equipment if necessary, to meet state air and water quality standards by the target date of December 31, 1972, and to do that they are required to include immediately in their budget planning the necessary funding."

> DAN RATHER: San Francisco Bay is an example, says Train, of federal government pollution. There are naval bases all around the bay pouring out pollutants. At the Mare Island Naval Base, for instance, where submarine batteries are cleaned, chemicals from the submarine cleaning process are diluted, but not totally; then they are placed into regular sewage, which winds up in the bay. The Navy has been working since 1940 to reduce such pollution. The President says that not enough is being done fast enough.
>
> The same applies to the naval shipyard at Hunter's Point on San Francisco Bay. Oil from ships' waste covers the water. The Navy has been ordered to institute new procedures against dumping such waste at this shipyard and all others.

Across the country, along the Great Lakes, the Great Lakes Naval Station is a major polluter. The Navy says it has plans to start pumping sewage inland, but needs money to do it. The President promises the funds.

Federal buildings are under orders to eliminate pollution from their smokestacks. Air Force training centers have been told to stop the black jet trails over metropolitan areas.

The President's get-tough, do-it-now anti-pollution policy applies to all federal facilities. The estimated price tag: a minimum one-third of a billion dollars over the next three years.

There is blame enough to go around. The guilty government is not just "those people in Washington." George Harlow, director of the Federal Water Quality Administration's Lake Erie Basin office, charged that 78 of 110 cities and 44 of 130 industries were behind the schedule aimed at cleaning up Lake Erie by 1972.

As Train put it, cleaning up the air, water, and land would be a vastly more complex job than landing men on the moon, at a cost involving both taxes and higher prices passed on to consumers by industry.

And so the environment is one of those issues all politicians agree all politicians can agree on as they proceed to make a political argument of it. Senate Majority Leader Mike Mansfield said of the battle against pollution that the Democrats "were there when no one else was," citing Senator Edmund Muskie, among others, as a leader. Muskie himself said that the President was "guilty in this budget of doing what in his State of the Union address he criticized the Democrats for doing in the past years: raising expectations and then not following through with adequate funding." The senator said that money spent on space and atomic energy, compared with environment projects, showed a lack of "reordering of priorities."

President Nixon called for an end to "sterile discussions" between the parties "as to who really deserves the credit for discovering the issue of dealing with pollution." Senator Muskie, author of much of the current environmental legislation, responded with an attack on administration timber-cutting policy, called for "a commitment from each of us to make sacrifices, to spend money."

Since the environment is a matter on which everyone has an opinion, now that it has been discovered the senator has run into difficulties of his own on the environment issue. Ralph Nader's Center for the Study of Responsive Law urged that he lose his title of "Mr. Pollution Control" because he co-sponsored the 1967 Air Quality Act, which was a "business-as-usual license to polluters." Muskie replied that the legislation had not been implemented as rapidly as it should have been, but he denied there was any conspiracy with industry to weaken it.

On November 17, 1970, the senator, widely regarded as the front-runner in the Democratic presidential sweepstakes, apparently stole a march on the administration by introducing an ocean-dumping bill that was called "almost a carbon copy" of one the White House intended to introduce later.

Amid the politicking that attends any great project in American life and the creation of superagencies and calls to arms by conservation groups, the Council on Environmental Quality issued its first annual report, after just three months of preparation.

Typically, the beauty of the report was in the eye of the beholder. Train hailed it as "a milestone." The report made recommendations on water and air pollution, the disposal of solid wastes, called for a new national land use policy. It supported the Nixon proposal of $4 billion in federal money in a $10 billion program for building waste disposal plants, enforcement of water quality standards, the phasing out of detergent phosphates, establishment of national air quality and emission standards, incentives for pollution controls in the electric power and automobile industries, and research into better ways of collecting solid wastes and salvaging valuable matter from mixed refuse.

Dr. Barry Commoner, director of the Center for Biology of Natural Systems at Washington University, St. Louis, saw the report as a kind of proof that cleaning up the environment was too important to be left to the government:

> I think it's a useful report, but perhaps not for the reasons that the government had in mind. It's not particularly useful as a source of information; there are much better government reports on that score. It's not particularly useful as a way of figuring out what we ought to do, because most of the recommendations are either inadequate or very vague. It is useful, however, in telling the public and particularly those of us in the scientific community that the government can't really handle this problem, and that the rest of us have to do something about it. Mr. Nixon says in the transmittal letter that the environmental problem is leading toward a possibility of ecological catastrophe. Now, ecological catastrophe involves human survival. If we are confronting an ecological catastrophe, then Mr. Nixon isn't acting as though he knew it.

But the first year of the war against pollution, the Decade of the Environment, involved interactions parallel to the nature of ecology itself—government, industry, labor, private organizations, and, perhaps most important, the individual taking on the matter of human survival, man himself having done so much to threaten it.

"Iron on the Water Shall Float"

the seventeenth-century English witch and prophetess,
Mother Shipton, is credited with some amazing prophecies, one couplet
forecasting, "iron on the water shall float/as easy as a wooden boat."
for centuries, man took this as an astonishing instance of
foreseeing the day of iron ships. it may be the old lady was more
prescient than that, for in our own day it was said of some polluted
lakes that you would dissolve before you drowned; the Interior
Department reported five thousand pounds of dangerous lead
pollutants and smaller amounts of arsenic dumped daily into a short
stretch of the Mississippi; Norwegian explorer Thor Heyerdahl
after a fifty-seven-day crossing of the Atlantic in a papyrus boat reported
oil slicks and "asphaltlike lumps ranging from the
size of rice to potatoes" in mid ocean.

It is not quite a case of water, water everywhere and not a drop to drink, but I Timothy 5:23 took on a new meaning for Americans in the opening of the seventies: "Drink no longer water, but use a little wine for thy stomach's sake." The Bureau of Water Hygiene reported that a survey of almost one thousand municipal water systems showed about one in six was "potentially hazardous" and another 25 percent were inferior—safe enough, but with a bad taste, odor, or appearance.

The $10 billion the President proposes should be spent within five years for water purification sounds like an impressive sum. But there is a lot of purifying to do. One of the world's most majestic coasts is that stretch of the Pacific shoreline that includes the fabled Big Sur:

TERRY DRINKWATER: In the 1940s John Steinbeck, who loved this coastline of Monterey and Carmel, said of it: "The sea is very clear and the bottom becomes fantastic with hurrying, fighting, feeding, breeding animals. Crabs rush from frond to frond of the waving algae. Starfish, mussels, shrimp, hermit crabs, a lovely colored world." But the sea is not clear anymore. Marine life no longer flourishes. That is because this part of the ocean is polluted with sewage. Warning signs for swimmers have been posted on some beaches. "Highly contaminated. No wading, swimming, or diving, by order of the Director of Public Health for the County."

DR. RICHARD FRASER, MONTEREY COUNTY HEALTH COMMISSIONER: The contamination in these areas consists of improperly treated sewage. Improperly treated sewage contains germs, disease-causing germs, of the germs typhoid, hepatitis, the intestinal infections. These germs are present, and people can become infected if they bathe or come in contact with the water containing these germs.

CORRESPONDENT: Some of the processed sewage is released on the beach itself. This pipe leads from the Army's Fort Ord sewage treatment plant. No funds have been appropriated to lay a pipe out to sea, so it simply flows into the surf. There are nine separate processing plants dumping into the bay. Four facilities are under cease and desist orders from the state Water Quality Control Board. The plants are old and too small. They were built when the population was a tenth of what it is today. Lab tests of their output show excessively high bacteria counts. Health officers are as alarmed as some boat owners, who say they often see pieces of human excrement floating in the bay.

Even worse is the flow from private cesspools in the Carmel section of the county. One can still find an occasional sea otter playing in a rocky cove. There is much beauty and sufficient marine life left here to be worth saving. Scientists and community leaders agree the solution to this problem is very simple: build a modern, consolidated sewage processing plant. But it's expensive, $5 million, perhaps, and so far neither the local taxpayers nor the state or the federal government has been willing to spend that kind of money.

A University of Kansas chemist, Dr. Ernest Angino, reported traces of arsenic in nine major brands of enzyme detergents. Detergent makers said they were aware of the arsenic presence—up to 2,333 times more than the Public Health Service's standards for drinking water—but that it was below dangerous levels. The Interior Department listed phosphate contents in twenty-two laundry and dishwashing products, ranging from a high of 74 percent to a low of 14 percent. Phosphates are accused by some ecologists of being a major cause of water pollution.

Perhaps the most celebrated case centered around Arthur Godfrey. The entertainer, long a leading and outspoken conservationist, made public his discontent with the presoak product Axion, for which he was a radio and television salesman:

> Now, I thought, and I had proceeded on the belief, that Axion contained none of this, that it was an enzyme-active presoak. Enzymes, as I understood it, are little things that eat the protein stains out of fabrics, same as the enzymes in our stomachs. And I talked to my ecologist friends about it and they said, nothing but enzymes, can't do any harm. But all of a sudden I find out that it's got all this phosphate in it, see.
>
> I said to them, I've now reached an untenable position. I cannot any longer talk ecology out of this side of my mouth and sell a pollutant over here. We've got to fix this and fix it quickly or you and I must sever our relationship insofar as Axion is concerned. I enjoy the association with them on the toothpaste—that's fine, that's a good product —but this one I can no longer sell unless you will permit me to tell the story as it is. . . .
>
> I don't like to talk about figures, but I was very proud of this when it came along a year and a half ago because at the end of my fortieth year in the business I had the largest contract—the way we measure things in America, by dollars and cents—that I'd ever had in my whole career. So it was a very nice thing to wind up my career with this association and—I'd thought—a spotless product.

The problem washed away two weeks later when Godfrey made a commercial in which he said that Axion, like all household detergents and presoaks, contributed to pollution in a small way and that the manufacturers were trying to improve the product.

Without waiting for that happy day, the Suffolk County government on New York's Long Island took a step believed to be a first: it flatly banned the sale of all detergents. Effective in March of 1971, anyone who sells detergents in the county faces a $250 fine and fifteen days in jail. The county has virtually no sewer systems, and detergents, after passing through septic tanks, were polluting groundwater, the sole source of drinking water for more than one million people.

But even as the battle to clean up cleansers continued, the larger job at hand seemed almost insoluble. While the debate centered on how much money to spend on construction of sewage treatment plants, ecologists pointed out that even the most modern snuffed out oxygen as they treated the more obvious objectional features of waste. "The modern sewage treatment plant," in Dr. Commoner's words, "simply substitutes one pollution problem for another."

It seems at times that mankind has been almost willful in his destruction of the environment; that is perhaps the saddest lesson of all. Posting warning signs, he ignores them.

Not until 1970 was there any major effort to legislate against oil pollution, to measure dollars against sense. If a single incident can be credited with impressing the dangers of pollution on the American consciousness, it would be the blowout of oil wells in the Santa Barbara Channel off California on January 28, 1969. At least 740,000 gallons of heavy crude oil leaked to the surface, much of it fouling the once golden beaches, killing marine life, turning up as far away as Santa Catalina Island, one hundred miles distant.

At an anniversary conference called Santa Barbara's Declaration of Environmental Rights, spokesmen broadened the theme beyond oil pollution:

> DR. ROBERT NASH: Moved by an environmental disaster in the Santa Barbara Channel to think and act in national and world terms, we submit these charges. We have littered the land with refuse. We have encroached upon our heritage of open space and wild land. We have stripped the forests

and the grasses and reduced the soil to fruitless dust.

DR. PAUL EHRLICH: As long as it's clear that the President is hooked on growthmanship and thinks that the quality of life is the size of the gross national product, as long as the cowboy economy which emphasizes production and consumption and waste—you know, foul your own nest and then move on west—our problem here in Santa Barbara is there's no place to go—then you can be sure, you can be absolutely sure, we've had it. Everybody who's looked into the overall population resource and environment picture comes up with the same kind of estimate of what would be required if we're to have a fifty-fifty chance of getting through the next couple of decades with civilization intact.

It boils down to an expenditure by the United States of a minimum of $50 billion a year on this problem and equivalent expenditures by all the other overdeveloped countries. As long as the President and politicians are talking about a few billion dollars here or a few billion dollars there, you can be absolutely sure that you're the cancer victim, and they're offering you aspirin. You are being kidded.

Santa Barbara, it was agreed, must never happen again, and President Nixon asked Congress to cancel twenty offshore oil leases and create a federal marine sanctuary in the channel. His proposal permitted continued production from three leases to empty deposits that continued to seep oil into the water. Conservationists were cynical:

AL WEINGAND: Well, it's an easy one for the oil interests. They're giving up nothing, nothing. They're getting—they're being repaid for any—any out-of-pocket costs that they have, and this is all right. But, further than that, they're being paid for leases that are not, that so far have not been shown to be productive. So we're—we're giving the oil—the government is giving the oil companies a lot of dough, or this is proposed in the bill, and sort of assuring all of us that this is a—a wonderful maneuver. This to me

is immoral, and—and—and it's a betrayal of the public interest.

INTERIOR SECRETARY WALTER HICKEL: There have been a couple of dry holes, as I recall, but in that whole twenty leases, we have stopped basically that exploratory drilling that is necessary to find out just what is there. Because what is the— what would be the use of going in to find out a—a geological structure, and then say hold it now. We're saying hold it right after the lease, and I think that's a wise decision. But they might say there is, they might say there isn't, but the fact is that we know there's lots of oil there, 'cause we're taking it out right now.

TERRY DRINKWATER: The administration plan called for releasing oil from the Elk Hills Reserve in partial payment to the oil companies. So the oil companies would be compensated partly in cash and partly in oil. Some, in the military, objected to the Elk Hills idea. The underground oil there, they said, should be used only in the event of a national emergency.

One part of the whole proposed administration solution which irked Santa Barbarans was that pumping would continue at Union's Platform A and at the nearby newly built Sun Oil platform. Department of Interior and oil company geologists said this was necessary to relieve undersea oil pressure; they called this drilling "remedial."

The government has proposed canceling twenty leases, but nearby, on either side of this sanctuary, vast areas are available for drilling. The administration will allow massive exploration and production here. The President's Council on Environmental Quality Control recommended that some of these leases be made part of the sanctuary, but the administration decided otherwise. Now, the oil companies have stepped up their drilling in these parts of the Santa Barbara Channel. Much new oil has been found. There is more activity, in fact, than at any other time since the original disaster a year and a half ago.

None of the oil companies involved would agree to interviews on the subject of the proposed sanctuary and what they would likely be paid for not drilling. Several spokesmen said any answers on the subject might be inappropriate because the amounts paid would be decided by the courts.

In the whole long Santa Barbara oil controversy, the companies have been under attack, but now the thrust of the conservationist criticism is directed at the federal government. What the administration proposes is too little, too late, and really of benefit only to the oil companies—that's what many citizens here say.

There was more, and worse, to come. The North American continent seemed ringed by oil slicks—off Alaska, off Nova Scotia, off Florida, and, most dramatically, in the Gulf Coast off Louisiana. A fire started in an automated platform that housed production controls for ten oil and gas wells owned by the Chevron Oil Company about forty-five miles off the coast. "Experts" estimated the fire might take a week to extinguish. It developed into the nation's largest oil spill, gushing an estimated maximum of 42,000 gallons daily into the ocean, creating a slick eight miles long and five hundred feet wide. After the month-long fire was extinguished, a federal grand jury indicted Chevron, a division of Standard Oil of California, on nine hundred separate offenses. The company pleaded no contest to charges that it had failed to install safety devices on ninety wells and was fined $1 million by a federal court. As a result of massive oil pollution in the Gulf, Secretary Hickel announced plans to double the number of federal inspectors in a crackdown on offshore violations. The government subsequently moved against five more major oil companies charged with failure to install safety devices.

This could all be regarded as confirmation of the old adage that oil and water don't mix, except that life seldom simplifies down to proverbs. As an almost explosive national awareness of the oil and chemical threat to water awakened, traditional values and traditional leadership came under fire. Situations at opposite ends of the Atlantic Coast crystallized the issues and interests at stake.

Machias Bay, Maine—rocky, breathtakingly beautiful, economically depressed. The community was talking about an oil company that wanted to bring prosperity there, erect a refinery, turn the bay into a port capable of handling mammoth hundred-thousand-ton supertankers, in an economic turnabout for northern Maine. But some people thought prosperity would come at too high a price—massive water pollution, the threat of gigantic oil spills, ruin for the coast and the fishing industry. One night, area residents met to argue the oil port:

FIRST MAN: Why do we worry about the birds and the trees? Main reason is because we're told by scientists who study the birds and the trees, and the people, and the animals, the ecologists, that the things that affect these, the way they go, are warnings to the way people are going to go. In other words, we have to recognize that we're all in the same boat.

SECOND MAN: I don't know what our trouble is, but I think it's chronic unemployment. I wonder how much longer the other people that is paying—paying on unemployment the year around is going to keep carrying the load. Some day they're going to wise up and just decide that they don't want the unemployment anymore.

THIRD MAN: We who have spent our lives on this coast and are familiar with its strong tides, its heavy fogs, its rocky shoals, and its frequent and severe storms believe it to be one of the most hostile stretches of ocean in the world and one of the riskiest places to handle oil. For this reason, we believe that oil spills are inevitable.

FOURTH MAN: I know that there are risks, but I believe that they do not outweigh the advantages of increased cash flow in this area. If we truly oppose oil development, would we not be morally responsible to use candles for light, wood for heat, and horses for transportation?

Twelve hundred miles to the south, a curiously similar conflict developed. Top South Carolina officials persuaded the giant German chemical combine, BASF, to build a $200 million dye and plastics plant on the shore opposite Hilton Head Island. The area, like Machiasport, is a remote, unspoiled corner of coastline and, like Machiasport, economically depressed.

The traditional southern prescription for such areas has been new payrolls, new industry. But this time the rallying cry was not "payrolls" but "pollution." And although the firm insisted it would make the plant pollution-free, thousands of South Carolinians banded together to block an economic bonanza. Their reasoning went like this:

MRS. MILDRED MITCHELL: I feel that this is the last place on the eastern seaboard that is really clean, and I think it is a shame to ruin what God gave us. And I feel like we have to work, and if we don't work, we don't deserve what we get.

CORRESPONDENT: Do you think you were as concerned about the issue of pollution, let's say five years ago?

MRS. MITCHELL: No, I don't think anyone was. . . . It has become such—such an issue, and we realize now that if we don't do something soon, our heritage is going to be in jeopardy.

MRS. JUDY BRAWNER: Well, it's something that involves all of us. We feel that this is—this area—is something very, very special, and we don't want it destroyed by pollution. And it's something that we can do, and we're the ones who will have to do it.

CORRESPONDENT: Do you think that you've always been aware of pollution or the problems caused by pollution? Why all of a sudden is everybody so concerned?

MRS. BRAWNER: Well, a few years ago, I didn't even know whether it had two l's or one. But now we're all very much aware of it because it's a national issue and our attention is being drawn to it, and it—it's something that really involves us. . . .

In microcosm, then, these two small communities faced issues confronting more and more Americans. This nation's economic success has been based on expansion. So far, that expansion usually has meant pollution. Can we learn to expand without polluting? Or can we learn to live without endless expansion? How much pollution will we trade for how much prosperity?

In Maine, the referendum supporting the refinery was approved by a small margin. In South Carolina, the German firm, reminded by Secretary Hickel that the government would act in the event of environmental damage, announced that it was abandoning its plans to build there.

There are no simple answers.

In what seemed less complicated days, the mention of mercury levels usually referred to temperature—your own, if you felt infirm, or that of the great outdoors. But the chemical mercury is used in seed as a pesticide and fungicide. It's in some plants. It's a frequent industrial by-product dumped in the nation's waters.

And in the human system mercury can cause severe damage of the kidneys and the brain, cause teeth to drop out, and eventually cause death. The symptoms of mercury poisoning are not easy to recognize.

In 1970, the first year of the Decade of the Environment, Americans discovered mercury.

The story started in Canada, when the Ontario government announced that it was banning fishing in Lake St. Clair, where pickerel had been found to contain forty times the amount of mercury regarded as safe by the World Health Organization. On April 1, Ontario ordered eleven plants to stop using mercury or discharging it into the water. A similar ban was imposed on commercial fishing in Lake Erie by Ohio Governor James Rhodes, for the same reason, although it was subsequently rescinded.

Suddenly, mercury seemed to get around with the speed of the god for whom it was named. An Associated Press survey showed potentially dangerous mercury levels in the waters of fourteen states. Secretary Hickel ordered a search for sources of "newly discovered mercury pollution" in the nation's waterways. The Justice Department moved in with suits against companies in seven states. The companies announced they were at work on the problem, but one executive was properly aggrieved:

"These problems of mercury pollution weren't even known by the government or industry until March of this year," he pointed out. And again, there were the conflicts. The government won its first victory in the mercury suits—others would follow rapidly—when a paper company agreed to close its plant on Maine's Androscoggin River by August 15. The cost: seventeen jobs.

Back at Lake St. Clair, where it all started, the issue was about as easily grasped as—well, quicksilver:

BILL PLANTE: To the nineteenth-century readers of *Alice in Wonderland*, it most likely came as no surprise that the Mad Hatter was, in fact, mad. It was common knowledge then that hatters worked with mercury, the white liquid metal, and that it did strange things to their minds.

These present-day fishermen on Lake St.

Clair, throwing their catch of bass and perch back into the lake, are not mad in the strict sense of insanity, but they are annoyed, put out, and upset by the state of Michigan ban that forces them to release their catch. The cause again is the white liquid metal, mercury.

DR. MAURICE REIZEN: A full-blown case of mercury poisoning may give you numbness and tingling in your arms and legs, difficulty hearing, tunnel vision, where your visual fields are restricted, inability to speak properly, leading eventually to total blindness and even death.

CORRESPONDENT: Primary sources of the mercury pollution in Lake St. Clair, the Detroit River, and Lake Erie were Dow Chemical at Sarnia, Ontario, and Wyandotte Chemical at Wyandotte, Michigan. The two companies were not exactly dumping their mercury—it's too valuable for that—but some was lost in various processes, as much as two hundred pounds a day at Dow, up to twenty pounds daily at Wyandotte. Both companies were told to stop polluting, Dow by the Canadian government, Wyandotte by the state of Michigan. They are now in the process of building recycling operations to capture the mercury waste.

At Michigan State University's Institute of Water Resources, Dr. Frank D'Itri and his staff traced the path of the metal through the waters to the fish population. Dr. D'Itri is in favor of even stiffer controls than those now required by the Food and Drug Administration.

DR. FRANK D'ITRI: In my opinion, the largest concern, or the biggest concern, should be that we're getting mercury from a variety of sources. We're getting it from the chemical plants that are using it in a manufacturing process, we're getting it through agricultural types of chemicals, for instance, sprays, there's mercury used in fruit—in fruit sprays. Mercury is also used as a seed dressing, a fungicide to kill off fungus that might rot the seed, and it's also used in lawn preparations, the types of materials that you can buy at your local nursery store.

CORRESPONDENT: A special commission in Michigan is now looking into the economic effects of the fishing ban. Preliminary reports indicate they will find that it has cost the state millions of dollars, and the same is probably true across the border in Canada. Ray Trombley has been a fishing guide on Lake St. Clair for more than twenty years. He and the Lake St. Clair Advisory Committee, of which he is president, are dead set against the governor's ban on taking fish.

RAYMOND TROMBLEY: We should be allowed to make up our own mind on whether these fish are dangerous to our health. If people don't— I'm not recommending eating fish to people. I would eat them myself, and I would have my family eat them—in small amounts. I would not—we don't live on fish, none of us do. Very few people in this country make a steady diet of it, and in the minute quantities that this mercury is in these fish, I don't think that—that the danger is as bad as is shown. The state cannot show us one clinically sick person.

DR. REIZEN: Well, I certainly can sympathize with them as a—as a fisherman of long standing having a—a virulent case of the disease, I certainly have a compassion for this. However, as a health professional, I feel we do have a dilemma here, and I feel that we certainly can't err on the side of allowing people to take the chance of eating the fish.

Meanwhile, ecologist Barry Commoner said he believed mercury contamination was far more widespread and dangerous than realized.

Although man is not yet up to handling all of nature's elements, he is not above adding a few of his own. And so the Army announced plans to bury at sea three thousand tons of the deadly nerve gas GB, less than a drop of which reportedly kills within minutes. (In the course of subsequent hearings,

it was revealed that one of the rockets, no one knew which, contained VX, a gas identified as deadlier than GB.)

Apparently some of the World War II nerve gas tanks in storage had begun to leak and the Army felt that the only answer was to wrap them in steel and cement, take them to the Atlantic Ocean about 280 miles off the Cape Kennedy coast, and dump them in 16,000 feet of water. Hopefully, the tanks would erode and the gas would be diluted in the sea.

Two trainloads of small rockets filled with gas and embedded in concrete and steel blocks were to be moved across fifteen hundred miles of track through seven southern states, bypassing large cities but traveling through twenty-one populated areas en route from Lexington, Kentucky, and Anniston, Alabama, to the Sunny Point Military Terminal near Wilmington, North Carolina. There the deadly cargo was to be loaded on an old navy hulk and sunk off the Florida coast.

The reaction was as predictable as the result. Florida Governor Claude Kirk called for a delay until he learned more details. Conservationist groups protested. The Pentagon spelled out elaborate safety precautions but asked hospitals along the route to stockpile an antidote in case of emergency. To show his confidence in the military, Georgia Governor Lester Maddox offered to ride the train.

Florida Democratic Representative Paul Rogers noted that a scientific committee had recommended destruction of the gas by nuclear means. "The Army doesn't do it," he said. "Instead they proceed in the old time-honored way they have of dumping it at sea." Rogers called the Army's handling of the matter the most incompetent he had ever witnessed. Two oceanographic institute scientists called it "sheer, unbelieveable inefficiency

and stupidity" threatening to "create a char-
nel house of dead creatures in the sea."

The plan was reluctantly endorsed at
Senate hearings by environmental adviser
Train. "Given the present set of circumstances, we agree that the proposed plan is
the least undesirable of available alternatives."

And, given the conflicting testimony, the
conservationist could conclude only that, even
on basic issues, there are times when doctors
disagree:

U.S. SURGEON GENERAL JESSE L.
STEINFELD, M.D.: Our department wishes
to take this opportunity to reassure the Congress and the American people that the transportation involved in Operation Chase is less
hazardous than that occurring daily in similar mass movements of chlorine, of phosgene,
of LPG, or liquefied petroleum gas, and of
anhydrous ammonia.

KENTUCKY SENATOR MARLOW COOK:
The confinement could lead to a high-order
explosion. Indeed, there is no positive assurance that further hazards could not result
from the possible sympathetic detonation of
adjacent rockets, thus involving about 630
pounds of explosives, including the rocket
motors. This could happen in the ocean as
well as it can happen on land.

THADDEUS BEAL: The point is we don't
care if it happens in the ocean. In fact, we'd
rather welcome it happening in the ocean,
that's the way this nerve agent will be released and then hydrolized. That's, I think,
the point that needs to be made here. This,
in our opinion, is one of the most efficient
ways of detoxifying this kind of—of gas.

According to oceanography expert Howard Sanders, the government had researched
the undersea dumping site for only ten days,
not nearly long enough, he claimed, to really
know the currents and conditions in the area.

The operative word in the case seemed

to be "reluctance"—on the part of just about
everyone involved. Did Train endorse the
plan *reluctantly?* Governor Kirk and a group
of scientists and lawyers calling themselves
the Environmental Defense Fund took the
matter to court, where a federal judge *reluctantly* backed the Army's plan. The Army
made it clear that it was disposing of the
nerve gas at sea *reluctantly,* promising never
to do it again. An appeals court upheld the
district court and, *reluctantly,* Governor Kirk
and the Defense Fund decided not to pursue
the matter to the Supreme Court.

The disposal itself was uneventful but
curious:

CORRESPONDENT: The Army, as if to remind everyone that it was in charge, moved
out at its leisure with a shipment from Anniston, Alabama. Dark skies and driving rain
accompanied the controversial shipment. Security and safety measures were elaborate,
the nerve gas rockets all but hidden in the
freight cars. Army experts made last-minute
inspections of the train carrying the 305
vaults that contained the deadly nerve gas
bombs. They confidently pronounced the
shipment safe for the trip to Sunny Point,
North Carolina. But just in case, disaster
teams carrying antidotes for the gas joined
the caravan.
    To protect the train against any of the
so-called subversives who might try to ambush the cargo, a pilot train pulled out ahead.
The men aboard the front train would look
for any land mines, snipers, or faulty track
which might cause problems.

Along with dirtying our water, we are
overheating it to a point that threatens the
entire cycle of the ecology of marine life.
The Justice Department in March, 1970, for
the first time filed a suit charging thermal
pollution. It cited the Florida Power and
Light Company for raising the temperatures
in Biscayne Bay "to degrees substantially

higher than their natural condition." New York State brought a similar suit against Consolidated Edison, seeking $5 million for fish kills in the Hudson River. The Federal Water Quality Administration proposed legislation barring activities that would raise by more than one degree at the point of discharge temperatures in the Great Lakes.

And so, given a late start, antiquated legislation complete with safeguards for industry rather than nature, the enormous costs in time and money, the awful damage already done, water pollution alone makes the environmental cause seem hopeless. There are times when, looking into the situation, you are ready to shrug and walk away from mankind as a bad mistake.

And yet there are indications that the world can save itself—if it will.

There is the example of Lake Washington in Seattle, the one sizable body of water in America that has been brought back from destruction. The beaches were open on Lake Washington in the summer of '70—twenty-four miles of sparkling recreational waters—and the fishing was fine.

Eight years earlier, half-treated sewage from a dozen different communities flowed to that lake through open trenches, twenty million gallons of effluent daily turning the once lovely lake into a sort of mini Lake Erie, the moon on slimy waters. James Ellis, that proverbial but rare concerned citizen, was the man most responsible for saving Lake Washington. He recalls the way it was:

> For a large number of the beaches on this lake, you'd have seen posted signs, "No Swimming." For a number of others that were swimmable, but just barely swimmable, you'd have seen water where you could barely see down a foot. You certainly couldn't see the bottom in most places. There was floating debris, there was floating algae, and

it was very visible, noticeable, sharply noticeable, and very repulsive. The lake is a beautiful lake, but it was disappearing on us.

In 1953, Ellis and others began to push for a superagency, the Municipality of Metropolitan Seattle, nicknamed Metro, which could take over all the sewage processing from all those growing communities around the lake and do the job none of them could afford. It took five years. One of Ellis's citizen campaigners, now governor of the state, says of those early days:

> GOVERNOR DANIEL EVANS: I was a member of the Muncipal League, and it was through the Municipal League and some other associated organizations we began to do citizen studies, luncheon meetings where we'd get together and—with a number of interested citizens, no one being paid, no one having any technical support, but just pure interest, began to initiate this effort. And it spread from there to actually getting out into the communities, talking to community clubs and organizations to spread the idea, the concepts, actually got down even to—to simple individual contact through doorbelling, people getting out and contacting their fellow citizens. It's plenty effective, but too often citizens don't take the first step.

After four years the state legislature passed a bill submitting the Metro plan to the voters, who, apparently leery of a powerful new governmental superagency with the authority to issue bonds, promptly voted it down. Refusing defeat, Ellis and his supporters mobilized the League of Women Voters, the King County Medical Society, local chambers of commerce, and five thousand doorbell-ringing mothers to change the voters' minds. And in the fall of 1958, the Municipality of Metropolitan Seattle was approved.

JAMES ELLIS: Well, I think the people

here have a peculiar love for the country, and for the beautiful country that they've been brought up in, and they could visibly see it disappearing on them. They could see this lake going, and they didn't want to see it happen. And it wasn't a question of believing what someone said; it was a question of observing, seeing it. And when they saw it, they said, you know, it does stink, and we'd better do something about it. And they did.

Today, Metro is a $120 million complex of sophisticated waste treatment plants, the largest single water pollution project in the world. The results are best seen in the laboratory of the scientist who first warned of impending disaster fifteen years ago:

DR. W. T. EDMONDSON: As soon as the first partial diversion of sewage was made, the lake stopped the deteriorating, and then pretty soon it began to improve. Year by year it's been better than the year—than the year before. It's been two years since the diversion program's completed, and the lake has shown a really dramatic increase in—in clarity. It's almost three times as clear now as measured by the disk transparency as it was in 1963.

ELLIS: They pay two dollars per month per single family residence, on average, more, for the Metro program. . . . That's the price of clean water in this area at this time. Now, I'm convinced that we were fortunate to move when we moved. We know that costs have risen on us and are going to rise on everyone else. But by the same token, personal incomes are rising, and rising sharply. And the proportion that we are asked to take of personal income to solve this kind of problem is going to be minor, just minor. And there's no way that an individual can do it by himself. There is no way. He's just got to join with his fellow people and say, "Okay, it's two dollars a month—I won't buy a carton of cigarettes, but I will clean up that stinking place."

By how fast it has come back, become clear and clean again, Lake Washington tells us all something.

The question, then, even for the mighty oceans: How many Lake Washingtons? How many Lake Eries? Have a glass of water and think about it.

The Earth and the Air

the ancients separated earth and air as elements, but today their interdependence is a matter we all live with. it is precisely because of the machines of the earth that we live in guilt over what we have done, are doing to the air. and there is growing concern that we are still not fully aware of the price we must pay. the president of the American Cancer Society warned this year that there are probably "scores" of unknown agents in the air which could cause cancer. and yet, regularly, man plunges ahead, loosing elements into the atmosphere with no knowledge of their long-term effects.

The Joint Committee on Atomic Energy has made public 1,108 pages of testimony indicating that nuclear reactors "could make a meaningful reduction" in air and water pollution as a replacement for conventional means of producing electrical power. Dr. Edward Teller, father of the hydrogen bomb, said that the dangers from such peaceful uses of atomic energy could easily be guarded against.

Others were not so sure. The American Civil Liberties Union charged that Atomic Energy Commission standards grossly underestimated the pollution dangers. While Paul Tompkins, executive director of the Federal Radiation Council, said that "hazards from nuclear power plants are being badly overpainted," two University of London professors suggested that allowable radiation from nuclear power plants be reduced by 90 percent.

The problems involved were pinpointed in a story from one of the nation's key atomic bomb plants outside Denver, Colorado:

BILL STOUT: The Rocky Flats plant run by Dow Chemical for the AEC makes plutonium parts for nuclear weapons. Denver is in the distance, sixteen miles away, with suburbs in between, in the path of the prevailing winds which blow down the face of the Rockies. Last May 11 two buildings were gutted by fire, causing $45 million damage to the plant, plus $20 million worth of plutonium, enough to make seventy-seven bombs of the size dropped on Nagasaki. After the fire, Dow and the AEC said there was no evidence plutonium had carried beyond the plant boundaries.

Several months later, scientists with the Colorado Committee for Environmental Information asked Dow Chemical to run soil tests in the Denver area, but the company refused. The scientists were concerned because, in terms of lung cancer, plutonium is one of the most dangerous agents known. So they went ahead on their own, with a number of soil and water sampling tests. In a report to the AEC, they now contend the plant has been releasing plutonium and they are sharply critical of its safety standards. They want greater safeguards for the 3,200 people who work here and for all the people of the Denver area.

Dr. Edward Martell is chairman of the scientists' Rocky Flats subcommittee. How much more plutonium do your samples indicate in the soil than the AEC has been willing to admit?

DR. EDWARD MARTELL: I would say that the amounts of plutonium that we found so far—and there may be more depending on hot spots and distribution in detail—the amounts we found so far are perhaps a hundred to a thousand times the amounts you should expect if there are good containment practices and good plutonium-handling practices at the plant.

DR. ARTHUR TAMPLIN, BIOPHYSICIST AT THE LAWRENCE RADIATION LABORATORY IN CALIFORNIA: Based upon the—Martell's original letter to the AEC, my colleague and I estimated that contamination might have been able to produce some two hundred lung cancers in the Denver area. This was an upper limit kind of an estimate. . . . Dr. Martell's recent information indicates that the plutonium is all on—essentially on the surface of the ground, and this suggests that the plutonium that he has observed in that area came from the fire that occurred at the plant. And as a result this material is subject to redistribution by the winds. It introduces more uncertainty into the calculations, but the net effect could be that the effects on—on the people could be ten times higher than we originally estimated. . . . This would be some two thousand cancers that might have been introduced—induced in the Denver area.

MAJOR GENERAL EDWARD GILLERS OF THE AEC'S MILITARY APPLICATIONS DIVISION: We have a continuous sampling system located both within the plant boundary and at various locations in the Denver area. These samplers sample the air continuously and are measured to find out how much radioactivity, plutonium oxide, is in the air. Therefore any material which is either falling down from the stacks or has been resuspended or blown around by meteorological conditions would appear upon our measurements. To date we find—the highest reading that we have seen is about one-tenth of our permissible limits, whereas about 80 percent of the time these measurement systems do not record any activity whatsoever, so we feel that the actual levels in there are well below the permissible limits at all times.

CORRESPONDENT: The burden of the Martell report is that Dow Chemical and the AEC have been neither strict enough in setting safety standards nor completely honest in reporting such accidents as the Rocky Flats fire. Dr. Martell and his colleagues are even more concerned about the long-term effects—what will the plutonium released do to the people of this area? Should all the existing standards of the so-called permissible levels of exposure to radiation be reevaluated? Should Rocky Flats, or any such facility, be allowed to handle the most dangerous nuclear materials so close to populated areas? All these questions raised by the Martell report, which must now be answered by the AEC.

The AEC denied that any health hazard was involved. It said Environmental Information samples showed the presence of "minuscule" amounts of plutonium. Dr. Martell, however, argued that "each plutonium particle in the lung produces millions of times more radiation in the tissue around it than a dust particle carrying natural radioactivity."

Subsequently the AEC, making public a report that 250 square miles of its Nevada atomic test site area had been sealed off to the public because it was contaminated by plutonium, said there was danger "only" if the plutonium was stirred into the atmosphere by winds. At the same time, the AEC noted that since the 1963 ban on atmospheric testing, one out of every twelve underground tests had leaked some radioactivity into the off-site atmosphere, at one-tenth the level considered safe by the Federal Radiation Council.

There are two points here that are beyond dispute. The first is that there is nuclear bleeding, safe or not, into the atmosphere, and that didn't use to happen. The second is that the AEC is not beyond criticism. It has been wrong before. It has seriously underestimated the amounts of nuclear fallout. In 1953, as an instance, it minimized the danger of atmospheric testing because, it said, the fallout would be evenly distributed over the globe in amounts so small no single area would be harmed. Five years later, test samples showed that fallout was highest in the northern temperate zone, where most of the world's people live—ten times higher than at the poles or the equator, five times higher than in the southern temperate zone.

But the dangers of radioactivity, real and awful as they may be, are rare compared to the older, more commonplace forms of atmospheric pollution, the kinds that just about all Americans live with.

This uncomfortable fact pressed down like a sweaty palm on East Coast residents the last week of July. A combination of high temperature and inversions—and, in New York City, where the effects were most serious, power cutbacks forced by the failure of two electrical generators—brought on near crises from Boston to Atlanta.

Any concentration of more than .1 part of sulfur dioxide per million parts of air is considered unhealthy. At .4 it is regarded as an "acute threat to public health." In New York, polluted air, trapped below layers of warm air, reached .23 in some sections of the city.

Strained by the demands of air-conditioners as temperatures hung in the middle nineties, power was ordered cut back by 5 percent. Subways ran at half speed. Office workers groped through darkened buildings. Operations of major municipal incinerators were shut down. For most people along the seaboard, it never got worse than eye-irritation levels—in Atlanta, Raleigh, Washington, Baltimore. But in New York, the Health Department warned people with serious respiratory diseases to stay indoors and advised joggers to lie down and think.

Environmental Action, Inc., the group that had coordinated Earth Day activities, charged that during the week of yellow gray smog "the strongest weapon any of our institutions responded with was rhetoric." President Nixon said that it was "perhaps fortunate, in a way, that the East Coast saw this problem in such a massive manner. Now we realize we don't have much time left, and it's time for Congress to get the environmental message." It offered New Yorkers a view of the kind of smog familiar to southern California, the President noted.

California conditions were described by a panel of experts. Their report on how to deal with problems of air, water, noise, and land pollution, authorized by the 1968 state legislature, concluded that it "is questionable whether major portions of the state will be capable of supporting human life within several more decades."

And for an eyewitness view going beyond doleful predictions that we may run out of fresh air in ten to fifteen years, with lung and bronchial disease increasing in smogbound cities, there is the Rim Forest, sixty miles from Los Angeles:

TERRY DRINKWATER: It used to be that only those who lived in the flatlands of the Los Angeles Basin choked with the smog, but now you feel it all the way up here, 5,280 feet, one mile above sea level. The trees are dying. That is the major effect. Some 1.3 million pines are dead or dying.

This ponderosa tree was a very healthy specimen undoubtedly fifteen years ago, but no more. The branches at the lowest level are already gone, and you have to go all the way up to the top to find the green.

Jim Asher, a former U.S. forester, has lived in these mountains for ten years and has seen the change. What happens when smog comes in contact with a tree?

JIM ASHER: Well, of course a tree must have its chlorophyll, or its greenness, in order to manufacture food and to grow. It cannot live without chlorophyll, the green, and so any time you have a color change in a green plant or tree, it has a problem. And the oxidants borne in the polluted fogs and weather apparently cause a chemical change in the surface areas of the needles, thereby destroying that chlorophyll, and that gives us this yellowish cast that we see on some of our trees. All of those needles that are yellowed are—are no longer functioning for the pine.

CORRESPONDENT: Only the ponderosas the Forest Service keeps in greenhouses with filtered air seem to grow well. It is the ozone in the smog that chokes the trees. Ozone is created chemically by the action of sunlight on car exhaust. Dr. Paul Miller calls this forest a disaster area. He is a noted tree pathologist with the U.S. Forest Service, and a leader in smog research.

DR. PAUL MILLER: As you can see here on this tree, the most visible symptoms are the dead needle tips and also, as you look back along the base of the needles toward the base, you have this distinct chlorotic mottle, a yellow mottled condition which we use as a diagnostic symptom for ozone injury. Eventually, these needles will fall off and eventually the tree will look like this one here, where you have completely dead needles. . . . In this stand we have about 30 percent of the total of the stand being ponderosa pine. We know that half of that population is—is doomed to death. We're probably looking at the top of the iceberg here. In other words, we're seeing a lot of dead ponderosa pine, and we're not really able to assess the total effect on the ecosystem, effects on other animals that depend on the trees as a habitat and as a food base.

The dangers come from a variety of sources with a variety of effects. Item: Thirty-one major airlines agree to install devices cutting down on jet exhaust, estimated to cause 1 percent of the nation's air pollution, by the end of 1972. Item: Papers at a New York Academy of Sciences conference indicate that the toxic effect of carbon monoxide, both from cigarette smoking and automobile exhaust, may trigger highway accidents because of effects on both heart and vision. Item: The federal government asks the airlines to stop dumping an estimated 6,700 tons per year of jet fuel into the skies near airports; the residue that seeps into holding tanks when the jet engines are stopped either falls to the ground as liquid or stays in the air as noxious mist.

Item: New York State's highest court sanctions air pollution by a Hudson Valley cement company; the court rules that the company can continue pollution-causing activities after it pays property owners for damage done to their land, suggesting no future suits for pollution may be filed against the company; a dissenting judge says the ruling amounts to licensing a continuing wrong. Item: A University of North Carolina home economics professor estimates after a two-year study that air pollution costs Americans $2 billion annually in damage to textile fabrics alone, through disintegration of fibers, discoloration, and fading.

But the answers to pollution control are further confused by the question of balancing the good against the bad. The matter of pesticides and herbicides, for example, some-times seems insoluble. DDT was hailed in the beginning as a kind of environmental penicillin, a wonder drug for insect control. But it has long been regarded with suspicion as being a danger to humans as such and upsetting to ecological balance in the bargain. It was a prime villain, of course, in Rachel Carson's *Silent Spring,* perhaps the first book to focus attention on pesticide dangers.

After DDT was found to build up in human tissues and to cause cancer in laboratory mice, the Nixon administration in November of 1969 banned the bug killer for a variety of purposes.

During 1970, the Soviet Union halted production of DDT. In this country, various states—Wisconsin, Illinois, Maryland among them—slapped restrictions or total bans on the pesticide. Secretary of Agriculture Clifford Hardin said he would not suspend DDT sales totally, although its use in four control areas was ended. But Secretary of the Interior Walter Hickel banned DDT, along with fifteen other pesticides, on the 534 million acres of public land controlled by his department.

On June 8, 1970, Olin Corporation, manufacturer of about 20 percent of the nation's DDT supply, announced it was halting production of the product. Three environmental groups had gone to court to enjoin Olin from dumping waste containing DDT into waters in an Alabama wildlife refuge. But a spokesman said the corporation acted on policy "to conform not only with present environmental standards but with those we believe will be in effect in 1974."

Meanwhile DDT continues to be manufactured elsewhere, sold, and used.

CHARLES KURALT: The blue spruce and Sitka spruce and hemlock are coming down. They're logging Alaska. And when a tree falls, what happens to the bird who lives in the top of the tree, the big, rare bird with the white head and tail feathers, the national bird?

Well, the fact is we have treated the American bald eagle exactly as we have treated the land he stands for—callously. Always, in our history, if an eagle's nesting tree was valuable as timber, then the tree came down, and the eagles moved on. They have moved as far as they can go now, to the coast of Alaska, the last place on earth where they're found in any numbers. And here too they would be facing eviction if it weren't for one man.

On the rolls of the Fish and Wildlife Service, he is listed as United States Game Management Agent in Charge. What Fred Robards is in charge of, by his own choice, is eagles. A couple of years ago, he perceived that at the rate logging was proceeding in Alaska, the eagles didn't stand a chance. He knew of a law, the Bald Eagle Act, which was meant to protect the birds. In the face of powerful lumber interests, Fred Robards decided to enforce the law.

Ever since then, he has wandered the waters of southeastern Alaska, going ashore in quiet places like Suicide Cove, with an incredible purpose in mind, to find every single eagle in the Alaska panhandle, and to mark their nests for preservation. What's more, he has won the agreement of the Forest Service that saving one tree isn't enough. Hundreds of trees around the nests must also be preserved.

The subjects of Fred Robard's passion are wary of man, and not easy to see, even here. But if you travel with him for a couple of days, you will be rewarded by the sight of one of these great birds soaring silently above your head, or fishing among the gulls on the distant, shining sea, or looking for food along the shore.

FRED ROBARDS: I think it's a great bird, very beautiful, one that's completely, totally able to take care of itself. . . . They're beautiful. All except the eye, and it's a fierce eye. . . . In fact, I have never seen an eye in my life that can have quite the amount of ferocity that an eagle's eye can have. . . .

They have vision that is beyond comprehension. I mean, if it's compared to my vision, and I have twenty-twenty vision, they have vision that's perhaps eight to ten times the clarity of my vision. . . . I don't think that he has any enemies other than man himself. . . . Disturbance of the habitat by felling of timber, this would destroy the nesting in certain areas. And . . . outright destruction by man, the shooting of eagles . . . and . . . pesticides. . . . We don't use pesticides to any great extent up here because we have very little agricultural area. . . . They come from the oceans of the world, and this seems to be building up, and we're finding DDT in the bald eagle here, not of the same level that we find it in the southern race of bald eagle, but we are finding it in massive amounts, really. . . .

It is not only a matter of DDT. Mercury poisoning caused the death of eagles in Minnesota; dieldrin pesticides are found in a growing number of dead eagles.

Whatever your feelings about the national bird, there are the threats to people. Parathion, hailed as a DDT substitute, came under Agriculture Department investigation when it was linked to three farm deaths and thirty illnesses. After a scientific committee approved a controversial spraying program involving the use of 2,4,5-T, saying that complaints that it injured plants and animals, the committee citing these as natural causes, the Agriculture Department banned its use as a weed killer around homes, lakes, and on food crops because it produced "an imminent danger" to women of childbearing age. The product allegedly causes "abnormal development in unborn animals." A defoliant of which it is an ingredient, "agent orange," was banned for use in Vietnam by the Defense Department. The Agriculture ban does not apply to range, pastures, forests, and other nonagricultural lands in this country.

And yet the matter of air pollution in

this nation at this time rests largely on the greatest polluter of them all—the automobile. The automobile is almost the symbol of our triumphant technological society, and it's the number-one source of air pollution in the world today.

Now at last, under growing pressure, the auto industry has begun to clean up its own product. Every year the new cars pump out less pollution than the year before. Yet every year we Americans add almost 3 million more cars and trucks to the 90 million now on the road. So that sometime—estimates range between 1975 and 1990—total air pollution will start going up again, just from sheer masses of low-pollution vehicles.

One easy, obvious answer: switch to electric cars; they emit no pollution. But then we find that batteries are made of lead, and there isn't enough lead left in the world to power all the cars in this country alone. We know how to make batteries of other metals, but there's not enough of them, either. Anyhow, we would discover that just to charge the batteries to run all the cars in America, we'd have to double our coal-burning power plants, which are already our number-two air polluter, second only to the automobile.

So, while industry leaders have said they are willing to consider other types of engines for the cleanup, Detroit's wagon still seems firmly hitched to the familiar internal combustion machine, more than a century old, widely criticized for inefficiency and pollution. As Dr. William Agnew, General Motors' pollution control chief, explains it:

> We think the internal combustion machine is going to be our best bet. We're the furthest along in getting low emissions for the internal combustion machine, and at the same time it performs the automotive function better than any other power plant we know right now. So we think . . . this is the best bet, with modifications it can do the job. . . .

We think it'll meet the 1975 proposed standards by both the federal government and the California regulatory authorities. This means the control of emissions to about 90 to 95 percent below the present, the uncontrolled values on a 1961 or 1960 car, let's say.

The industry, maintaining it will clean up without government intervention, concedes that some legislation might be needed to keep its antipollution equipment in shape. It is now developing kits, costing around fifty dollars, to clean up the exhaust of older cars, but the cheerful optimist concedes that it would take laws to make drivers buy the kits.

Detroit seems convinced that it has broken the back of auto pollution, that the private car will no longer make any significant contribution to the brown cloud of filth hanging over our cities, that petroleum reserves will hold out or new power sources be developed—in short, that in spite of arguments from environmentalists, America can continue adding millions of new gasoline-burning vehicles to its highways far into the future.

Doubtful about that proposition, fifteen states have to date filed suit to force General Motors, Ford, Chrysler, and American Motors to produce pollution-free engines "at the earliest feasible" date. The suit, charging conspiracy among the manufacturers to block competition in developing such engines, asked the Supreme Court to order the defendants to install antipollution devices at their own expense on every car sold during the last seventeen years.

There are wheels within wheels in the matter of environment and auto pollution. Ralph Nader, the self-styled consumer's advocate, announced early in 1970 "Campaign GM," aimed at pressuring General Motors to be "more responsive" to the public interest. The group sought expansion of the company's board to add three consumer-oriented members and to establish a "Committee for Corporate Responsibility." At the annual stockholders' meeting in Detroit, Robert Townsend (author of *Up the Organization*) offered a battle plan:

> Now, the only way to get to these people is through their dealers. Don't buy any cars made by GM until they produce a clean one, and they could produce one very rapidly, and if enough Americans did that they'd produce a clean car in three years that wouldn't pollute the air. And don't—don't patronize their dealers with your old car. You know, everybody's hurting in their budget. Just say, all right, as a, you know, as a token to my own budget, I'm just—I'm going to make the old car last, and I'm going to take it to the mechanic at the Shell station, not back to the GM dealer.

"Campaign GM" representatives around the nation spoke with bankers, investors, and university trustees who held General Motors stock. The aim was to persuade them to vote their shares in favor of the campaign's demands. The project, in the words of one adherent, "is not to try to grab control of General Motors in any way. It's mainly to, let's say, insert a little bit more public responsibility where the public comes before the profits, not profits before the public."

And yet even those likely to approve of the campaign found themselves in a dollar dilemma. The trustee of an educational institute spoke about it:

> There is an honest difficulty in my . . . position here. It's our job to look out after Merrill-Palmer. Now, let's say that your group resulted in General Motors spending all of its excess moneys on pollution, and I know this is an absurd position, but there would be no dividends for Merrill-Palmer, which is already running at a deficit, and that is a problem that we have.

But, like many others, he said that while

he would cast the vote of the institute's shares with the management of GM, he would be willing to consider the campaign's demands again next year. The group of young lawyers generically referred to as Nader's Raiders did not expect to win the battle of proxies, and they didn't. They saw the campaign as a new form of dissent, to be directed at many major corporations in years to come.

General Motors was chosen "simply because it was the biggest company in the United States" and "who are they to run their business in a manner that doesn't take into account the massive public impact that they're going to have by running their business?"

General Motors saw "Campaign GM" in quite another light: first, government intervention if the Nader group attacks persist; second, an attack by the political left on American big business. As one spokesman put it, "This movement against GM is not just against one, General Motors. I think it's a move against the auto companies. I think it's really a move against the free enterprise system."

And so the matter of auto pollution gets lost in a political, social, and economic smog.

The oil companies, gearing up for the 1975 emission standards, are pushing a massive but somewhat confusing advertising campaign:

> TERRY DRINKWATER: Low-lead Chevron with F-310. No-lead Shell of the Future with TCP. Union low-lead regular. Enco's Big Plus, Arco's Lead-Free. Gulftane Low-Lead with Agent 724. Texaco's Lead Free, and a score of others. The new gasolines have bewildered the motoring public.
>
> For all of us, there are really three questions. First, should you use a non-lead or low-lead gasoline? Lead in the gas raises its octane, makes it more powerful. But like all heavy metals, lead is a poison. In the

polluted air of the cities, there are high concentrations of lead, thanks largely to leaded gasoline. As yet, there is no conclusive medical evidence linking illness to atmospheric lead, but there may be a connection.

As potentially serious as this poison aspect of lead is, it is not the primary reason that the gasoline companies are taking the lead out. The lead is coming out mainly because of the catalytic muffler. It is the device Detroit has decided to put on cars in the years to come to meet 1975 emission standards. The catalytic muffler, which removes large quantities of pollutants from the exhaust, cannot work with lead in the gasoline. . . .

The second question: what about the additives? Massive advertising campaigns are now selling detergent additives. Do they do any good, or any harm?

The Federal Trade Commission accused Chevron of false advertising. . . . The claim the commission objected to was that F-310 significantly reduces air pollution. How either Chevron or the FTC defines the words "significantly reduces" isn't clear. . . .

The experts we've consulted say detergent additives do not add anything harmful to exhaust. Your car probably will run a little better with them, and some pollutants in your exhaust will be reduced slightly. So, detergent additives? Yes. Buying gas with them is advisable.

Up to this point, we know the answers. The third area is a lot more controversial. As the lead in gasoline is removed, other chemical compounds can be put in to keep the octane up. These additives the companies aren't advertising. They are a class of chemicals called aromatics. Some of them have been in some gasolines for a long time, but in sufficiently greater concentrations they are known to cause cancer in animals.

Fond as we seem to be of blaming the automobile for all our ills, there is no indication that it will go away, or even that it should. Much fouling of our land and air and waters results because man, to put it inele-

gantly, is a slob, and Americans, having the most matter to dispose of, are the biggest slobs of all. If this seems strong, take a look around on your next drive through the countryside:

CHARLES KURALT: . . . 85, 86, 87, 88, 89, 90, 91, 92, 93, 94, 95, 96, 97, 98, 99, 100, and 1, 2, 3, 4—just counting beer cans. You can do the same along any highway in America, and you'll find that you have to be on a back road in a dry county before you average much less than a hundred, a hundred and fifty beer cans to the mile. The only thing wrong with this as a traveling game, in fact, is that along most roadsides of America the beer cans are too numerous to count.

America produces 48 billion beverage cans a year. That is about 230 cans for every man, woman, and child. If our population keeps going up as it is, and our consumption of beer and soft drinks goes up with it, thirty years from now there won't be 48 billion cans a year to worry about—there will be 155,664,000,000 every year. That will be almost enough to tinplate the country and be done with it. Go for a walk up any country lane or wilderness trail in America and you will find the beer cans of those who've gone before you.

There is something about beautiful places that makes people want to throw beer cans at them. The more beautiful—the more beer cans. This rule of nature occurred to us one day on the banks of the Chattahoochee River. With a stray dog who wandered by, we cleared a spot among the beer cans on the bank and sat down to watch the beer cans float by. There isn't a stream or a lake or a river in America that isn't full of beer cans.

The tin cans, of course, eventually rust away, although they may take ten or fifteen years to do it, but the new aluminum cans may be expected to last literally forever. They will no doubt be excavated by archaeologists of the future, still shiny bright— the ritual urns and vessels of twentieth-century America.

In the beginning, the earth, the good

earth, seemingly inexhaustible storehouse of all the needs of life—air, water, food, minerals. In the middle, us, modern technological man, whose hand now holds the world, and in no very gentle grip. And at the end, a billion battered beer cans, symbol of the garbage heap we are making of our planet.

It's a law of nature—nothing is created, nothing is destroyed. Every pound we carve from the flesh of the earth is going to wind up somewhere, probably as pollution. So even as we find those "inexhaustible" resources beginning to dry up, even as we discover that twelve of our twenty basic minerals may not last through the lifetime of our own children, we are threatened with destruction by mountains of our own waste. And that paradox gives us the beginnings of a glimmer of an answer.

Suppose you owned a stockpile with these resources: carbon, 25 percent; oxygen, 21 percent; glass and ceramics, 9 percent; metals, 7 percent; hydrogen, 3 percent. Why, you'd probably think you owned something rather valuable, and you would be right. What we've just listed is a partial chemical analysis of a municipal dump. To an extent this effluent society has not yet begun to understand, pollution is simply resources out of place.

How do you get them back into place, and into circulation?

How do we restructure our whole economy so that the manufacturer who pollutes no longer turns a bigger profit than the one who cleans up after himself, so there's more profit in reusing those out-of-place resources than in throwing them away to poison the most precious resources of all, our earth, our water, and our sky? In recent years, a new, maverick breed of economist has been breaking with traditional laissez-faire business thinking and coming up with techniques that

would take the profit out of pollution. Dr. Allen Kneese, of Resources for the Future, explains:

Without question, the best way is to put an actual price on those resources that are being used. Now, in my organization we have done quite a lot of research on how one might do this, especially in connection with rivers and lakes—water bodies. We call this device of putting a price on the use of the common property resource an effluent charge. This means that if, for example, a paper mill discharges a certain amount of waste into the water body, a government agency, representing us all, would put a price on that discharge.

The idea would be that this price should reflect the social costs of using that resource. Now, when that kind of a procedure is used, some very desirable things happen from the point of view of the environment. One is that the company then treats this like a scarce natural resource, just like labor is scarce, or like the pulp that it uses is scarce, and so forth, and it tries to economize on it.

That's a new thing, you see. Before, it's been treated as though it was completely free, so there wasn't any reason to economize on it. You just threw everything away that you found had no immediate value to you. And it was costless to throw it away and put the cost on somebody else.

Some of the cost will be passed forward to the consumer in higher prices. Now, many people kind of rebel against that, but there's a good reason why it should be, because these commodities that use a common property resource so heavily really are much more costly to produce than the current consumer prices would suggest that they are. And that means that the consumers don't have the proper incentive to economize on them, or to substitute other things which cost less for these which cost more. So that it's very important that an appropriate share of the cost be passed forward to the consumer.

The price of the cleanup is astronomical. Probably the only thing more expensive would be not cleaning up. Dr. Athelstan Spilhaus, one of the world's authorities on waste management, who wants big federal subsidies to encourage waste recycling, sees an outlay of $50 billion by 1975. Dr. Kneese, who sees the government's role in the cleanup as more policeman than partner, puts the total cost at $10 billion a year, but says only $3 billion a year should come from Washington. Even that is triple the amount President Nixon has proposed spending.

Certainly, if we are to rescue our environment, and the quality of our own life, we must live with another of Dr. Kneese's ideas: the individual must wind up paying for all of the environmental improvements in one way or another.

Or, as biologist Paul Ehrlich puts it, "There is no such thing as a free lunch."

The industrial ingenuity required to dispose of the 200 million tons of garbage dumped annually by opulent America may seem beyond us. There is literally no place to put it. Bury garbage and it ruins the underground water; burn it and it pollutes the air. It carries germs. It is, in one of those side effects of any war that are seldom noticed, a frequent trigger for ghetto disturbances by people who become inflamed as it piles up, uncollected.

But attach a profit to it and even garbage takes on a certain attraction:

MORTON DEAN: The idea of turning mounds of garbage into barrels of oil sounds a bit daffy, but scientists at the U.S. Bureau of Mines say that there's oil in them there hills of garbage, that from every ton of garbage you can draw one barrel of crude oil.

The discovery that you could produce a high grade of oil, low in air-polluting sulfur dioxide, was made at the Bureau of Mines Facility in Bruston, Pennsylvania, where each week a truck arrives loaded with bags of ground-up garbage, glass and tin cans already removed. As the stuff is wheeled into the laboratory for the great transformation, it is almost irreverent to call it garbage. Some scientists here speak of it as urban refuse, meaning wood, paper, cardboard, grass, as well as leftovers from the dinner table. . . . Dr. Herbert Appell reveals that at first he discovered he could coax crude oil out of ordinary paper towels, the kind found in rest rooms the world over.

DR. HERBERT APPELL: As part of this project we studied a number of compounds, including cellulose. These paper towels are mostly cellulose, and to our surprise we found that we could convert this cellulose very easily to an oil under pressure with carbon monoxide.

CORRESPONDENT: And then came the garbage experiment?

DR. APPELL: Yes. Some of our staff in Washington was interested in waste disposal. They suggested that I try an experiment with the garbage . . . it certainly worked very well.

CORRESPONDENT: The garbage is funneled into a heavy metal cylinder, part of what the scientists call an autoclave, and what the dictionary says is an apparatus using super-heated steam under pressure. The garbage is heated to 700 degrees Fahrenheit, carbon monoxide is forced into the system, pressured at 5,000 pounds per square inch. And, two hours later, there it is, a thick black liquid smelling very much like oil laced with garbage.

No one believes this new approach will compete with the more traditional way of producing crude oil, but Dr. Irving Wender, who years ago worked on the atom bomb project, proudly expects that one day soon garbage will become a national resource.

DR. IRVING WENDER: Well, we've figured out that a person, one person in the United States, is responsible for about a ton of garbage per year, and that we can convert a ton of garbage into a barrel of oil. That's about forty-two gallons. And you can almost think of a pipeline being built in a large city where somebody would take their garbage over to the—to some opening . . . in this pipeline, and then it would be funneled to a central plant where all of it would be converted to oil and water, and a very, very small residue . . . the residue is mostly clay and silica, which is the same as dirt, anyway, and would make no problem . . . if dumped somewhere.

The question of pollution control, the larger question of whether the world can be saved, centers on two rival philosophies—two wholly different and antagonistic ways of attacking the environmental crisis.

Detroit represents the philosophical party in power, the certainty that the same

technology that has gotten us into such terrible trouble can, by an extension of the same ideas, get us out again, and that nothing really has to change very much. Consumption, and gross national product, can continue to burgeon, world without end.

The second school of thought is out of power, centered on the campuses. It's broad and it's deep, not among the radical fringe but among the most creative elements of the emerging generation. It's a reaction against the endless multiplication of cars, highways, cities—of *things*, not only as environmental problems in themselves but as a kind of mystical heresy against the earth and against the human spirit.

A Turning of the Tide

even the most pessimistic concede that there exists today some recognition of environmental problems unrecognized short years ago. whether we possess the moral nerve and stamina to act on that recognition is another matter. the staged destruction of an automobile may simply be another happening popular among the decade's young; and so, perhaps, were the Earth Day ceremonies, a herding together of proper thinkers. but there is increasing evidence that the long, hard war against waste and despoliation is under way. you can fight city hall.

More than most Americans, conservationists know that the price of liberty is eternal vigilance. At the opening of the decade's first year, an agreement was reached between federal and Florida officials banning construction of a major international jetport near the Everglades National Park. The Dade

County Port Authority had already spent almost $14 million on the site.

For decades now, at least since the great land boom of the twenties, Florida has been fair game for real estate developers to buy virgin land and use it as the site for everything from modest apartment houses to the gilded joys of Miami Beach. But, in a new spirit of the seventies, Florida developers are running into effective resistance from conservationists:

FOSTER DAVIS: Honeymoon Island, Florida. It nestles in the shallow water just off Florida's Gulf Coast. It's about two miles long, and right now there's not much on it but sand dunes, sea oats, and birds.

A few years ago, a familiar Florida story —developers moving in with plans to expand Honeymoon Island to five times its present size, scooping out nineteen million cubic yards of gulf bottom to create nearly two square miles of brand new, highly salable land, one of the largest landfill projects in Florida's history.

All this is fill, like the public beach back there. A year ago all of this was under water, or, in the developer's language, submerged land. Now the developers want to finish dredging and filling here. They want to put motels along here, and houses over there, on the other side of that tree line. The developers put in over a hundred of their planned fourteen hundred new acres, but then their dredging permit from the Army Corps of Engineers expired. And this time, when they went to renew the permit, they found the atmosphere in Florida had changed.

FIRST WOMAN: I think to put condominiums and high rises on these glorious nuggets of sand is just a desecration to the land we put them on.

FIRST MAN: To take nineteen million cubic yards of fill would be one of the most calamitous things that could happen in this time. To fill eleven hundred acres would make not only one of the largest island fills, but would also be one of the most damaging ones. We need every inch of this bay.

SECOND MAN: We're simply asking for you to maintain a quality of life where a man can go out and fish, have a place to go outside of his business, and relax, maybe sit there with his son when the dawn comes up in the morning, talk over matters that might be of importance to those two people.

SECOND WOMAN: Much of our activity, and that of our children, is centered around this environment. Swimming, boating, fishing, and the pleasures of watching our priceless seabirds—these are the things that give our area its unique character, and are an irreplaceable heritage for our children and grandchildren. We appeal to you today to help us preserve this way of life.

CORRESPONDENT: A year ago it was the federal government that blocked the Everglades jetport, but this year the Honeymoon Island resistance is coming from Floridians who, rightly or wrongly, are convinced it would make their area a poor place to live.

The concerned environmentalist must steel himself for a hard look at seemingly incurable wounds, like a surgeon in the midst of bloody battle. Cleopatra's Needle, in Central Park, shows more damage after a half century exposed to New York's industrial and automotive fumes than it did after a millennium of African sun and sand.

And yet, even with living creatures, the damage, if it has not gone too far, can be reversed, like an illness caught before the terminal stage. The crucial point is the interaction of ecology. As a demonstration, one of nature's elder citizens and the entire life cycle of a magnificent southern wilderness appears saved, in large part because of a law passed in New York City:

CORRESPONDENT: The Everglades, a river of grass through which fresh, cool water trickles slowly to the sea. The amount and variety of life in this one-and-a-half-million-acre park are scarcely to be believed. Fish teem in its shallows; water birds fill its skies. Almost every bush, every bank, every rock, reveals something alive. But much of that life depends on the 'Glades' least lovely creature, and until this year the creature that seemed most likely to become extinct.

The alligator, unlikely star of what's starting to look like a major conservation success story. Assistant Chief Ranger Richard

Stokes, a great fan of the alligator, details its comeback and its critical role in preserving the 'Glades.

RICHARD STOKES: One of its most important functions is to preserve the wildlife during the drought periods in the Everglades. They dig holes out in the Everglades where the fish survive, the birds feed, the alligators feed, the animals feed, and also get water. And then, as the water rises in the Everglades, these fish come out of the holes and repopulate the Everglades. In addition to that, they help control the rough fish, the turtles, and keep the sloughs open, and they're just a tremendous value to us here in the park; in fact, probably the one most important critter we have in the whole park is the alligator. . . .

We started working on saving the alligator a number of years ago, and we now have federal legislation, new state legislation, and city legislation even as far away as New York City, which is helping us to preserve the alligator, do away with the market. And our alligator populations are looking good. But, of course, there is no tremendous increase because they haven't had a nesting season since the laws have been passed. But we're seeing them in places where normally if they were there they would be poached, along the canals on the borders of the park, we see alligators there all the time, and a year ago if an alligator got out there, he wouldn't last over two, three nights.

CORRESPONDENT: Not long ago, one of these alligators would have been worth five dollars a running foot in New York City's garment district, but the demand is drying up. By next month it will be illegal to ship him interstate, and illegal to sell his hide in New York. The Florida alligator appears safe to be fruitful, multiply, and thrash about in the cool mud, digging the holes that will help keep the whole Everglades alive through the next drought.

One of the reasons we find ourselves in such desperate environmental trouble today has been man's sheer inability to predict the consequences of his actions. If he sees a traffic jam, he decides to build a freeway, but the freeway generates more traffic than it can handle, destroys a series of possibly healthy neighborhoods in the process, and perhaps a whole city falls into decay.

Just beginning now is a movement to predict the future, actually to simulate the future, using the vast capacity of electronic computers to work out all the consequences of a given action before we inflict it on the landscape. The most advanced program of the kind is in progress just across the border in Canada.

North of Seattle, in the Strait of Georgia between Vancouver and Victoria, British Columbia, lie the Gulf Islands, the Misty Islands, forty or more of them, remote stands of Douglas fir and wild lilac, of Tom Sawyer and Izaak Walton coves, a last great natural reserve, with only here and there a few summer cabins beginning to alter the landscape.

A team of specialists from the University of British Columbia decided to probe the future of the Gulf Islands on a computer, correlating whole libraries of data on what has happened to land in the past, in an attempt to simulate, or "model," what will happen to the islands from here on:

DR. C. S. HOLLING: The model is an attempt to identify all the various actions and interactions that occur when a mass of land like the Gulf Islands that's largely used for recreation is under exploitation.

The computer attempts to predict the future by taking note of the past. It is programmed with details of what has happened to other communities when given types of action have taken place. The function of the computer is to weigh the variables, note which factors are the same and which are different, sort out the interrelationship of forces, and make a prediction of probable results. The process can be incredibly complex. A typical application: Charles Wakelin, head of the Capital Regional District, which is charged with planning the area's future, requested a computer run simulating the impact of a bridge to the island:

> DR. MICHAEL GOLDBERG: We can see, with the introduction of this hypothetical bridge, that there's a very large increase in speculation, and that the number of developers getting into the market to develop land increases and the amount of land that's released as a result of this speculation is very, very spectacular, and that puts that little blip into the land system.

> CHARLES WAKELIN: So all the best land really is being used up, and really the islands have become . . . covered by a sea of houses, I guess, almost as if it were in the Vancouver area now, solidly urbanized.

When such simulations showed the islands on the verge of a real estate boom that could destroy them, the provincial government promptly banned all trading in small lots, perhaps the first significant political decision to be based on a computer warning of a resource in peril. Now scientists and government planners have launched a vastly more ambitious project, a computer model for the future of the entire Vancouver area:

> DR. HOLLING: What would happen if a freeway system went into the Vancouver region? What will happen when the superport down at Roberts Banks goes in? How will this distort the agricultural patterns, the recreational pattern—what will this do to wild-fowl, for example? What will it do to the poor citizens of the community? Will this enrich them, or will this just exaggerate the separation between the rich and the poor?

Vancouver is as beautifully sited as any city on earth, its head in snowcapped mountains, its feet in blue water. In the fashionable West End, whole neighborhoods in flower, streets alive with cherry blossoms, immaculate $50,000 homes. Downtown, the subtle beginnings of urban sprawl, of traffic jams, smog, of sheer asphalt ugliness. In other words, a city like all cities. The attempt to formulate this city's future on a computer has snatched the Holling group out of the groves of academe and plunged it into the middle of real world politics. At City Hall, Alderman Arthur Phillips saw computer simulation as a valuable legislative tool.

"My business is investment management in the real world," he said, "and I'm used to a lot of data, a lot of information, and we just don't have it on cities. It's a great gap which I think this would help fill."

In Vancouver's squalid East End, Harry Rankin, avowed Marxist and gadfly of the establishment, was the only alderman to vote against the attempt to forecast and guide Vancouver's future with Dr. Holling's computers. But he expressed a reservation that, translated from Marx, is shared by some others:

> HARRY RANKIN: A computer is not a rational instrument. A computer is simply a machine, or whatever you want to call it, where you put your ideas into that machine. Middle-class values will come out middle-class values, working-class values will come out working-class values, and upper-class values, whatever they may be—come up—will come out as upper-class values. There is no neutral instrument, and that's really what they're trying to put over on people, that here we have a completely neutral instrument that will solve the problems of the community—technocracy, the engineering society, the professors running society.

> ARTHUR PHILLIPS: I think you have to be conscious of this sort of possibility, but the real protection against that sort of thing is to—is the elected people. I think you're going to find that the elected people are still responsive to the public, very human in their reactions, and so on, and aren't going to

necessarily completely trust any computer anyhow, so that they will be there to override, if you like, any dehumanizing effect that a computer might have, or that the technicians that operate it . . . might acquire.

There are dangers in computer simulation of the future, the danger of establishing an elite class, high priests of the machine, the more mundane likelihood that politicians, realtors, or other vested interests might use inside knowledge for enormous gain at public expense, and even the basic problem that we know far too little about what really constitutes the good life for human beings to be certain what directions the future should take.

But whatever the drawbacks, and despite America's traditional suspicion of large-scale government planning, there are many who believe we would do well to take a long look at electronic simulation and the chance to make our mistakes on a computer. Up to now we have made all our mistakes on the landscape, and that landscape—our country and our world—cannot absorb many more mistakes.

The knowledgeable agree that the public is aware of the environment now and acting on that awareness. But the biggest problem is not pollution, no matter what its importance. Pollution is only a symptom.

The illness itself is so basic, so wrapped in man's deepest nature and inmost beliefs, that until recently it remained pretty much a closed-door topic. Dr. Rene Dubos puts it succinctly: "The population cannot continue to grow. It should not; it cannot. There will be disasters."

For most of man's two million years on earth, our history has looked like that of any other species—a high birthrate, a high death rate, combining for a very slow expansion of the population. Not until the year 1830 were there a billion people on earth. But that slight upturn, starting around the end of the eighteenth century, became one of the most remarkable events in the history of life—the medical revolution.

As science kept more and more of us alive longer, we reached our second billion in just one hundred years, our third in thirty years. Today, human population is shooting up almost at right angles, so that by the year 2000 there will be twice as many of us on earth as there are today, 7.5 billion people, with another billion every five years.

A further reason why ours may be the last generation that can begin to save the future: by some estimates, one-half of the world is undernourished today. Ten or twenty million people starve to death each year. But the danger is from those who live.

It's now clear that some forms of malnutrition in the unborn child and the infant can permanently impair development of the brain. In effect, the human race is frantically producing more and more people and of lower and lower intelligence, when what is needed is fewer people and of keener intellect.

And if you ask those population authorities where in all the world you can find an effective, broad-scale program of population control, the answer is: there is no such place.

Consider the matter of abortion reform. Last year, advocates of abortion reform pushed their measures with the fervor of persons who believe the time for their idea is at hand. They achieved some success— major reforms in Hawaii and New York, assurance that a similar sort of reform is near in Maryland, strong challenges of existing legislation in Wisconsin and other states.

But both advocates of reform and its opponents bring tremendous pressure to bear on this most emotional of issues. The New

York reform bill passed by one vote on April 10, 1970.

State Assemblyman George Michaels of upstate Auburn cast the deciding vote on a bill legalizing abortions, *for any reason,* up to the twenty-fourth week of pregnancy, the decision to be made between a woman and her physician. Under the old law, legal abortions were permissible only if the mother's life was in danger.

On the roll call, Michaels had voted against the reform bill. His district is predominantly Roman Catholic, and he knew the voters' beliefs on the matter. When it became clear that the bill would fail unless one vote was changed, George Michaels, his voice breaking, was clearly a man in torment as he asked for the Speaker's attention:

> Mr. Speaker, I ask your indulgence. Just before I left for Albany this week, my son Jim, who, as you recall, Mr. Speaker, gave the invocation to this Assembly on February 4, and he said, "Dad, for God's sake, don't let your vote be the vote that defeats this bill." I cannot go back to my family on the first Passover Seder and tell them that George Michaels defeated this bill, so, Mr. Speaker, I fully appreciate that this is the termination of my political career, but I cannot in good conscience stand here and thwart the obvious majority of this house, the members of whom I dearly love and for whom I have a great deal of affection. I'll probably never come back here again to share these things with you, Mr. Speaker, but I must have some peace in my family.
>
> I therefore request you, Mr. Speaker, to change my negative vote to an affirmative vote.

Michaels was right. The voters of his district did not return him to the Assembly.

Population control, before or after conception, is the touchiest of political subjects. It hits head on against certain religious beliefs. Beyond that, entire cultures are based on the premise that large families are a form of wealth, insurance against diseases that used to wipe out the young, proof of masculine virility and feminine fertility.

The earth mother broods over ancestral myths. The childless woman through the halls of literature and drama serves as a figure of fun or tragedy; to make her a heroine, as has recently been suggested, requires breaking a cultural mold dating back through centuries.

For those women who wanted to limit the size of their families, or to delay childbearing, the pill, an oral contraceptive, seemed the answer to a dream when it came on the market in 1960. Women turned to it slowly at first, and then in rapidly growing numbers, until at the opening of this decade almost nine million women in America and ten million elsewhere were taking the pill each day, in the words of one expert, "as automatically as chickens eating corn."

Eight U.S. pharmaceutical houses produce twenty-nine varieties by the thousands every minute, and the pill is a $300 million industry. The pill is also linked with starting a sexual revolution, freeing women from inhibitions caused by fear of unwanted pregnancy. But the safety of the pill became a public question in 1970, as a Senate subcommittee opened hearings on the subject.

The first witnesses expressed alarm over the pill's potential hazards. Dr. Hugh Davis of Johns Hopkins University testified that the pill's side effects were so great that if it were a food product it probably would be taken off the market:

> It is medically unsound to administer such powerful synthetic hormones in order to achieve birth control objectives which can be reached by simple means of greater safety. It seems to me extremely unwise to officially license, sponsor, and encourage a long-range experiment such as we now have in progress on the effects of chronic ingestion of these

synthetic hormones. Even if one ignores the findings of altered metabolism in the direction of diabetes and the elevated serum changes suggesting a serious potential hazard or arteriosclerosis, a nagging specter of cancer remains.

This is not to suggest, however, that the oral contraceptives should be withdrawn from the market, despite the mounting concern regarding their safety. These agents are extremely valuable for the treatment of many diseases and incapacitating conditions in gynecology. There are also certain women who cannot or will not use effectively other methods of birth control. It would be tragic not to have these agents available for the treatment of disease, just as it may prove equally tragic to continue dispensing the pill in an almost completely permissive atmosphere.

Other witnesses before the subcommittee, chaired by Senator Gaylord Nelson, described dangers in oral contraception, one specialist saying that synthetic estrogen, banned for fattening chickens because it caused cancer in some laboratory animals, was allowed for use in the pill.

One hearing was disrupted by women describing themselves as Washington supporters of women's liberation:

FIRST WOMAN: All the women here have suffered ill effects from the use of the pill, and we were told by the doctors, while suffering these effects and afterward, to go on taking the pill.

SECOND WOMAN: I got pregnant when I was on the pill, and you should know that every . . . woman . . . in our group, which is about three hundred women, had some kind of side effects while they were on the pill.

Robert Finch, then health, education, and welfare secretary, said he hoped that "scare talk" would not cause women to stop using the pill:

And we are continuing to study the side effects. We know there are some side effects

in a relatively small percentage of women, in the various kinds of pills that are on the market. But by and large, pending these studies that we have coming up, there is no question but what . . . the greater good to the . . . woman in terms of her own physical health and avoiding unwanted pregnancies is much, much higher than any possible danger. We can make that general statement.

By February, 1970, when the Senate reopened its hearings on the safety of the pill, it was charged that earlier testimony had created a worldwide panic.

The head of Planned Parenthood said the hearing spread "unwarranted and dangerous alarm" throughout the world.

A specialist in population control, Dr. Allen Guttmacher, told the senators that statistics show that pregnancy is more dangerous to women than the birth control pill.

Mrs. Phyllis Piotrow, mother of two and a member of the Population Crisis Committee, said the hearings would result in "Nelson babies," unwanted children born after frightening statements of earlier witnesses:

From a woman's point of view, there are several issues which stand out in this controversy and which have not been sufficiently emphasized, perhaps because most of the initial witnesses were men. First and foremost, it is a biological fact that all of the mortality associated with human reproduction is borne by the female. There are no male fatalities from pregnancy or childbirth.

A Louisiana program called Family Planning, Incorporated, has drawn the interested attention of observers from such states as New Jersey, Texas, and California, and from other nations, including India, Argentina, and Poland. One of its aims is to space out or limit the number of children born to those poor who cannot adequately feed or clothe the children they already have.

Founded five years ago by Dr. Joseph Beasley, a pediatrician, when it was still a felony in the state to distribute birth control information, the organization has seen that law erased from the books and now operates without active Roman Catholic opposition, an important factor in a state that is 36 percent Catholic.

"We have never had their support," says Dr. Beasley. "But certainly we've been able to agree on a set of principles by which we could operate."

The program is strongly backed by the federal government with contributions totaling more than $4 million. An additional million has come from such foundations as Ford and Rockefeller. The state offers no money but provides the use of existing health facilities.

Each participant is given the opportunity to make up her own mind. If she's a Catholic, she is asked whether she knows her church's position on birth control. If not, she's referred to a priest. But if she decides she wants to use something other than the approved rhythm method, the clinics provide it free of cost—the pill, the intrauterine device, the diaphragm, foam.

Family Planning, Incorporated, however, is more than a pill-pushing program. There is prenatal care for pregnant women and a program for children already on this earth. A total health concept, it involves doctors from Tulane and Louisiana State University and in private practice.

The program has done away with the myth that the indigent will not respond to family planning. The rate of illegitimate births can be dramatically reduced—in one parish (county), such births declined 40 percent in a single year. These are valuable lessons, especially to an underdeveloped nation with a population growth as much as seven times that of the United States.

But there is a shortcoming. The program is aimed at the poor, and it is not the poor of this country who are the major contributors to population growth. Of the 3.5 million new babies born in the United States each year, fully two-thirds are born to the middle class and the well off.

The Food and Drug Administration told the senators it had prepared a leaflet to accompany each box of pills warning women of possible side effects. But for all the hearings and the accompanying arguments, it cannot be said that there was any meaningful advance toward population control in this first year of the decade. We have yet to take that first step, as Eric Sevareid analyzed:

At the time of that giant leap for mankind last summer, the popular reaction was that if we can so magnificently do something so complicated as reaching the moon, then we ought to be able to clean up our environment and make our small space on earth fit for human habitation. But reaching the moon is a far simpler operation, for one reason: there are no people between earth and moon.

Here on earth the problem that people face is people. Destruction of our living space is directly connected with the creation of more human lives. The greatest threat to the human race is its instinct for perpetuating itself.

When the secretary of health, education, and welfare spoke to an environment meeting here the other day, he suggested that government might have to offer "disincentives" to keep families small. And today Senator [Robert] Packwood of Oregon . . . announced . . . a bill that would forbid a taxpayer to claim tax exemption for more than three children.

That's a disincentive. There could be direct incentives to accomplish the same end. One idea is to provide a direct payment of, say, $500 to families in low income brackets for each year they do not have a child, and to grant the same amount in tax relief to higher income families who don't have a child during the year.

A good many such proposals are on the way and will produce serious debate. Two things are beginning to dawn on many people of potential influence: one, that we can't diminish the poisoning of the earth's waters and air and the various associated malfunctionings of life unless we diminish the birthrate sharply; and two, that voluntary birth control, without the prod of direct economic incentives or disincentives, is not going to diminish the rate sufficiently.

Some people, looking far ahead, foresee the day of not only free and legal abortions, but compulsory sterilization as these things get truly desperate. The more immediate stage will be these financial devices. Other peoples in the world, even those more desperately crowded, see the American problem in a different light.

They see that with only 6 percent of the world's population, America consumes 35 percent of the raw materials produced every year on the entire globe. In terms of raw materials, food, power, living space, and general stuff, each American baby is a threat to the world's livability some fifty times bigger than each baby born in India.

At times most of us have probably felt an impulsive wish to isolate this country from the rest of the world and its troubles, but the rest of the world can't isolate itself from us and our effects upon the world.

Neck-deep in "garbage," the environmentalist looks beyond the obvious symbols of ravaged field and polluted stream trampled by unwanted and hungry children, beyond the automobile graveyards slicked over by soot and fallout.

Of all the creatures on this earth, none is more generally revered, feared, and wondered at than the whale. He is, along with man, woman, and firmament, in the Book of Genesis: "And God created great whales."

This far along the road toward whatever ultimate end, the whale—his symbolic servitude not yet over—offers himself as an embodiment, a vast and archetypal monarch as symbol of the deeps that were all our beginnings, being edged toward extinction by a creature more cunning if less wise.

The story of the whale in our time is almost too perfect an analogy: he is mighty, ageless, and in great trouble. Man, a conqueror seemingly unaware how close he himself is to the same fate, wages his war through a technology he cannot control. We can save the whale or kill him; save ourselves or commit suicide.

We know the alternatives; we have the means.

From waters off Japan:

ED RABEL: We are sailing out of the Japanese port of Ayukawa into the North Pacific aboard a whaling ship equipped with a cannon high upon the bow. Within the barrel there is a whaling harpoon with a bomb in its head. Soon it will be fired into the body of the largest of all sea creatures, and there it will explode, and the leviathan will die.

Standing there beside the powerful gun, the wind at your face, there are recollections of a time when men died while stalking whales, of small harpoons piercing the sides of giant spouting mammals. But aboard the diesel whale catcher *Tashimaru*, capable of seventeen knots and equipped with electronic eyes and ears and a cannon mounted at its peak, even the great white sperm whale, the hero monster of *Moby Dick*, with the largest brain of any animal, would be no match.

Soon we are upon the whales, a dozen or more swimming and spouting. Koki Huntuwa, who has stood for fourteen years at the trigger lever of a harpoon gun, has taken command. While directing the movements of the highly maneuverable boat using a small microphone mounted in the gun, Huntuwa's squinting eyes are fixed on the now frightened animals.

Huntuwa has killed his first whale of the day. But he has made a mistake; the mortally wounded animal is a female with her calf alongside. Whaling rules prohibit killing females with calves. As the whale is pulled nearby, the calf swims protectively around her. Then, almost as if sensing the hopelessness of the situation, the calf swims away. A huge rubber float, a radio buoy, and a radar reflector with the whaling company's identifying flag are shackled to the corpse. The dead whale is then set adrift, to be picked up when the day's hunt is done.

The gunner commands the ship to return to the hunt, for the whales have taken flight. Whales, like humans, must breathe, and these frightened whales, like frightened humans, gasp for breath. But they cannot outrun the fast boat, and the killing resumes.

At the end of the hunt the *Tashimaru* returns to pick up the catch. One of the whales, thought to be dead, has survived and is swimming away with the attached radar reflector pinpointing its location. The boat must pursue. The whale is overtaken and harpooned once again. It is learned the whale has swum six miles from where it was originally harpooned.

Working quickly, the crew picks up each whale, lashing them to the side of the boat. The floats and flags are also retrieved and stowed for another hunt to come the next day.

For the crew of the *Tashimaru*, the hunt has been a big success. Two and a half hours after the whales were spotted, ten of them had been harpooned, and in less than a day from our departure we are headed back to port, the whales at our side.

Fears that whales are being hunted to extinction are reinforced by observing the efficiency of this whaling ship. In the past decade alone, 607,000 whales have been slaughtered, mostly by the Japanese and Russians. Altogether, the three major whaling companies killed 61 sperm whales on this day. The number slaughtered by the Tayo Company's three boats was 29 sperm whales. It is estimated the day's catch is worth $11,000.

Whales are processed into margarine, soap, hand cream, suntan oil, lipstick, paint dryer, cat and dog food, shoe polish, and fertilizer. But of all the products of whales, meat is the most important to the Japanese. They will eat 127,000 tons of whale meat this year. It would seem the laws of economics would eventually force the Japanese to stop whaling, but, although the international demand for whale products is dropping and substitutes for most whale products are readily available, Japan's whalers insist they must go right on killing whales, just to satisfy their country's demand for the meat.

Today a whale is killed every twelve minutes. So intensive is the slaughter that some scientists say no sperm whale ever dies of old age. The argument is frequently heard that our environmental crisis will solve itself because, as industry faces the end of its raw materials, it will become more careful, will conserve and protect the resources it now destroys. The recent history of the whaling industry offers little hope for that theory.

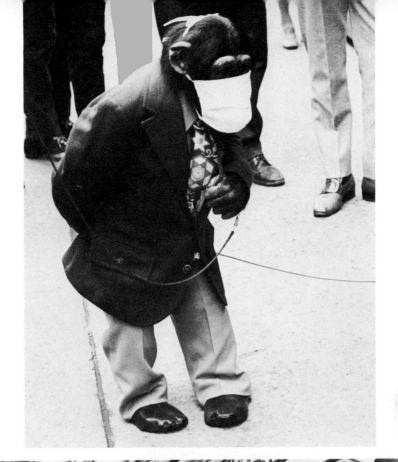

Polluted stream.

Helicopter hovers over flaming platform following explosion and oil leakage from offshore oil well into the Gulf of Mexico.

Members of the Martha's Vineyard Eco-Action and Catastrophe Committee protesting destruction of hundreds of ducks and other water birds from oil slick off the Vineyard coast.

Oil-soaked waterfowl off New England coast.

Oil-soaked seabirds rescued from their nesting ground at Hoe Point, Cornwall, England.

Sorry, son, no fishing today;
all the fish are dead.

The Ceaseless Fire

the new decade saw new American concern with the Middle East. for the first time since the mid-sixties an area other than Southeast Asia was the stage for confrontation between the superpowers. the Middle East, of course, has been a powder keg since about the time that cliché was invented, a kind of permanent Balkan situation. the stakes are as large as they are obvious: the fourteen touchy members of the Arab League, none of them out from under foreign rule more than a generation or so, control much of the known major oil supplies of the world; Israel, feared and hated by most of them, represents what United States foreign policy traditionally regards as a pressing spiritual debt. so interests in the Mideast—both monetary and moral—continue to clash.

For the United Nations, "keeping peace" in the Middle East is an ambiguous term. Middle East peace is a relative matter.

Egypt, ideologically spoiling for a fight, was shaken in 1970 by the death of President Gamal Abdel Nasser, the major Arab surrogate figure in the past five hundred years. Yet even Egypt in its shock and anger seemed a calming force on the Arab side compared to the fiery leaders of Syria and of the Jordanian guerrillas.

The war simply goes on, a kind of toothache of the world. A ninety-day truce, supervised by the United Nations, is extended —and violence continues through it all.

Some observers, including President Nixon, have said the conflict in the Middle East is more serious than the situation in Indochina. In midyear of 1970 Eric Sevareid had observed:

> The last thing the American government wants and the last thing the general American nervous system could stand would be direct involvement in a Mideast crisis on top of Vietnam and Cambodia. The President has called the situation in the Mideast terribly dangerous, and American diplomats are trying once again for direct private talks with Soviet diplomats.
>
> The immediate danger involves control of the air over the Suez Canal area and what the Egyptians or the Israelis will attempt on the ground when that control shifts or seems about to shift.
>
> Beyond that lies the unhappy prospect of an escalation of both Soviet and American military power in the eastern Mediterranean, and even if this stays within peaceful bounds, as both powers obviously wish, beyond all that, in the more distant future, lies the prospect of stronger Soviet influence over that arc of small countries which provide the basic means of industrial existence for most of the non-Communist world.
>
> Nobody is thinking in the stark terms of all the Arab nations suddenly shutting off their oil at the behest of Russia or anybody else; they must, after all, sell to live as others must buy to live.
>
> But the current drift of events and emotions there is seriously alarming virtually everyone here who understands the meaning of oil. Soviet influence has grown in Aden and Yemen, oil installations have been nationalized in Algeria, production has been cut back in Libya, and the power of the extremist do-or-die Palestinian Arabs steadily grows in various countries. There is now the greatest anxiety inside the oil companies for the safety of their employees and installations. It would not take much to set off mob actions, one reason Washington prefers to quietly replace Israeli aircraft losses a few at a time rather than issue any dramatic announcement of a big plane shipment.
>
> Several new studies have been made about world oil supplies and the future, and the facts look bleak. Nothing in sight will alter world dependence on the Mideast, from which both Europe and Japan draw more than three-fourths of their oil.
>
> The eight-billion-barrel reserves recently discovered under the North Sea could supply the non-Communist world for less than six months. The North Sea, the Alaskan North Slope, and all else combined cannot replace

Mideast oil. In fact, Mideast oil production must be drastically increased by 1980 if the needs of the non-Communist world are to be met.

The Soviets are quite aware that those hot, sandy little countries with their unstable regimes constitute the Achilles heel of half the industrialized world. What they will try to do with this knowledge is the name of the diplomatic guessing game.

Raids, then, and counterraids. No major war since the 1967 Six-Day War, although the threat exists and is real. And the strangest tactic of all—hijacking.

Diplomacy by Hijack

the practice is new enough to strain the resources of word coiners: "skyjacking" is a bad kind of pun, "air hijacking" almost redundant. the politics of war always involves the innocent. soldiers do not start wars; failed politicians and generals do. the "grunt," the GI of all nations, begins his military career as a hostage of the soul, forced to risk his life because his leaders have blundered. war is nothing more than a failure of diplomacy. today it may involve nothing more dramatic than an air travel credit card.

Few people in the world are more troubled than the three million Arab refugees of Palestine. Like many desperate men everywhere, they take to desperate measures. The concept of airplane hijack is not new. Back in 1968 an El Al Israel aircraft had been diverted for political purposes; on April 21 of 1970 a Zurich-to-Israel plane was bombed with forty-seven persons aboard, the Palestine Liberation Organization claiming credit which it later repudiated.

But four days in early fall saw the boldest, maddest attempt ever to call the world's attention to the plight of the Palestinian refugees whose home seemed to be nowhere.

Starting on Sunday, September 6, four Arab guerrilla hijackings were attempted and three of them worked. What had been regarded as the senseless act of the baggy-pants ideologists brought the world to the edge of war in a bizarre move by the Popular Front for the Liberation of Palestine, a Marxist group not to be confused with the larger Palestine Liberation Organization.

The synchronized attacks involved an El Al flight from Tel Aviv to London—the male leader killed by armed guards, a charismatic woman named Leila Khaled subdued. It appeared that Israeli airline officials had the right idea, since the other hijackings worked: a Pan American 747 flight from Amsterdam to New York, a TWA flight out of Frankfurt, and a Swissair DC-8 from Zurich. Two of the three hijacked planes were flown to a desert airstrip in Jordan, where they were joined later by a hijacked BOAC plane. The Pan Am 747 was flown to Cairo, where it was blown up moments after those on board had disembarked.

These were the most demonstrably irresponsible acts of recent politics, and yet the drama itself, personae representing idea, commanded world attention. This was an example of being able to see events happen that could spell out your own future. The guerrillas threatened to blow up the hostages along with the aircraft unless their demands were met, including the release of convicted terrorists by Great Britain, Switzerland, West Germany, and Israel. Passengers were told that the multiple hijacking was what the world deserved for ignoring the Palestinians and for not realizing that "twenty-two years of misery" in refugee camps, after they were pushed out of what is now Israel, would someday produce a hard core of desperate men and women. The Popular Front had prepared the desert airstrip days in advance, planting mines and fortifying what it called the "revolution airfield" against an expected attack by the Jordanian army.

Americans were held captive on the airstrip in the most dramatic and frightening series of hijackings in history, and President Nixon prepared to announce plans for armed guards aboard international flights of U.S. planes.

For some of the hostages' families in the United States the ordeal was a remembered hell. Alexander Herman of Brooklyn spoke of his seventeen-year-old daughter, Miriam. "My wife was four years in Auschwitz," he said, "and I was four years in a concentration camp in Hungary, and I lost four children by Hitler, and now I am going through the same thing again."

So, too, did Nathan Leser of New York, whose wife and two children were hostages. In his words: "We went through five years in a concentration camp, and we never expected in our lives that our children would be exposed to similar types of mental torture."

The drama played itself out under a tension unusual even for this century. President Nixon was described as incensed about the international kidnapping nightmare, determined to keep his tongue and his temper only as long as hostages were still held, more than three hundred of them, in spite of moderating arguments from Arab leaders. The International Red Cross said that the planes, loaded with dynamite, could be destroyed at any time. And, on September 12, they were, after the passengers were removed.

It was the most curious of situations, the world watching as the debate went on, the tenseness of the situation revealed in the statements of the participants:

While the hostages remained in the desert, two Popular Front spokesmen, identified only as Comrade Basam and Comrade Ibrahim, discussed the hijackings with newsmen.

CORRESPONDENT: Can you tell me—can you tell me what is being done for the passengers out there in the desert?

COMRADE BASAM: What is being done now? They are in very good health, and they are treated very well by our fighters.

CORRESPONDENT: How long do you plan on keeping them?

COMRADE BASAM: Till our demands are met.

CORRESPONDENT: Suppose they—suppose they don't—if you don't get the demands, what will you do?

COMRADE BASAM: The officials and authorities know what we shall do.

CORRESPONDENT: Are you planning any more hijackings?

COMRADE IBRAHIM: As I said, this is a political line. And when we say political line, we don't mean it is an interrupted line; it is a continuous one. The world public opinion did not help us in a single inch in twenty-two years, so we don't care about the public opinion. We know, we request those people who try to understand our code. Nevertheless, we know exactly that through such operations, although it is a severe injury to their mind, but nevertheless it is an injury that will create the big question, why. This big why would be because shame, in order to understand exactly the problem of our people.

CORRESPONDENT: The Jordanian chief of staff, General Mashur Haditha, had been negotiating with the commandos. He succeeded in getting them to release the women and children, all except Israelis. . . .

WOMAN: Well, we weren't aware that we were being hijacked, but we knew our flight was from Zurich to New York, directly over France, and we looked down and we saw this mountain range, that was definitely snow-capped, and we knew there wouldn't be that kind of a range; immediately after we had noticed that our plane had taken a different course, the announcement was made that the Palestinian Liberation Organization had taken over the plane.

CORRESPONDENT: And how were you treated in your time in the desert?

WOMAN: Very well. Very well, they were very courteous.

CORRESPONDENT: What about the men who are left behind?

WOMAN: Well, they—I—I certainly hope they'll be all right. I wanted to stay, and they said an order is an order, meaning all women and children had to go.

SECOND WOMAN: One thing we must say is that pilot came in without knowing where he was coming in to. He said for all he knew there were mountains ahead of him, and he crash-landed in the desert with absolutely no lights and no runway, and he just did a mag-

nificent job. We were just glad to be alive, and then after that, lights all went out, we had to manage the best we could to sleep. We had—could use only the water that was left on board, and we weren't given any food until about six or seven o'clock this morning. . . .

CORRESPONDENT: Were you traveling alone?

GIRL: Yes.

CORRESPONDENT: Did you have any friends on the airplane at all?

GIRL: Well, I—I made friends after I—after this all happened, everybody was talking to each other.

CORRESPONDENT: Did you have any one friend in particular?

GIRL: Yes, she's—she's still at the plane. I'm not sure what's happened to her, because she's Jewish.

CORRESPONDENT: The Popular Front has a policy of destroying American aircraft. This time they say the kidnapped Israeli men, women, and children, along with male passengers from the United States, Great Britain, Switzerland, and West Germany, will be blown up with the planes if all the commando demands are not met, including the release of three thousand Palestinians allegedly imprisoned in Israel.

While the guerrillas played checkers with the hijacked hostages, moving them about the nation, the major concern of the United States became the safety of some four hundred American citizens, including the hostages. President Nixon said he was prepared to "preserve the proper interests of the United States" in Jordan, where the commando movement mounted a strong challenge to King Hussein. The hijacking simply symbolized the stresses within the Arab states; but it did not seem that way to the hijacked passenger. Symptomatic of the confusion was a report by the Red Cross that an American woman hostage had given birth on one of the hijacked planes. After offering all sorts of information about the condition of mother and child and the efficiency of its medical teams in the desert, the Red Cross subsequently explained there had been no such birth and it didn't know how the error was made. In a way, that confusion exemplified the Mideast story.

Sporadic Action Is Peace

technically, there had been no major war in the Middle East for three years. realistically, the war there never ends, preoccupying national budgets, energies, priorities, and hopes for the future. under prodding by the United States, a cease-fire was initiated in August, renewed for a second ninety-day period in the autumn, and almost constantly violated. within Jordan alone there were two assassination attempts on the life of King Hussein and four cease-fires called between the government and the Palestine Liberation Organization before the dark days of September.

Even as the world watched anxiously for news about the fate of fifty-four hostages, including thirty-four Americans, removed from the planes by the Jordanian guerrillas before the aircraft were destroyed, there was an even more threatening development. Jordan collapsed into civil war on September 17, Syria invaded the nation in an attempt to bring about the downfall of the Hussein government, the United States dispatched men and ships to the Mediterranean, and, for the better part of a week, it seemed touch and go that the Middle East would indeed see the armed showdown between the big powers predicted for so long by so many.

As early as February, reports indicated the extent of Palestinian resentment of the government:

DON WEBSTER: The trouble in Jordan leaves no doubt whatsoever who is the real power in the country. It is not the king, it is not his government, it is the commandos. In the heart of Amman they brazenly set up roadblocks. Every car that passes must acknowledge their authority. When they confront the police, it is the police who turn and run.

Of the two million persons in Jordan, two-thirds are Palestinians. Many of them consider themselves just temporarily residing here while they wait for the problem with Israel to end. As this confrontation shows, many of them look on King Hussein and his government merely as an impediment to their radical solutions to the problem.

This is a Palestine refugee camp called Wahdad. Troops of the Royal Jordanian Army occupy a citadel-like building in the center. The commandos decide to attack the Jordanian army troops.

King Hussein can't rely on much of his own army, either. Many of them are also Palestinians. Inside the citadel are Bedouins serving in the army. They are more loyal, as is the King's Royal Guard. Many of the refugees who live here stand back and watch the action. Most of the commandos were born and raised here, during the twenty-two years of Israel's existence.

The purpose of all this is not to depose King Hussein, or defeat his army. Lately the Arab states have been getting their share of military humiliation from Israel. They don't need it from each other. Rather, every once in a while, the guerrillas want to make sure everyone knows who's boss.

After several hours the fighting subsides. Some of the energy and ammunition will be saved for fighting Israel.

Outbreaks of open warfare continue. A thirty-four-year-old American military attaché, Major Robert Perry of Chicago, is killed in a cross fire at his home; thirty foreigners, including seventeen Americans, are held hostage by guerrillas in an Amman hotel, warned that their lives are in jeopardy if Jordanian troops continue shelling Palestinian refugee camps. Twists multiply in the Levantine labyrinth, the guerrillas charging that the U.S. Central Intelligence Agency is deeply involved on the government side, in an effort to turn the army against King Hussein and engineer a right-wing coup headed by Crown Prince Hassan, thus easing the way for a Jordan-Israel settlement. Evidence of such a plot is not forthcoming.

In an effort to avoid full-scale war, Hussein apparently accedes to the guerrillas' demands by firing his top military advisers, shortly after an unsuccessful attempt is made on his life. He says he will take over command of the army himself. The Americans and other hostages are released. The bitter fighting in Amman, not as widespread as

what would follow, demonstrates the seriousness of the situation:

BOB ALLISON: During the first twenty-four hours of fighting, the commandos seized the Jordanian capital and forced the army to take up positions on the outskirts of the city. They have held Amman ever since. They have snipers on rooftops all over town. They did it without too much trouble. As Palestinians they outnumber the native Jordanians by two to one. They control the economy of Amman, and it is today pretty much a city which they built by themselves, after they lost their lands and homes to Israel twenty-two years ago.

But while the commandos control the capital, they don't have sufficient strength to protect the Palestinian refugee camps which are outside of Amman, and army troops have poured a lot of shells into these camps in an effort to bring the commandos to heel. Nearly all of the commandos were either born or raised in these camps, and their families are still in them. This is why the guerrillas seized dozens of foreigners as hostages, in an attempt to stop the Jordanian army from shelling the refugee camps.

By way of reasserting his authority and in the face of continued guerrilla intransigence, Hussein puts the government under the control of tough military commanders strongly opposed to the guerrilla movement. The guerrillas almost immediately announce they have come together under a unified Palestinian command that will not accept the new military authority. In Washington there are real fears that the Palestinians might take complete control of Jordan, a prospect that depresses and alarms top officials for at least two reasons: first, the Palestinians' violent opposition to any peace settlement with Israel would quickly kill all diplomatic efforts in that direction; second, Israeli leaders have privately indicated that they will not tolerate a Palestinian-controlled Jordan and might launch a preemptive attack if that appears a possibility.

At the beginning, the situation does not appear any more threatening than the usual internecine clashes that have bloodied the sands of the desert since the tangled political and diplomatic establishments of the various regimes developed over the past quarter century.

Although casualties on both sides are reported heavy, the government claims victory after only a day of fighting. United Nations sources are confident that Hussein will win any climactic showdown with the Palestine guerrilla organizations, and that neither the eighteen thousand Iraqi troops in Jordan nor the Syrian army will move to help the guerrillas, although both governments have earlier hinted such action.

The customary split among the leadership of Jordan's armed forces does not now exist; elements favorable to Nasser who might earlier have broken with the government now side with the king because Nasser and Hussein are working together in search of a peaceful Middle East settlement. And in spite of the spectacular propaganda results, the hijackings have antagonized the responsible blocs in the guerrilla organizations who fear a take-over by the radicals. In spite of the presence of more than four hundred Americans in Jordan, the need to intervene on their behalf seems unlikely.

But the picture changes with dramatic suddenness. The United States dispatches Atlantic Fleet units to the Mediterranean to aid in the possible evacuation of those Americans. Included is a landing force of fifteen hundred marines. Soviet commentators concerned over the possible American military intervention call on Jordanian troops and the guerrillas to halt what they call this "fratricidal" fight. But the guerrillas show no sign of laying down their arms, and the government modifies its earlier claims that it has broken the back of the resistance. Heavy fighting takes place in at least six cities and casualties mount into the thousands.

And as the first eyewitnesses make their reports to the outside world, elements of the vast tragedy become clear, although its extent remains unknown. Some put the dead and wounded at five thousand, some at fifteen thousand, others say many more. For most of the wounded, even in the national capital of Amman, there is no place to go. Not enough hospital space, not enough drinking water— some hospitals do not even have enough water to boil their surgical instruments.

In the words of a Swedish news photographer who lived through the beginnings of the Amman holocaust:

> The situation right now is terribly poor. Civilians are lying all over the streets. They can't get to hospitals because they're shooting at the ambulances. The Red Cross can't get through. Today, when we went with a Red Cross car out to the airport, we had to change to an armored car because we were hit by twenty bullets. . . . They are shooting without any reason. They are shooting on everything, everyone who moves. Today, at the hospital where I was, one woman came in, and she was hanging up her laundry when two soldiers passed by and shot her . . . and the kids. It's awful. It's awful. For no reason at all. Yesterday, during the lift of the curfew, two nurses tried to go home. They were shot at.

Other reports confirmed the particular horror of the civil war:

> BERT QUINT: All-out war came suddenly to Jordan with a ferocity peculiar to those wars in which brother kills brother. I've covered scores of wars and revolutions, and I've never seen such concentrated fire-power over such a long period of time.
> When they opened up on the limestone

houses and the buildings and the refugee camps of Amman, the generals told foreign diplomats: do not worry, this will be over by teatime. Seven teatimes have come and gone; no one knows how many people have died. The guerrillas say that there have been thousands; at times it's easy to believe. In any case, certainly, many, many more than all of those Arabs who died in fighting against Israel since the Six-Day War of 1967 ended.

BOB ALLISON: The commandos claim that 90 percent of their casualties are civilians. It's clear that the toll has been high. Most of the sniper fire comes from rooftops, or inside buildings. The army troops answer it with a barrage of artillery and machine gun fire. By then the sniper has usually slipped off to another location, but the occupants inside of the houses have no place to take shelter. The morale of the commandos in this area is good. They feel they are winning the war. They claim to control most of the city. King Hussein makes a similar claim. What seems to be closer to the truth is this: at this point Hussein cannot take complete control without killing several thousand more civilians. The stone houses give the commandos as good protection as the thickest jungle. The only way Hussein can destroy the commandos is to destroy most of Amman.

IKE PAPPAS: While there was plenty of activity right outside the hotel for newsmen to cover, getting at it was often a frustrating process. The 120 newsmen from all over the world were unable to move because of martial law. Particularly perilous was a peek out the window. The Bedouin troops of the Jordanian army had orders to shoot anyone who attempted to take a picture. One Swedish cameraman was wounded doing this. Virtually every photographer's frame was taken at the risk of his life.

CORRESPONDENT: For six days the hotel and those of us in it withstood the barrage. Damage to the building was extensive.

Arabs from other countries have been meeting, trying to stop this war, at least to keep it from spreading, telling the Jordanian government and the guerrillas that their guns should be trained not on each other but on the Israelis.

But as we left Amman today, they still were firing. If there is any likely winner in this war between the Arabs, it is the Israelis, who from a distance are watching the Arabs kill each other.

Threat is piled on tragedy when Syrian troops invade Jordan on the guerrilla side and are reported to have quickly captured the nation's second largest city, even as Hussein announces a series of cease-fires designed to clear the way for medical treatment of thousands of casualties lying in the streets of Amman. The king immediately appeals to Russia, Britain, France, and the United States to help him repel the Syrian attacks. United Nations diplomats describe his mood as one of desperation, as clutching at any straw as the tide seems to turn against him.

For critical days, the possibility of American military involvement grows stronger by the hour. Hussein's top armored regiment is reported routed by Syrian troops and the king dispatches thousands of troops to the northwest to try to stop Syrian and Arab commando advances in what appears a showdown battle with cheerless prospects. Russia seems powerless in efforts to restrain the Syrians. Thousands of American paratroopers and infantrymen are put on the alert as President Nixon calls a meeting of the National Security Council. In an apparent reference to the safety of the four hundred Americans in Jordan, he says he is prepared to "preserve the proper interest of the United States" there. This serves to heighten speculation that American forces might move in the bloody conflict. The situation is further complicated by a lack of allied bases in the Mediterranean area available for any United States military intervention. Spain, used as a staging area in the Lebanon landing of '58, says no this time. A good many factors have changed in the Mideast, as Eric Sevareid pointed out:

> Syria has turned the Jordanian civil war into an international war and the problem for President Nixon is a familiar one—how to deter an aggressor without going to the brink, and if you have to go to the brink, how to keep from going over it.
>
> When the Syrians tried to knock out the pro-Western Lebanese government in '58, President Eisenhower sent in fourteen thousand marines, ordered American warplanes to fly near the Syrian border, and Britain sent troops into Jordan. Things are different today, with tens of thousands of armed Arab Palestinians all over the place, with our European allies possessing no stomach for getting into the Mideast, even though Mideastern oil is vital to Europe's life, not to ours. One can add the little item of a Russian military presence in Egypt for the first time.
>
> And theories of the cold war have changed. The Eisenhower Doctrine of '57 said we'd use force to help nations threatened by countries controlled by international communism. Since then most people have given up trying to define what international communism is, and the Nixon Doctrine is approximately the reverse of the Eisenhower Doctrine. Under the Nixon Doctrine we can help with money and arms, but client states are to use their own bodies, not ours.
>
> The Eisenhower Doctrine is a dead letter. The 1950 tripartite pact between America, Britain, and France to guarantee Mideastern borders died with Suez in '56. The '54 Baghdad Pact, which Secretary Dulles fostered but would not join, is another dead letter. To top the weird story of our Mideast relationships, the most binding commitment is to Israel, and that isn't even written down.
>
> Events are much more likely to determine what Washington does now than any doctrine or pact, present or past. There are those who see the shadow of World War III in what is now developing, but it is surely a very distant shadow. Both Moscow and Washington are determined to avoid any direct confrontation. Yet it remains true that what the Balkans were to the world of 1914, the Mideast is to the world of 1970, and it will remain the tinderbox for as long as anybody can now see ahead.

To paraphrase a comment about the weather, however, there is always this to say about the Middle East: If you are faced with a major crisis, stick around. The situation will change. Apparently rocked back on his heels, Hussein was shortly claiming victory in his civil war. He proclaimed a peace agreement negotiated by a four-man committee of leaders from neighboring Arab lands. This was repudiated by the Palestinian guerrilla leaders.

But it was clear that government troops, backed by armor, artillery, and planes, had dealt a smashing blow to Syrian units in a pitched battle that reportedly lasted six hours, saw Syrian soldiers forced out of Jordanian territory, and resulted in the government's recapture of its second largest city, Irbid. As quickly as that, American military involvement was no longer considered a likely possibility, and the Sixth Fleet was taken off alert status.

It was clear that American involvement with Hussein was strengthened by his performance under the pressures of two weeks in September. There would be no official explanation for the sudden withdrawal of Syrian tank units from battle. But the principal reason, according to State Department explanations, was the first-rate performance of government tanks and air force units, which reportedly inflicted heavy losses upon the Syrians.

There would be continuing charges, particularly from the guerrillas, that the always tenuous cease-fire was being violated. But in the main, the worst of it was over, and it is only on looking back that we see how close it seemed to us at the time. For the Jordanians, of course, it was not over. Even as buildings continued to blaze in parts of Amman, another bad moment began: the time for counting the cost. The Jordanian government, trying to play down the fact that it had turned tremendous firepower on its people, talked about casualties of a couple of thousand. The guerrillas claimed tens of thousands were killed. And a concerned Jordanian doctor offered a medical opinion:

> The people there have lived and are still living in terror, I'm sure, without water, without food, without electricity, without anything. And those who have not died from the shooting, I'm sure are now exposed to death from starvation and thirst. And I appeal to the conscience of the world, wherever they are, all creeds, all, all the world, to think of helping the people of Jordan at this time. The Good Samaritan was there, and the Good Samaritan is still there, and I don't know when the Good Samaritan will arrive in Amman to help the children, the thirsty and hungry children, the thirsty and hungry women and old people.

Ironically, the first major relief supplies entered Jordan in International Red Cross vehicles from the Israeli side of the border. The convoy was the largest group of vehicles ever to cross from Israel to Jordan. Two weeks earlier, that kind of mission could not have been possible, but the changes wrought at such awful cost by the civil war made it possible to bring help along the shortest and most direct road.

In the Middle East, sporadic action is relative peace and acts of violence as routine as a hyperactive child's war games. A close-up of major recent developments, first in military terms:

THE PALESTINIANS—I have noted their role in a civil war that many feared would spark World War III, and in the hijackings protesting the "American peace plan" for the Middle East.

By any account, they are at once the most pitiful and terrifying group in the Middle East, scattered through much of the Arab world, encouraged by some leaders in their determination to regain their homeland, tolerated by others simply as a handy way to harass Israel without accepting responsibility.

The influence of the small radical wing, once minor, now plays a major role in the politics of other Arab nations than Jordan; indeed, in all the nations of the world, for a part of their determination is to sabotage any peace settlement that does not return them to the homeland they believe is theirs, even with the coincidental destruction of Israel:

JOHN SHEAHAN: The squalid refugee camp is the common memory of every Palestinian family since the creation of the state of Israel pushed more than a million Palestinians out of their homes. The Palestinian commandos . . . are no longer only the young lions of the refugee camps. Now there are thousands of urban commando families.

Liela, for instance, is a normal, fourteen-year-old Palestinian girl, with normal, fourteen-year-old Palestinian girl pursuits. The Chinese-made Klashnikov automatic rifle has been commonplace in the home since about a year after the Six-Day War. Liela's little brothers—nine-year-old Calid and seven-year-old Nema—train every day under an adult commando cadre at the school playground.

In cities like Amman, Jordan, the commandos control the streets and the neighborhoods. The boys are called cubs, and are taught that they must fight for places called Haifa, Jaffa, and Jerusalem in a magic land called Palestine. Calid has never seen an Israeli, but he has heard they are cruel, evil people who took his father's house away before he himself was born, and two years ago wounded his big brother, Labib, with cannons and tanks at Al Karan. Nema is not yet sure what killing means, but he knows that if you do it, even in make-believe, everyone likes you and praises you.

He knows he's not just an Arab, but a

Palestinian and a commando. For him it is perfectly normal that his big sister, Liela, is home only one day a week and lives the rest of the time at a training camp, like many of the other neighborhood girls her age. Commando leaders say they are insuring that if they fail, their children and grandchildren will see to it that Israel never has peace.

Liela's father spends most of his time on commando operations in Lebanon and Syria. When he sees his daughter in the field, they maintain the traditional Arab distance. Of growing concern to her is the fact that her father will someday choose a husband for her. She knows the choice will be a commando, but she hopes he won't be one of those still living in a refugee camp. She says she would go out in the desert alone rather than have a baby in a refugee camp.

For twenty-five-year-old Labib, personal ambitions are subordinate to the goal of liquidating the state of Israel and replacing it with a Palestinian republic made up of Moslems, Christians, and Jews.

Now the girls are taking part in some of the military operations for the first time. Do you ever think about the fact that your sister, Liela, might be killed?

LABIB: I think one who has to fight against —against the enemy—maybe he will—he will kill and he will die. So one who—who fight to return back to his homeland and to his house, so it's normal to put in his—in his mind that he will die, maybe—maybe this night and all the other nights. So it's normal to—to lose our life, to—to gain—to gain up our—our homeland.

WINSTON BURDETT: Is it worth it to you for Liela to die?

LABIB: Yes, of course, I have—it's worth it to see my sister die, to fight and—against our enemy.

ISRAEL—One of those dramatic Israeli escapades—a safe return home of five gunboats supposedly securely embargoed by France:

CORRESPONDENT: The Israeli gunboats on their final dash for home. The boats that slipped unnoticed out of Cherbourg harbor on Christmas morning 1969 and made a mockery of a French arms embargo. Six and a half days and three thousand miles later, they are heading into the Israeli coast and the port of Haifa. Six and a half days of mystery, controversy, and suspense. But at no time during their journey were the Israeli boats intercepted or molested.

Soviet intelligence ships kept close watch on their voyage, but no Egyptian submarines tried to shadow them, no Soviet-made Egyptian torpedo boats appeared on the horizon to challenge their passage. Now they are only forty miles from home. From start to finish, a perfectly calculated operation, a triumphant gamble.

The port of Haifa, shortly after dark on New Year's Eve. All of Israel feels the thrill of pride and elation as the first of the five boats makes its way into the harbor. For two days Israelis in Haifa had been waiting and watching for their runaway ships to come in. Swift, ultramodern, 250-ton boats made in France, and designed to carry surface-to-surface missiles made in Israel. The Israelis insist that the boats are for civilian use only, to help supply and protect their oil drilling operations off the Israeli coast. The boats are apparently unarmed. They carry no recognizable insignia. Their crews are ostentatiously civilian, in their assortment of civilian dress, shirts and sweaters. They are skeleton crews, and they worked double shifts throughout the voyage to bring their craft safely home.

The Israelis know that these powerful little boats are a major addition to their country's midget fleet, and will be vital if one day their conflict with their Arab neighbors moves from the land and air onto the sea. For the Israelis, bordered by hostile states, and seeking modern arms wherever they can find them, the arrival of this flotilla of five boats means one of the happiest New Year's Eves in their country's history.

Reaction to the incident was sharply different in France, whose preferred position as Western middleman to the Arab nations was won largely by its total arms embargo against Israel. The French public seemed to regard it as largely fun and games, but outraged—and embarrassed—officialdom did about the only thing it could under the circumstances: ask for the recall of the two Israelis who had signed the gunboat contract.

The Israelis almost topped the gunboat affair by a daring raid in which they captured and airlifted back to their territory a seven-ton Soviet radar installation from Egypt. The Israelis also hit United Arab Republic camps within nine miles of Cairo, the closest raids to the Egyptian capital since the 1967 war, and their commandos romped over the Egyptian island of Shadwan at the Gulf of Suez entrance. The fighting was more or less continual, Israeli and Egyptian jets attacking each other's positions across the Suez Canal, reports of gains by one side usually denied by the other. Defense Minister Moshe Dayan said "all of Egypt is a field of battle."

The Israeli feats of daring were often born of desperation. Looking at it one way, there is not much else you can do, surrounded by belligerents. The day before the "daring" raid on the Egyptian-held Shadwan, for example, there had been a "daring" foray into Jordan.

An Israeli potash plant on the south end of the Dead Sea had been the target of guerrilla shells. So Israeli armored units rolled into Jordan for a twenty-hour stay, claiming they killed five members of the Al Fatah guerrilla organization as the strike force advanced across the border but otherwise meeting no opposition.

The loot was Japanese-manufactured jeeps, equipped with recoilless rifles and anti-aircraft guns, but the cause was the shelling of the potash factory. And, as is often the case, the nationality of the foe was indeterminate: a Jordanian military spokesman said the Israelis were engaged by Hussein's troops; other Arab broadcast announcements said Saudi Arabians fought alongside the guerrillas.

Such raids along the border are not expected by Israel to end the fighting there, but there is constant hope that they will someday convince Arab leaders that the activities of their guerrillas will cost them dearly.

New heights of bitter fighting with Egypt are paralleled by stiffening diplomatic moves. In late January, 1970, France announces an agreement to sell one hundred planes to Libya, one of the most militant of the Arab nations. The Israeli press charges the Paris government with pro-Arab bias, even suggesting the deal was influenced by right-wing anti-Semites in Paris. Other reaction concerns the political and psychological reverberations through the Middle East, encouraging Arab extremists to ask for more French hardware and the Israelis to demand that the United States speed up American arms shipments. For in the Middle East every action has its opposite reaction, not always equal.

Then the Soviet Union sends a series of notes to the United States, Great Britain, and France expressing, more as a warning than a threat, its concern over the escalating warfare in the Middle East. Soviet Premier Kosygin makes it obvious that the message is intended chiefly for the United States and Israel. He warns that unless the United States convinces Israel to ease up attacks on Arab nations, the Soviets will be forced to step up help to the Arabs, an escalation of the kind the Soviets claim to want to avoid. The note also applies pressure on the United States against sending more modern weapons to Israel, particularly more jet aircraft.

The immediate response to this call for a quieter Mideast is an exchange of air raids between Israel and the United Arab Republic, an invasion of Elath harbor by Egyptian frogmen who sink a five-hundred-ton supply ship and damage another Israeli craft, and a retaliatory air attack "within hours" by the Israelis that hits more than fifty Egyptian targets, including a seven-hundred-ton mine-layer in the Gulf of Suez. An Israeli spokesman describes the retaliation as taking "an eye for an eye."

Sometimes both cause and retaliation seem childish. There is that day when Syrian aircraft are sent over Israel's port city of Haifa to create sonic booms. This is successful. So, that same day, Israel retaliates, sending two jets over Damascus, thus producing war's newest weapon—retaliatory sonic booms.

The extent of the Middle East fighting is reflected in the record Israeli budget of $2.8 billion, 40 percent of it devoted to military spending. Officials say that paying for the war has made the Israelis the second highest taxed people in the world, coming only after the Swedes.

The Soviet Union indicates strongly that it will give substantially more arms to all Arab nations unless Israel stops "attacking them." Prime Minister Golda Meir, emphasizing that she wants to see an end to the bloodshed, accuses Egypt of waging a war of attrition and says that Israel has no intention of halting military operations until Egypt agrees to a total cease-fire.

Faced with reports of increasing Soviet aid to the UAR, including ground technicians and pilots, Israel steps up its appeals for more jets. It was receiving about 4 a month; its initial order would be filled by June; it wants an additional 125.

Basing the decision on hopes that the Soviet Union would agree to come to some kind of arms limitation deal in the Middle East, the United States turns down the Israeli request for jets. Secretary of State William Rogers, admitting he has nothing specific on which to place his hopes, comments, "In our judgment, Israel's air capacity is sufficient to meet its needs for the time being. Consequently, the President has decided to hold in abeyance for now a decision with respect to Israel's request. . . . In doing so, he has instructed that close watch be kept on the military balance in the area. . . . We have evidence that the Soviet Union has been taking recent steps to strengthen the air defense of the UAR by the introduction of SAM-3 missiles and additional Soviet personnel."

Those "recent steps," according to the usual "reliable diplomatic" sources in Cairo, are accompanied by a reported fifteen hundred USSR troops to operate the missiles. Rogers notes the SAM-3 is "a defensive weapon . . . and we have to assume they'll be used defensively." The report is they are to block low-flying Israeli aircraft. And in spite of a $100 million grant in U.S. economic aid, Israeli Ambassador Yitzhak Rabin believes the decision is a mistake, likely to encourage the Soviets to go further:

> There is no letup in the Russian efforts to improve the military situation—position of the Arab countries, especially of Egypt. The history of mankind is filled with miscalculation about balance of power. For us, a mistake about the balance of power means our destruction. It endangers the very existence of Israel. I believe that the decision not to supply us arms today, it's a wrong one, and I am afraid that it will affect future developments in the Middle East in a negative way.

But Russia faces difficulty in maintaining the UAR air force. By April Egypt has lost more than half of its MIG fleet since the 1967 war, according to the Israelis. For whatever the reason, Russian pilots are committed to the defense of Egypt, according to an Israeli charge and U.S. intelligence. The Russians promptly deny that at least 150 of their pilots are flying for Egypt, but the State Department calls it "a serious, potentially dangerous situation," which could affect the decision on jets for Israel.

While Israeli Foreign Minister Abba Eban calls repeatedly for cease-fires and presses Washington for more jets, Oregon Senator Mark Hatfield says that peace in the world could not be maintained through a balance of power, such as sending more jets to Israel. And he calls on both Israel and the United States to recognize that the Palestinian Arabs were dealt an injustice when Israel became a nation in 1948, calling the Arabs' loss of their homes the central grievance in the Middle East.

The deadly games continue to play themselves out, with air raids, retaliatory air raids, shellings, commando raids, the undramatic endless little battles of the undeclared war.

On June 25, the United States advances a new proposal for peaceful settlement of the Middle East impasse, revolving around a ninety-day cease-fire. United Nations mediator Gunnar Jarring enters the picture after the cease-fire begins. And, most importantly, the proposal stresses Israel's recognition of the principle of withdrawing her forces from territory occupied during the 1967 war, with the Arab states' "acknowledgment of Israel's right to exist within secure and recognized borders." Initial reaction from all concerned is negative. By the end of July, however, first Egypt, then Jordan, then Israel accepts the United States peace formula.

Within days of the American proposal and a presidential warning that the Arab-Israeli conflict is more dangerous than the war in Indochina and could result in a clash between the United States and Russia, a new threat arises. Israel charges on July 6 that SAM-3s have been fired at Israeli jets near the Suez Canal, and that there is every reason to believe the surface-to-air missiles have been fired by Russians.

Confirming the essence of the Israeli report, the United States fears a new cycle of violence in the area, in which direct Soviet-Israeli conflict is likely to expand. In spite of appeals from the United States, it is clear that the Russians and the Egyptians have moved the missile installations to within fifteen or twenty miles of the canal. Israeli Ambassador Rabin assesses the situation:

> What they want at present is to eliminate the freedom of activity of the Israeli air force, and then if they achieve it, of course, they'll be free to use their masses of artillery, tanks, firepower, from the west side of the Suez Canal to harass our forces on the east side, and even to mount their raids on a larger scale than they used to in the past. . . . Israel, once we get the means, can cope for any foreseeable time, from the military point of view, with the total strength of the Arab world . . . with a very limited Russian military intervention. We don't pretend to be able to cope with a massive Russian military intervention against Israel.

The Israelis, claiming to have knocked out a third of the newly emplaced missiles, plan to knock out the others in spite of U.S. concern about bombing deeper in Egypt. Israel says that there are eight thousand Russians on duty in Egypt, including three thousand soldiers and pilots of missile systems, although the Egyptians deny that Russians serve any direct military role. Egypt charges that the Israelis are trying to build up a case for more military assistance from the United States and, in the face of the latest crisis, there are indications that they are getting additional American weapons.

There is continual violation of the old cease-fire, supposedly in effect in the Middle East since 1967. And the action is not confined to air attacks, of course; Israeli artillerymen shelling Egyptian positions across the canal have their reasons:

LARRY POMEROY: These weapons and the soldiers who fire them have been a leading factor in Israel's frontline defense against Egypt's army, and in Israel's view the soldiers should continue to fire their guns until Egypt is ready to resume the United Nations permanent cease-fire it accepted three years ago. The American peace initiative's limited cease-fire proposal would silence the guns along the Suez Canal, but Israelis suspect Egypt would resume the Middle East war on an even greater scale at the end of the truce.

In the middle of the Suez Canal battle are the cease-fire observers of the United Nations. They have been left to oversee the discarded truce. Most of their time is spent counting air strikes and artillery barrages. There has been speculation a UN emergency force might be sent to the canal to supervise a new cease-fire if the American plan is accepted by Israel. The smoke billowing across the canal marks the target of an Israeli air strike. Thousands of tons of bombs are dropped every week to keep Egyptian shelling of Israeli fortifications at a minimum. But the limited cease-fire proposed by the United States, Israel's chief ally in the Mideast war, has raised fears that the air force's achievements will be wiped out in a matter of months, and once the temporary truce ends, Israelis believe, it may be another three years before Egypt is ready to talk peace again.

The American-proposed cease-fire went into effect August 7. While things quieted down along the canal between Israeli and Egyptian forces, the Palestinian guerrillas had refused the truce agreement, so sporadic action continued on its ceaseless way, particularly in the Jordanian, Syrian, and Lebanese sectors:

CORRESPONDENT: At this cease-fire line, on the Arab side of the River Jordan, the cease-fire is a sometimes thing. Placid days are contrasted with death by night. Israeli occupation forces on the West Bank allow truckloads of farm products to come over into Jordan, and allow the Arabs back and forth across the Hussein Bridge, called the Allenby Bridge from the other side, to visit relatives.

But at night the Palestinian commandos cross the river, to strike at a village or a kibbutz, and these terrorist raids have increased since the new Middle East cease-fire. The Israelis, of course, retaliate against suspected commando bases on this side. Sometimes even the 105-degree daytime calm is broken by gunfire.

JORDANIAN FRUIT INSPECTOR MOHAMMED KAYED: It seems to be a little quiet, but yesterday there was a little bit of firing from the north and south front.

CORRESPONDENT: Could you tell which side started the shooting?

KAYED: I don't know exactly which side, really.

CORRESPONDENT: Well-placed Jordanians say peace negotiations will fail, that the American peace plan is an illusion based on a naïve American hope the Israelis will withdraw from the occupied areas in the same easygoing way they now let traffic across this bridge. Here on the Arab side, in the Jordanian capital of Amman, and especially right here at the cease-fire line, there just isn't much confidence the Israelis will give up the easily defensible high ground as long as the nightly commando attacks go on.

The talks themselves were exacerbated by Israel's discovery of Russian-Egyptian missile movement during the truce in August, by truce violation charges leveled by Egypt against Israel, and by divisions between Arab leaders and within the Israeli cabinet.

But the peace talks, interrupted, did not seriously interrupt the truce. Israel continued to react to guerrilla attacks with shellings and commando raids but there seemed a genuine interest in keeping the peace.

EGYPT—For the senior member of the United Arab Republic, there was major tragedy in the loss of Nasser, small indignities on the battlefield, little progress on the home front, and, at the end, a bellicose tone promising enlarged and renewed attacks on Israel some time after the extended cease-fire was scheduled to end early in 1971.

And through it all, an increased reliance upon the Soviet Union, whose interest in the Mediterranean, one of the few sections of the world still up for ideological grabs, was never so patent.

As Israeli bombing raids pocked the country, Ahmed Esmat Meguid, chief spokesman for the Egyptian government, called them futile efforts to "achieve political and psychological effects."

But other developments were not so easily dismissed: the Israeli hijacking of a radar station at Ras Ghereb and the Israeli attack on the island of Shadwan, a military base. After Israeli jets attacked targets only six miles from the center of Cairo, the Egyptian government announced that the state-owned television would show the film *Battle of Britain* to help prepare Cairo residents for further raids. A spokesman said the World War II scenes of destruction in London and other British cities would serve, among other things, to alert Egyptians to take shelter during the air raids.

President Nasser's government, along with Jordan, Syria, Iraq, and the Sudan, assailed the Nixon administration for "a hostile attitude" toward the Arabs and indicated that major U.S. oil interests in the Middle East should be liquidated.

Ordinarily, communiqués about air strikes in the Mideast are simply clashes of statement: "Egypt claimed today that its air forces struck hard at Israeli positions in the western Sinai Peninsula, inflicting heavy loss of life. The Israelis mentioned no casualties but did say one Egyptian MIG was shot down."

There are times, though, when the conflicting claims are a little more difficult to dismiss, as when the Egyptian government said that Israeli warplanes had killed thirty children and one adult civilian in a raid on a primary school in the Nile Delta. Another forty-six persons were reported wounded. Israeli Defense Minister Moshe Dayan said that attacked targets were strictly military and "if the Egyptians installed classrooms inside a military installation, this in my opinion is highly irresponsible."

The Egyptians denied there were military targets nearby. The Israelis offered what they called photographic proof. Both sides disputed the location of the target. The Egyptians took newsmen to a hospital to see the victims of the raid, but denied them a visit to the stricken location itself.

Somewhere in all this, as in all wars, the victims themselves—in this case, children—come out forgotten.

There was no argument about Russia's increasing involvement in Egypt, only about the numbers. And there was growing concern, as Eric Sevareid noted, that United States preoccupation with the Far East left the nation losing out in the Mideast, with strong indications that Egypt had slipped beyond the ring of Western influence:

When the principal political capital of the world becomes a one-subject town, as Washington has since Cambodia, then it's hard not only for individuals but for sovereign governments to raise other subjects, however urgent.

70

Israel's foreign minister has come and gone once again. He now sounds slightly, but only slightly, more hopeful that his country will get those American jet planes. He warns that if the planes are not forthcoming, Russia will go even deeper into its Mideast involvement. In Moscow the Communist paper *Pravda* assumes Israel will get the planes and hints that that will push Russia in deeper. The Nixon administration has not decided against the plane delivery; it has merely decided not to decide.

If there has been any movement inside the inner councils here, it seems to be a new leaning by two or three presidential advisers in the direction of the Israeli argument that the big Russian military presence in Egypt has altered the Mideast balance of power. But President Nixon remains very much his own secretary of state. The decision is now up to him alone.

The immediate action, and the headlines, concern the fights across the Israeli-Lebanese lines, but the main show is with Egypt, centered on the forward defense lines of Egypt and Israel west and east of the Suez Canal. Peace or intensified war in the Mideast centers on Israel's relations with Egypt more than her relations with all the other Arab countries.

But Egypt is now pretty far inside Russia's political grasp. In the military sense, at least, it seems fair to say that Egypt is no longer an independent state. Large numbers of Egyptian military specialists are being trained in Russia; about a hundred Russian pilots are flying defense of the Egyptian heartland; hundreds of other Russian specialists are present; more and more surface-to-air missile sites are being installed. The Soviet Union is now unquestionably a major power in the Mediterranean world and can become the dominant power. She moves a step at a time, testing the ground and the wind, watching for every reaction.

The present question is whether she will try to establish Egyptian control of the air over the forward defense zone, which the Israelis say they cannot allow. If that question comes to the real test, then a lot of people will have to make a lot of decisions. This government will make its own with a clearer head if Cambodia and its accompanying uproar can be made to subside.

A major fear of the Russian-Egyptian alliance was that it would put Russians into direct confrontation with the Israelis. That apparently happened over the summer, when State Department officials were quoted as saying Russians had manned two of four MIGs shot down over the Suez Canal. Previously, there had been indications that Russians were flying for Egypt but not in combat situations. A report that a Russian had shot down an Israeli plane added urgency, in Washington's view, to acceptance of the U.S. cease-fire proposal.

The major Soviet contributions were construction and operation of the missile bases in Egypt, but a Russian hand seemed to be in everything Egyptian. Following nineteen days of high-level talks in mid-July, the joint Russian-Egyptian communiqué blamed the Middle East crisis on "unceasing armed attack by Israel," an "aggressive, expansionist policy" possible only because of United States support.

And the long-discussed Aswan Dam went into full production for the first time during the year. Built with Soviet aid, the dam was expected to give Egypt five times its power output and to convert one million acres of arid land into fertile soil.

For all its belligerence toward Israel, Egypt offered the first positive indication that there was light developing in the Middle East crisis when it offered a favorable response to the deliberately vague American peace plan. It was the first nation to act on the proposal.

And even before the talks began, Egypt made its first move against the Arab commando groups, which fiercely opposed the peace proposal. The Nasser regime put a temporary ban on the nightly Cairo broadcasts of the Palestine guerrilla organizations. But even with the peace talks and the moderating influence on Arab firebrands, Nasser remained locked into the policy of recovering land now occupied by Israel.

And so his death left Egypt as strongly as ever committed to the same policy. For Nasser was not only revered; he had put together a political organization of potency and dedication.

Nasser's successor was little known outside Egypt, a friend and comrade of Nasser and vice-president at the time of his death, fifty-one-year-old Anwar Sadat. The ritual was as formalized as a religious ceremony. Sadat served as interim president, was recommended as president by the nation's only political party, then was elected president for a six-year term by the national assembly, confirmed by a national plebiscite—6,432,580 yes votes to 711,252 no—and in his first presidential address made a promise to fulfill Nasser's goals: recovering Arab lands occupied by Israel, uniting Arab lands, defending the gains of Egypt under socialism.

But Sadat, although an ardent Israeli foe, was largely unpolitical, an ideal compromise man to follow a dictator, considered neither pro-West nor pro-East. Nothing changed in the Soviet friendship society, however, and the Russians continued to move more firepower, including sophisticated missiles, into the restricted area west of the Suez Canal. Estimates placed the missile and anti-aircraft power in that area at more than the Soviet Union had supplied North Vietnam at the height of the air war.

And so, as the lines hardened between East and West, a Mideast heating up of the cold war, Sadat developed an increasingly tough tone toward Israel, Egypt rattling its SAMs toward a threatening spring. But an eyewitness account, even during a restricted tour of the area, made it clear what the war had cost, was costing, Egypt:

CORRESPONDENT: This is the front, from the Egyptian side. The Israelis are just across the canal, about four hundred yards away. This trench is the last Egyptian defense before you reach the occupied territory across the canal. The trenches we've seen here today might have been dug by World War I doughboys. They offer no protection from close or direct hits.

Looking at the destruction the Israelis have left behind makes it clear that the casualties at the southern end of the canal here must have been very heavy. This rail line was blown apart by Israeli planes attacking anti-aircraft guns hidden from view by that embankment. Amid the wreckage and destruction of what were once two thriving canalside cities, Suez and Port Taufiq, we could find no signs of modern underground bunkers where troops could take shelter during air raids.

Just across the canal there, Israeli troops have waited out the Egyptian artillery attacks in underground bunkers with roofs of steel railings. On this side the Egyptian soldier can only keep his head down.

We are not permitted to take any pictures of the Egyptian soldiers here, but we can report that they are happy to be out of their trenches and walking around without worrying about planes overhead. None that we talked to was optimistic about the cease-fire. Repeatedly the soldiers told us: we don't trust the Israelis. They could, though, learn something from the Israelis about how to survive during war.

A Longer Fuse

there is no estimate as to how many peace proposals have been put forth for the Middle East. the option is available to any dreamer and the Mideast seems particularly attractive to global problem solvers. following are only a few of the more prominent proposals, with most of the attention centering on the only one that has become operable. the United States peace initiative did little more than get the sides to agree to possibly, perhaps, talk. a CBS News colleague, looking at the Mideast picture, said, "the fuse is still lit, but it's a little longer now."

"I think the Middle East is now terribly dangerous, like the Balkans before World War I," said President Nixon in midsummer. "The two superpowers, the United States and the Soviet Union, could be drawn into a confrontation that neither of them wants because of the differences there."

Within the week, the President and his advisers were warning Moscow that if it increased its military intervention in the Middle East, it ran the risk of direct confrontation with the United States. Instead of adding to the number of pilots and missile experts in Egypt, so the warnings ran, the Soviet should be withdrawing the ones already there.

The Russians, in turn, warned that if the United States intervened further in the Middle East " it might not get only its fingers burned but its whole arm." And both sides continued to furnish Mideastern allies with aid.

Amid all the threats—and it was too serious a matter for mere blustering—the step off the edge was never taken. Why? For one thing, because neither of the superpowers wanted war. And, most important, because just about all concerned were, at crucial moments, to make the delicate shade of adjustment leading to consultation, not confrontation.

As the Mideast adversaries went at each other sporadically, the United States and Russia were working on peace plans. But it was not a joint venture—each nation was pushing its own.

Details of the Russian plan were not spelled out, but it reportedly called for "a formalized state of peace" only after the first stage of Israeli withdrawal from occupied territories had been completed. There was more, but this was enough for a flat turndown by Israel.

The American plan, short on specifics except in its call for a UN-supervised cease-fire, seemed destined to suffer the same fate. Nasser scored it for not mentioning Israel's withdrawal from Syria's Golan Heights; Russia called it "further support of the Israeli military"; and the Israelis objected to the temporary cease-fire feature, which they feared would be used by Egypt for a missile buildup while Israel was grounded.

One by one, they relented. A Soviet newspaper echoed Nasser's critique of the Golan Heights feature but said the plan "seems closer to the legitimate aspirations of the Arab countries." Nasser, in July of 1970, accepted "the basic provisions of the plan"; the Soviet Union accepted those same provisions —a ninety-day truce along the Suez Canal while talks started under UN auspices. Israel was odd man out for the better part of a month, accepting only, in Prime Minister Golda Meir's phrase, "after we had reached the conviction that the cease-fire would become effective under conditions which would prevent its being abused."

Now, for any of the parties involved to announce acceptance of the truce took courage. Israel acted only after a stormy cabinet session. The 17–6 vote reflected the split; all six negatives, members of the right-wing Gahal faction, resigned. Iraq led the pack of Arab extremists blasting Nasser's acceptance. He answered that Egypt "has not indulged in the luxury of fighting from platforms" and would "continue to be in the vanguard of the liberation movement."

But the meetings were almost stopped before they got under way, when Israel charged that Egypt was moving Soviet-made missiles closer to the canal, in defiance of the truce. It offered photographs alleging to show the violations. Defense Secretary Melvin Laird reflected the official Washington position when he said, "I think the important thing for us now is to move forward toward negotiations and not debate what went on twelve hours before or twelve hours after" the cease-fire. Israel's Foreign Minister Abba Eban said the talks would go on as scheduled but, "on the one hand, our adversaries endanger our security; on the other, our friends impugn our accuracy and sincerity."

United Nations mediator Gunnar V. Jarring opened the talks on August 24 in New York City. He held "separate, preliminary discussions" with Egypt, Jordan, and Israel. But the talks stalled within a week as Israel filed charges of further missile movements on the Egyptian side of the canal and Egypt charged that Israel was moving soldiers into the thirty-two-mile standstill zone and building new fortifications.

Meanwhile, relations between Israel and

the United States reached a new low, Israel angry over Washington's refusal to pressure Russia to halt the missile movements, the United States impatient over what it regarded as Israeli foot dragging. Israeli Defense Minister Moshe Dayan said, "The Americans bear a heavy responsibility. They initiated the cease-fire, and we agreed to it only after they had informed us that the Russians would abide by the standards."

The pressures, of course, centered on Moscow and Washington:

MARVIN KALB: There is a myth afloat about these hot, sticky August days that barely a leaf ripples. This is not so. In August, 1961, for example, the Russians built a wall through Berlin. President Kennedy gasped, but did nothing. In August, 1968, the Russians nipped the promise from Dubcek's liberalization drive. President Johnson gasped, canceled an earlier session of strategic arms limitations talks, but essentially did nothing. Earlier this month, the Russians and the Egyptians moved a substantial number of ground-to-air missile batteries closer to the Suez Canal. This forward deployment reportedly continued after the start of the cease-fire. The Nixon administration gasped, too, but it has done little to dispel the impression that it will not challenge the Russians and the Egyptians.

Formal representations have been made by quiet American diplomats in Moscow and Cairo, but no complaints have yet been registered, no cry of concern. Why? Not, certainly, because the evidence does not exist; there is much evidence privately conceded. The reason is threefold.

First, the administration believes that this may be a last chance for peace talks before major hostilities erupt once again. Second, it thinks Israel knows, deep down, that the U.S. will give her more military hardware if war again threatens. And finally, this chance for talks is part of a larger diplomatic mosaic, the complicated launching of the President's era of negotiations with the Communist world. There have been some hopeful signs recently: the progress on strategic arms talks in Vienna, the possibility of an East-West security conference next year, the cooling off of the Indochina war.

The chips are big, but in a way the irony of America's Middle East position today is even bigger. President Nixon wants to lower America's profile, yet in the Middle East the profile has never been higher. He is clearly learning that the role of the peacemaker, while politically rewarding, is not only a visible and a vulnerable one; it is risky, too.

Riskier approaches were offered: Senator J. William Fulbright offered a plan which, subject to United Nations mandate, called on the United States to protect Israel's borders, with the guarantee that Israel would not violate them. The British offered a detailed peace plan based on "the inadmissibility of the acquisition of territory by war."

Israel announced it would boycott the Jarring *talks* until the missile installations were moved. But, importantly, the Israelis said they would continue to observe the *truce* through expiration of the cease-fire.

The day of the boycott announcement was also the day of the three-plane hijack by the Palestinian guerrillas. Within a month Nasser would be dead. Civil war would break out in Jordan. Any of these convulsions could have been enough to upset the delicate balance of the flag of truce fluttering over a boycotted conference. As an instance, Nasser died as President Nixon undertook an eight-day, fifteen-nation tour of Europe. One of the presidential stops was Belgrade, and the diplomatic reason centered on peace in the Middle East:

MARVIN KALB: Nasser's death has robbed this presidential stop of one of its principal private purposes: to use Tito's friendship with Nasser to breathe new life into the stagnant American peacemaking effort in the Middle East. Tito helped once before this year. In February, Secretary Rogers met him in Ethiopia and asked him to explain America's evenhanded policy to Nasser. Tito did, and this helped set a climate for the current cease-fire along the Suez Canal.

President Nixon wanted to persuade Tito of America's goodwill, and indirectly to suggest that he could salvage the American peace effort in the Middle East if he, Tito, could quietly suggest to Nasser that a good way out of the current dilemma would be for Nasser to withdraw his missiles from the Suez area. But with Nasser's death this American plan died, too. Of course, chatting seriously with an important Communist leader, showing the American flag in Eastern Europe, and being cheered by East European crowds, all of this is good policy and good politics, but really just frills. The possibility for serious diplomacy here died with Nasser's death.

As for the talks themselves, the expiration date was extended through February 5, 1971, under a United Nations resolution, which Israel opposed but went along with.

Saying, "It is more honorable to die fighting than to live in surrender," Egypt's Sadat spoke of "all-out battle" following the end of the truce extension. Dayan was quoted as saying that Israel did not have to abide by the truce, since Egypt had violated it, a statement he later denied.

And so, uneasily and armed to the teeth, the Mideast's two major antagonists spent a third of a year in a truce without talks. Israel agreed to return to the peace meeting it had boycotted for four months, apparently confident it would continue to receive American arms to counter the flow of Soviet weapons to Egypt.

Israeli soldier passes piece of candy to Lebanese child.

Israeli Premier Golda Meir.

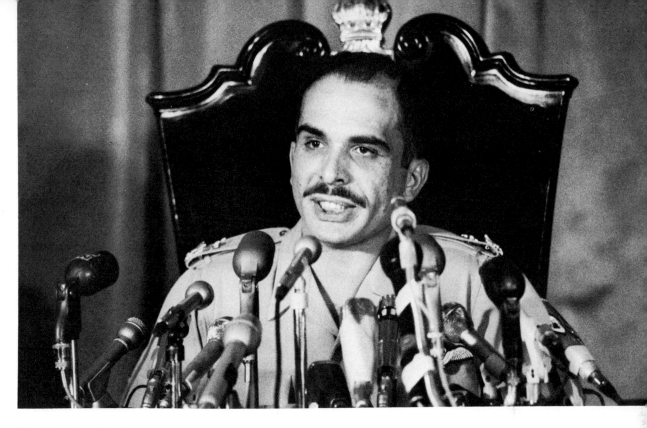

King Hussein of Jordan.

Yasir Arafat, head of Al Fatah, with Mayef Hawatmeh, leader of the Popular Democratic Front for the Liberation of Palestine.

Arab refugee camp in Jordan.

Passengers debarked in
Jordan desert airstrip
from jetliners hijacked by
Arab guerrillas.

Women and children
released by Arab captors
being transported to
safety in Amman, Jordan.

Hijacked BOAC jetliner blown up by Arab guerrillas on desolate airstrip in Jordanian desert.

A Beginning, a Middle, an End(?)

the three former French Indochinese states were a matter of indifference to most Americans until well along in the 1960s. the first American died in what had become Vietnam in 1961. before the decade was out forty thousand more would die there. but what child of 1960 would believe a story like that? Vietnam became the longest war in our history, our costliest foreign war in terms of lives lost; it banged up the national economy and psyche, dominated two presidential campaigns, overturned priorities, and caused the deepest division in the nation since the Civil War. and in 1970, it was no longer Vietnam alone—that seemed only a beginning. a place called Cambodia became the middle piece in the jigsaw, and another place, Laos, an end (?). Americans of all persuasions seemed determined that there would be no more Vietnams in the decade of the seventies.

The battle names no longer made sense. Duc Pho. Dakseang. Quangnai. We had been there before. Americans learned in other wars to adjust to unfamiliar names: Argonne, Verdun, Iwo, and Anzio. But those names meant victory or defeat in a nation interested only in winners and losers.

The Vietnamese names meant six years of no-win, two of them since General William C. Westmoreland's farewell speech concession that the war would not end in a military victory. So the battle names meant about as much as assurances from visitors that Vietnamization was proceeding smoothly: too many recalled too many earlier visitors who had seen "light at the end of the tunnel"—the very phrase had become a national joke. The war went on being fought, brave men went on dying.

As in any war, the stories ranged from the ridiculous to the unspeakable, although with a quality seemingly peculiar to Vietnam. A U.S. general received a Silver Star for an action he had nothing to do with; two dogs were among twenty-one members of the Twenty-fifth Infantry Division to receive Bronze Stars for valor. Embarrassed army authorities revoked that entire award.

An instance of the unspeakable followed a congressional tour of South Vietnam aimed at assessing the course of the war and the progress of the Thieu regime to win over the country:

BOB SCHIEFFER: Congressmen Augustus Hawkins of Los Angeles and William Anderson of Tennessee broke off from a congressional inspection party and went to the Vietnamese prison facility on the island of Con Son, off the South Vietnamese coast. With the South Vietnamese prison commander in charge, they got the usual VIP tour. But they had been tipped in advance to look for a secret passageway at the prison that led to an area never before seen by outsiders, the door to a hidden prison where political opponents of the government were kept in open pits called tiger cages. Anderson and Hawkins got through the door when a guard opened it by mistake. They found themselves on a walkway.

CONGRESSMAN WILLIAM ANDERSON: And from this walkway, you would observe down beneath you the cages in which the prisoners were kept, the top part of the cages being covered with a series of iron bars, so that the cage amounted to an enclosure, I estimated roughly five feet by nine feet, with no windows, no—nothing but a solid wall and solid door, and nothing open to look out to, except through the top, through the cells.

CONGRESSMAN AUGUSTUS HAWKINS: In this case, there is hardly room for one or two persons, but there are actually five prisoners. There is a vertical bar that is across the cage about a foot off the floor, and to this bar are tied shackles. These shackles are used for containing the feet of the prisoners, so that an individual lies stretched down on a cement floor shackled to this vertical bar and lies in that position sometimes for months and months, and as a matter of fact almost continuously for several years in many instances. The effect of this is to paralyze the prisoner, and most of those that we interviewed through the interpreter that we had with us indicated that they were completely paralyzed in their legs.

CORRESPONDENT: The congressmen said they saw about five hundred prisoners, both men and women, being confined in the cages. The prison receives some American money through the AID program, and there is an American civilian stationed there as an adviser. Told that the adviser described the prison as "better than some in the United States," Anderson said tonight: "The man should be sent home on the first plane."

There was great furor, an announcement that the tiger cages would be removed, and a final revelation that they were being repaired by the Saigon regime to make them more comfortable.

The personalities of the war remained the same: South Vietnam President Nguyen Van Thieu repeating that he would oppose any coalition government including Communists and that those favoring such a course were "cowards and defeatists" who must be eliminated; Vice-President Nguyen Cao Ky finally calling off an on-again-off-again appearance at a Washington rally demanding a military victory in Vietnam (he later visited the United States to "inspect" the Vietnamization program, touring military bases where South Vietnamese soldiers were being trained).

An "end-the-war" amendment sponsored by Republican Senator Mark Hatfield of Oregon and Democratic Senator George McGovern of South Dakota was rejected by the Senate by a 55–39 vote. At that, the size of the vote backing the measure indicated the growth of sentiment calling for an early pullout. Some doves who voted against it said they did so only because they did not want to tie the President's hands in negotiations with the Communists.

But through the year there was a growing sense of impatience and behind it a philosophy whose time had come, as Eric Sevareid noted:

There seems every reason to assume, as the autumn begins, what one had to assume as the summer began and the spring began—that the longest war in American history is going to go on for a long time yet.

Year by year, stage by stage, the cutting edge of the leading arguments for this intervention has been blunted and discarded. At first the argument was that the security and vital interests of the United States were at stake in the outcome of this civil war in a strip of East Asia. The specter was raised of a threat to the whole power position of America in the Pacific if the northerners won instead of the southerners. Very few suggest that anymore. Then the commitment argument was made, that the SEATO treaty somehow obliged us to send in American forces. It says nothing of the sort; other signatories have remained passive, and this argument has faded away.

For two or three years it was claimed that more men, more planes, and more tanks would finish the war. This prevented defeat of the South, but did not finish the war. Then it was said that the enemy was realistically beaten but hung on only because he was encouraged by the protest movement inside the United States. But the protest movement has ebbed and flowed, and the enemy behaves the same.

Now we are at the point where even Mr. Nixon, the original hawk—he suggested intervening in Indochina back in '54—no longer claims this war was necessary for American interests. He offers no program, manageable by Americans, for ending the war, but does offer one for reducing the American part of the war.

So the basic argument now is on the pace and the method of extrication. This is not going to be determined by intellectual debating points, however sharp. It will be determined by events—what happens inside the Saigon government, the course of battle in

Cambodia, the enemy's ability or inability to increase American casualties.

As time wears on, American opinion is likely to be less and less responsive to the number of men brought home, more and more responsive to what happens to the men still there. And their fate will not be under exclusive American control.

As to the pace of American withdrawal, President Nixon announced in the spring of 1970 that 150,000 American troops would be withdrawn from Vietnam in the following year. At year's end, the tempo was slightly faster. The troop level of 337,900 was the lowest since 1965.

And in October, President Nixon offered a five-point peace plan, two points of which were new: a "standstill" truce and expansion of peace talks to include Cambodia and Laos. Hanoi rejected the proposal, saying that an "immediate" truce would concede that Americans had the right to be where they were in the first place.

But the most extraordinary episode in Vietnam at that time was revealed shortly before Thanksgiving by Defense Secretary Melvin Laird:

On Friday, November 20, shortly after 2:00 P.M. eastern standard time, which was about 2:00 A.M. in North Vietnam, a small rescue team successfully landed by helicopter at a reported prisoner-of-war compound at Son Tay, approximately twenty nautical miles west of Hanoi. The operation was under the overall command of two distinguished officers, whom I would like to introduce to you at this time. They are Brigadier General Leroy J. Manor, United States Air Force, who was in overall command of the operation, and Colonel Arthur D. Simons, United States Army, who led the team in the search and rescue attempt. They arrived in Washington early this morning.

Operating in darkness, Colonel Simons and his men landed, entered and searched the compound where the prisoners of war reportedly were being held. Regrettably the rescue team discovered that the camp had recently been vacated. No prisoners were located. The SAR [search and rescue] team, according to its well-rehearsed plan, searched every building, broke the locks on doors of rooms which had been used as detention cells. They successfully returned to safety without suffering a single serious casualty.

BOB SCHIEFFER: The officers said it appeared the camp had been vacant for two or three weeks. They refused to speculate why the prisoners had been moved, but they ruled out the possibility that the North Vietnamese had been tipped in advance that a rescue attempt would be made.

LAIRD: It might be well to point out that the mission did receive quite a bit of fire. There were over thirty SAM missiles fired, and some of them were fired at rather low altitude, and I believe that they resulted in considerable damage. Firing a SAM missile at such a low range, the explosion would take place over occupied territory in North Vietnam. There of course were diversionary actions taken along the coast in lighting flares by navy planes to divert the attention from this SAR mission, but . . . these diversionary actions did draw off fire as well as fire upon the helicopters involved.

CORRESPONDENT: More than 250 American bombers bombed in the area for more than seven hours, striking at antiaircraft sites and related facilities. . . . Initial reports indicate that more than a hundred trucks were hit, and that several missiles were destroyed on the ground. . . . Pilots reported about a hundred secondary fires and explosions. All the planes got home safely.

A principal purpose of the raid, Secretary Laird said, was to "show our dedication" to American prisoners of war, "and we will do everything in our power to accomplish their early release."

The raid was carried on at the same time as were the air strikes at military targets near Hanoi, and the two became confused in spite of Defense Department efforts to explain that there was "no direct connection." Officials also denied Hanoi's claims that the bombing raids hit that city, killing forty-nine civilians.

But subsequently the story changed:

CORRESPONDENT: Confirmation of the air attacks on the outskirts of Hanoi came from the Pentagon's top spokesman, Daniel Hankin. He said the raids were carried out only to protect the American commando helicopters as they moved toward the North Vietnamese prison camp. He indicated the American fire was directed at North Vietnamese ground troops and antiaircraft installations in the area around the camp. He also said that some flares and dummy explosives were dropped to divert attention from the commandos. Hankin avoided the use of the term "bombing." He preferred the words "protective actions with appropriate ordnance." He also added he would not rule out flatly that no bombs were dropped in the area. Until Hankin's admission, the Pentagon had indicated that American bombers struck only south of the nineteenth parallel, far south of Hanoi. Now Hankin is saying: obviously we would not send those men in without protection.

And still later, a department spokesman described that "appropriate ordnance" as "about a dozen" Shrike missiles launched near Son Tay. The arguments over the bombing centered on an alleged agreement made by the Johnson administration and Hanoi in connection with the November, 1968, bombing halt in North Vietnam to the effect that U.S. reconnaissance planes would not be fired on. If they were, air attacks could be launched as a retaliatory or protective measure.

Disputes about the existence of the agreement and its meaning cleared up a little, but President Nixon in a news conference in early December warned that the United States would resume bombing North Vietnam if necessary to protect American forces. The following day Secretary Laird appeared before the Senate Foreign Relations Committee:

MARVIN KALB: The President's tough comments about the bombing chilled most senators on the committee, some of them quickly charging that the administration, Laird included, was really escalating the war. Laird did little to ease these frequently expressed concerns. In fact, in discussing the famous 1968 "understanding," which ended the bombing, the secretary seemed only to add to them in referring to the North Vietnamese.

DEFENSE SECRETARY LAIRD: They can't have it both ways. They complain that we violate some understanding when we use air power to the North. That understanding runs both ways. And if there is no understanding then they can't complain about bombing missions to the North. Now I believe there was such an understanding, and I have tried to do what I can as secretary of defense to abide by that understanding, but it goes both ways. And I think it's—if the understandings want to be discounted and thrown out, then the bombing to the North would eventually follow.

CORRESPONDENT: Chairman Fulbright seemed deeply disturbed, not only about this bombing possibility, but also some problems with the recent prisoner rescue mission in North Vietnam.

SENATOR J. W. FULBRIGHT: You stated that there was no failure of intelligence, that your intelligence was for all practical purposes perfect, I guess. You reiterated that there was no failure of intelligence. If there was no failure of intelligence, then you knew there were no prisoners there. You can't have it both ways.

LAIRD: As far as the intelligence was concerned, all intelligence agencies were consulted for all information, and intelligence information was taken from all agencies before the decision was made by me, or by the President of the United States.

FULBRIGHT: Well, I think that is—is not a very accurate response, with all deference, because it's been reported by several sources, and I personally asked the director of the CIA if he had been consulted about the—the raid itself, and he said no.

LAIRD: I would approve the kind of actions that I have approved in the last few months, as far as prisoners of war are concerned. Every effort must be made in the court of world opinion, with all of our allies, with the Communist bloc countries, to see that the Geneva Conventions are lived up to, and that these men are made free men. The Vietnamization program cannot be completed as far as I am concerned until there has been a resolution to the prisoner-of-war question.

SENATOR CLAIBORNE PELL: Right. In other words, Vietnamization will not be considered a success unless we get our men back. Is that correct?

LAIRD: That is correct.

CORRESPONDENT: And so, for the first time, the administration has revealed that unless the prisoners are released the troop withdrawal program from South Vietnam cannot be complete. Laird did not say how many troops would have to remain.

As for the raid itself, the participants were hailed and decorated by President Nixon on their return. The raid was criticized abroad and some at home called it "Operation Numbskull" or "harebrained," but General Manor said the operation was "a complete success with the exception that no prisoners were rescued."

The Unforgotten

American prisoners of war are called "the forgotten men," but this has not been entirely true. the Son Tay raid was an exclamation point to a year of highly publicized efforts to free them from the silence of imprisonment. in December, 1970, North Vietnam released an "official" list of 368 names of captured Americans; the Defense Department puts the number at 462. the President has offered an "even-up" prisoner trade, the Pope has intervened, four American wives flew to Moscow in a fruitless attempt to ask the Russians to pressure North Vietnam, a newspaper in Pottstown, Pennsylvania, carried a front-page appeal in Vietnamese asking a prisoner release. and, as always, figures alone do not tell the whole story.

Early on, the United States government told families of men captured in Vietnam that silence was the best policy, that speaking out would do no good, and that criticism of Hanoi's treatment of prisoners might mean an even harder life in the POW camps. But now nearly four thousand wives and parents of presumed POWs are joined in the

National League of Families of American Prisoners in Southeast Asia, their aim being to publicize the prisoner-of-war issue, urging citizens to write Hanoi and Washington, urging a higher priority on the issue.

The league has not secured the release of any prisoners. It certainly has centered some attention on the captured men, however, and may have been instrumental in the granting of selective interviews with the men.

Mrs. Sybil Stockdale, whose husband was captured in 1965, is the league's national coordinator:

> Back in 1966, when Hanoi marched the prisoners through the streets, the world—there was an outcry from all of the people in the world, and they were offended about that, and Hanoi seemed to respond to an outcry from all peoples of the world. And therefore I came to the conclusion that they did care about world opinion, and did want to be known, and do want to be known, as a respectable government in the world community. Now, the people of the world could not condemn Hanoi for their treatment of the prisoners if they didn't know the truth about what was happening. Therefore, it seemed to me that we had to let people know the truth.

Most of the wives are not asking much— only to find out if their missing husbands are living or dead:

> MRS. CAROL HANSEN: I have a little boy who has never seen his daddy, it's most difficult to try and teach a little boy what the word daddy means. It's hard on all of the children, and I think this is one aspect that hasn't been brought up. There are thousands of children growing up in America today not knowing if they have a father or not. Just the other day a little boy across the street told my little boy, Todd, that his father was dead. When they come back with a question like this, what do you tell them?

> MRS. PAT MERSE: There's no way of expressing that kind of heartbreak and there's

nothing I can say to her, either. Our youngest child has gone from a toddler to kindergarten, and enters first grade this year. I don't know how to put it. It's heartbreaking.

A Swedish camera crew interviewed two American POWs, Mark Gartley, a pilot from Greenville, Maine, and Bill Mayhew, a navigator from New Manchester, West Virginia. As is always the case, it was emphasized that, while the captured men were not told what to say, it was obvious they did not want their remarks to produce an unfavorable reaction toward them or their fellow prisoners:

> BILL MAYHEW: My treatment has been very good ever since I got—since I was captured. It's been much better than I'd ever— it's been much better than I ever expected it to be.

> MARK GARTLEY: And when you look at the country as—as it's been bombed by our aircraft, and it is a poor country materially, in goods, the standard in which we are—in which we are kept is very good. It's very good.

> INTERVIEWER: Is there anything you would like to add to this interview?

> MAYHEW: I'd like to say to my mother and father that I'm in very good health. I have a small head cold right now. It'll pass in a few days, I'm sure. I'd like to tell my three nieces to study hard in school and play hard, and tell my folks that I have learned to play the guitar since I've been here, and probably will drive them out of the house when I get home, and I'm not worried, and my hopes are high for the future, and that's good, thank you.

> INTERVIEWER: How about you?

> GARTLEY: Also I'd like to say hello to my family, and hope that they are in good health, and assure them [indistinct] that I am in good health, that I'm receiving good treatment, outstanding treatment here, and that— for them not to worry, that things will have a way of working out and to keep their hopes

up. And also I want to thank you for allowing us to talk to you. It's been a privilege for us, and it makes us feel good to see you and to talk with you.

While deep concern is expressed about treatment of war prisoners in North Vietnam, Saigon officials are eager to suggest that at least one of their camps, at Bien Hoa, is practically a recreation center:

BRUCE DUNNING: Bishop Henri Le Maitre was making his second visit to the camp at Christmastime. Six hundred prisoners, 300 adults and 300 boys under the age of seventeen, were lined up to represent the camp's population of 4,300 in receiving gift packages from the bishop.

The visit of a delegate from the Vatican provided an unusual opportunity for a carefully arranged tour of what the South Vietnamese consider a model prisoner-of-war camp. Bishop Le Maitre praised the camp's appearance and admonished the prisoners to prepare themselves diligently for the day when there would be peace, and he urged them to have courage and patience.

The prisoners applauded vigorously, as they had been instructed to do by the South Vietnamese guards. And as the bishop handed out their individual packets, they responded with smart military salutes. The gifts included drums and electric guitars for the camp, and individual packages containing a towel, shirt, soap, cigarettes, candy, cookies, and a picture of Pope Paul.

The gift giving was followed by a brief tour of the camp, a tour carefully directed by the South Vietnamese and their American advisers. The tour included Mass celebrated at the camp chapel, at which about a dozen of the young boys took communion.

Everywhere the tour went, the prisoners in other compounds gathered to watch silently through thick rows of barbed wire. The tour moved into a selected compound where the papal delegate visited an infirmary where men sleep on individual beds, unlike the regular shedlike barracks where the overwhelming number of prisoners spend their days on hard benches covered with straw mats.

About a third of the men in this camp, a small one by South Vietnamese standards, are permanently disabled, amputees, or blind. Several of the amputees had an unusual treat because of the VIP visit. They were allowed to wheel themselves around in circles, in wheelchairs which were provided just for the occasion. Brand-new they were, this very morning, one official admitted.

The tour ended with a visit to a special compound. Here eleven women, captured by the South Vietnamese, live in a tiny hooch, three of them with babies, one only a few days old, born in prison of a Vietcong officer and his wife captured by the South Vietnamese, a child who may well grow up in prison if peace does not come soon to Vietnam.

When Hanoi had released its "official" pre-Christmas list, Secretary of State William Rogers blasted it as a "contemptible maneuver" aimed at raising false hopes among the relatives of men missing in war. The administration was clearly committed to expand an offensive aimed at generating the worldwide sentiment spoken of by Mrs. Stockdale in the direction of a prisoner release before the general peace settlement Hanoi insists on. There was particular concern over the wounded. One of them, Lieutenant Commander John McCain III, son of the commander in the Pacific, was interviewed in a Hanoi hospital after his capture three years ago:

I was on a flight over the city of Hanoi, and I was bombing, and I was hit by either missile or antiaircraft fire, I'm not sure which. And the plane continued straight down, and I ejected, and broke my leg and both arms, and went into a lake, parachuted into a lake, and I was picked up by some North Vietnamese and taken to the hospital.

It is grandly called "the prisoner-of-war issue." This is what it meant to one family, the McCains, last Christmas:

CAROL McCAIN: Christmas has no meaning for me. I do it for my children, but for me personally it has no meaning because John is not here.

JOHN LAURENCE: Mrs. John McCain goes to the mailbox outside her home in Orange Park, Florida, six times each week. She is one of the wives who wait. She has been waiting since October of 1967.

Mrs. McCain has three children. The two older boys, Doug and Andrew, are hers from a former marriage, adopted by Commander McCain. Doug, who is eleven, plunges himself into sports he once shared with the daring navy pilot he remembers as having peculiar eyes that changed color from blue to green. Andrew, at eight, is not as big as the older boys, and as a result gets left out a lot. It is one of the concerns of his mother.

MRS. McCAIN: I worry about the boys. I don't know what to tell Doug to do with football, if he—what position he should be trying out for or how to get him up for a game. Or Andrew, if—he's gone from a little boy while John was here to a young man. And there are really problems that come up with him emotionally that I don't know what the man's reaction would be.

CORRESPONDENT: Sydney McCain, age four, is a mascot, budding cheerleader, and flag carrier for one of the Orange Park boys' football teams. Her father left home for Vietnam when she was eight months old, and she knows him now only from his photographs.

Sunday morning, the family of John McCain goes to church, the Grace Episcopal. Do you have a special prayer?

MRS. McCAIN: Well, strangely enough, the family prayer is really the fourth verse of the Navy Hymn: "Lord, guard and guide the men who fly through the great spaces in the sky. Be with them always in the air, in darkening storms or sunlight fair. Oh, hear us as we lift our prayer for those in peril in the air." And that's really kind of our motto.

CORRESPONDENT: Doug, how long do you think that the Vietnamese are going to keep your daddy prisoner?

DOUG McCAIN: Probably till the war's over.

CORRESPONDENT: How long will that be?

ANDREW McCAIN: Probably until summer.

DOUG: Maybe another year or two.

ANDREW: It may be in summer.

CORRESPONDENT: Mrs. McCain has received several letters from her captured husband, but none in six months.

MRS. McCAIN: The most recent one I have was written last June. It says: "Dear Carol, I hope you can still think of the really great times we had together. It is time for our fifth anniversary this year and I am hoping I will see you soon. Boys, please keep working hard in school and I promise we will really have fun when I come home. Love, John." He sounds okay; he sounds kind of depressed to me. When he says, "I hope you can still think of the really good times we had together," it sounds like he, you know, he's worried that I might forget or something. That bothers me: it makes me feel very badly. There isn't any way I could possibly forget.

It is the hardest thing to remember about war. Not all the casualties are killed in action.

The High Cost of Winding Down

ground troop withdrawals from Vietnam are up, casualties dramatically down—"only" 4,229 in 1970, a 55 percent drop from the previous year. it seems an encouraging thought, whether you agree that President Nixon is following the wise course toward an honorable peace or you believe in some more immediate or dramatic program. if you examine the casualty lists issued each Thursday through the year from the U.S. command in Saigon, you find the comforting figures disquieting. war winds down, but not like a toy.

On January 1, 1971—a Friday—the figures issued were "more than 40,000" Americans dead, a quarter of a million wounded in nine years of Vietnamese war. Enemy deaths over the same period were put at 586,000. No figure were issued on South Vietnamese troop losses and, it not being the military's business, civilian deaths were not estimated:

BOB SCHIEFFER: More Americans have been wounded in Vietnam than in all of World War I, twice as many as during the Korean conflict. What the statistics do not show is the seriousness of the wounds—how many bodies have been damaged beyond repair.

Since the summer of 1965, when the American buildup got under way, more than 17,000 Americans have been disabled in the war. In all cases, the wounds were serious enough to cause separation from the service. The total includes 1,928 men who have lost at least one limb. Four hundred and seventy-three men have been blinded or rendered deaf. Three hundred and thirty-five men are paraplegics, paralyzed from the waist down.

Of the wounded, one man in a hundred will come out of the war an amputee; eight of that same one hundred will be disabled in

some way. In all cases, because of better medical care and helicopter evacuation from the battlefield, the figures are lower than those of previous wars. But many of those who do survive must live out their lives with broken bodies.

The Pentagon disputes claims that men in this war suffer worse wounds than those of other wars. However, an army spot check of wounded men's medical records in 1966 and 1967 shows that of all men discharged from service because of disabilities received in Vietnam, 53 percent were amputees or suffered paralysis of the limbs. In World War II and Korea, those categories accounted for 21 and 27 percent.

As U.S. disengagement continues, South Vietnam death tolls are increasingly higher than those of American soldiers:

BILL McLAUGHLIN: The casualties are low, but the enemy hasn't disappeared. He's still here, in the mountains and in the valleys. According to U.S. Army Intelligence, there are just about as many enemy troops in Vietnam—about 250,000—as there were five years ago.

The enemy is betting that when the U.S. forces finally leave, he will be able to move out of the mountains, and everything will be right back to where it started five years ago.

Charlie Company

*Company C, Second Battalion, Seventh Cavalry, First Cavalry Division—
"Charlie Company." for weeks, reporter John Laurence and a television
camera crew covered the activities of that unit in War Zone C, near
the Cambodian border. Laurence's coverage, subsequently expanded into
a special broadcast, was hailed by the press as "both objective and
compassionate," bringing "sharply into focus the human condition."
this is the look and sound of men at war.*

After five months of almost continuous action, Charlie Company at springtime had suffered the lightest casualties of any in the area, just two KIAs—men killed in action— a fact attributed to the caution and wisdom of Captain Robert Jackson.

Jackson said, "It just kills me if one of my people gets hurt, and they may get upset 'cause I make them work a little harder or move a little farther or move a little later. But . . . I'm super cautious when the time comes to be cautious."

SOLDIER: I don't know—maybe—you can call it luck or just fate, but out of the whole battalion, since we got Captain Jackson out we have been the company that has hit the least amount of—made the least amount of contact, and if we do make contact, we're coming out the best, and since Captain Jackson took over we've only lost two guys, actual KIAs, whereas the rest of the companies of the battalion have been losing quite a few more, and it seems like with Captain Jackson we've just kind of lived an almost charmed life, and, boy, I'm not for knocking that.

SOLDIER: Like a father to a big family. I don't know, it's just that you get used to the ways of one man, and then you have to change all over again. I don't know, it's sort of like moving from one house to the other, and having a different father. It doesn't work right for a long time.

SOLDIER: Now that we're going to lose him, in my opinion, I don't think we'll ever get another CO as good as he is. There could be contact all over, but behind Captain Jackson, we aren't even worried, and it's going to, it's going to take a little, really getting used to, get your new CO.

The replacement of one lower-grade field officer by another is not the stuff of headlines, not even when it brings a unit to the verge of mutiny. But it is the stuff of war:

JOHN LAURENCE: Charlie Company had been on patrol in the field since March 24, and as the men were being resupplied this time, it was becoming apparent that no one knew clearly what they were doing now or what their mission was. Privately, the men were complaining about the seeming lack of organization and coordination Charlie Company was now experiencing since the loss of its former commander, Captain Robert Jackson, and the critical injury of its battalion commander, Lieutenant Colonel Robert Hannas. "Flaky" was the word heard most often now, a GI expression meaning that the company and the battalion did not seem to be operating as efficiently as before.

The next day the new company commander receives orders to move his men nearly a mile, the plan calling for them to be picked up by helicopters to make a combat assault. The orders also say to move down a road, something the veterans in Charlie Company had been taught by their former commander never to do.

Second Platoon, in the lead, refuses to walk down the road. To them, it is too flaky, too risky, too much of an opportunity for the North Vietnamese to ambush them. But Captain Al Rice has received orders from higher up in the command to move down the road.

CAPTAIN AL RICE: We're going to move out on the road, period. Either we're going to move out and they're going to be left behind, or I'm going to take point and they can follow me if they want to. Now, it's that simple. Now, we got a job to do and we're going to do it. It's not half as dangerous as doing some of the crap we've done out here in the boonies a while ago. At least we can see what we're doing. They'll either move out or else I move out and they sit on their butt right here. It's that simple. All right? Okay, let's move out. Tell them to make up their mind. Just tell them to sit here and then— then I'll send some people back for them, which won't go over too big at all. We can't have this. This is extremely safe; it's the safest thing we've ever done.

SOLDIER: I'm not going to walk down there. Nothing doing. Never going to do it.

SOLDIER: Going to walk down the trail?

SOLDIER: My whole squad ain't walking down that trail.

LAURENCE: What's the problem?

SOLDIER: Well, we just don't want to walk down the road. This is one of the things I told you about when we were wondering what the new CO was going to be like. These are the kind of things that you don't want to have him be like.

LAURENCE: Like what?

SOLDIER: Walking down a road.

SOLDIER: Like a shooting gallery.

SOLDIER: Like sitting ducks.

LAURENCE: Suddenly, a compromise appears. A helicopter pilot spots a possible landing zone closer to Charlie Company's position, about three hundred yards down the road in the other direction. Captain Rice changes his orders.

RICE: You go with—move out—going to be okay. That's right, the longer we sit here, the worse it gets. Okay, let's go.

LAURENCE: The rebellion begins to recede. Reluctantly, Charlie Company moves out down the road. The men are angry now and afraid.

SOLDIER: In my opinion, if he was a little more cautious, he wouldn't take us down this trail. These foot tracks look a day or two old. This trail is used quite often, you can see it, with tracks all over it.

SOLDIER: I think it's crazy.

SOLDIER: It's senseless, walking down the road.

SOLDIER: Well, they always told me not to walk down no trails.

LAURENCE: But the enemy is not waiting, and Second Platoon, in the lead, reaches its destination and begins clearing the brush around two bomb craters for the helicopters to come in and take them out. The mission accomplished, Captain Rice calls a conference among his platoon leaders and the other officers, and a discussion about discipline under orders.

RICE: I can't run around and kick everybody in the butt. I can't run around and build everybody's ego up, so you have to back me up if I say something. And believe me, if it's bad, I'll know it's bad, and you'll just have to make it out what you can—make out the best you can. Any question? Okay, let's get this LZ [landing zone] built and get out of here. I'm glad we didn't have to walk, too.

LAURENCE: The helicopters come in slowly, one at a time, lifting out the men of Charlie Company to a staging area nearby, where they'll take off for the combat assault. Waiting to make the assault, the men in Second Squad discuss the day's developments.

SOLDIER: That road was suicide walk, right there. This road clearing was about maybe six, seven feet wide, big enough for a vehicle, and on both sides of the road there was nothing but thick brush. You could have had a gook three feet inside that wood line and you couldn't have seen him for love nor money.

SOLDIER: And that is about the flakiest thing I've ever done since I've been in the Army, and I won't do it again. Come hell or high water, I won't do it again.

LAURENCE: Was there a rebellion today?

SOLDIER: You might call it that. Back in the world they call it rebellion; here it's just downright refusal. We had there the whole company—CO says okay, we're going to walk through it, and the whole company says no, negative. We've heard too many companies, too many battalions want to walk the road, and that's why they aren't what they are now. They get blown away.

SOLDIER: I don't think he knows his stuff. Hasn't been a captain but maybe two weeks, three weeks, and he's got a lot of stuff to learn before he can manage the company like Captain Jackson could.

SOLDIER: Today I found out what happens when the whole company refuses to do something.

LAURENCE: What happens?

SOLDIER: Puts everything in a big, fat bind. And I'll tell you, somebody's—heads are going to roll when this whole thing's over with. I don't know whose, maybe mine, but heads are going to roll. And it's about time. You can't—you can't do what we did this morning and get away with it. We happened to be lucky, and I'm not going to try that one again. I don't feel that lucky.

LAURENCE: If there is another dimension to the minor rebellion of Charlie Company, it is that a hundred experienced soldiers, most of whom believe in the biggest picture of all, the political reasons for the Vietnam war, veteran soldiers who are not afraid of combat, normally brave and obedient men,

would not walk down a road that to them was symbolic of the way forty thousand other GIs had gone before.

Only later did high-ranking officers tell Laurence that Charlie Company was ordered to go down the road in order to move quickly out of the way of an impending B-52 strike. There was no time to explain this to the soldiers, the officers said, because of the urgency of the mission.

But later, the deputy commander of the unit's brigade said there would be no punishment of the men who balked at going down the trail. He said the men showed good sense: "Thank God, we've got young men who question."

By mid-April, as Charlie Company made its fifth combat assault in nineteen days, it was within a mile of the Cambodian border, although the U.S. troop offensive in Cambodia had not yet been ordered:

JOHN LAURENCE: Sergeant Gene Dunnuck, the leader of Second Squad, Second Platoon, known to the company as "Killer," was anxious to "get me some gooks" on this patrol. The first problem was getting through the fire touched off by the artillery barrage before the combat assault. The flames encircled the landing zone, burning up the dry leaves and brush baked by the Southeast Asian sun for the months of the dry season.

The men were getting along better with their new company commander after the brief rebellion the previous week. He was carefully calling frequent rest breaks now and exercising more caution.

CAPTAIN AL RICE: Eight, one, delta. You were supposed to give me a read-back. I have not—yet to hear from him. I'd like to know. We could use it. Over.

LAURENCE: Captain Rice is talking to his men on observation. They have spotted enemy movement nearby and he is advising them. Sergeant Dunnuck sits nearby, waiting for an opportunity to engage the enemy. You got a nickname of "Killer." What are your feelings about killing?

SERGEANT GENE DUNNUCK: Don't have any. Doesn't mean nothing. I guess you could say it was a job to do, that's all. Either you get killed or you kill him, so better off him than me, any day. You really don't have no feelings about it, you know. You see a dead gook it don't mean anything. The only time you really feel anything is when you see a GI messed up. Then it sort of hurts you, you know. But them gooks, it don't bother you none.

LAURENCE: How'd you get the nickname?

DUNNUCK: "Killer"? Killed a couple gooks in a bomb crater one time.

LAURENCE: How?

DUNNUCK: Claymores. Threw a couple of Claymores over them. Put a few .60 rounds into them. They was taking a—they was taking a bath. Just proves not to take no baths while you're in the field.

LAURENCE: Not all of the men in Charlie Company are as enthusiastic about fighting the war as some of the others. Doc Howe, one of the four medics, is opposed to killing. Yet, as the men say, Howe has guts. He and Sergeant Dunnuck ran up to the point to bring back a wounded buddy the last time Charlie Company was in contact, braving bullets to help the GI, who died three days later.

PFC. RICHARD HOWE: I like to say that I won't, you know, fire, or shoot anybody. But then you always got the little thing back in your mind, what if all of a sudden one day there's a gook and he's got his AK pointed at you. I mean, wow, if I ever do have to kill somebody I think I'd go insane afterward, though, because of the conscience thing, wow, I killed somebody, you know, wow. I just hope it never happens.

LAURENCE: Others in Charlie Company—only a few—are unwilling to fight at all. Chess is the most serious contest Glenn Hindley will engage in, for he has not fired a shot in his nine months in the field with Charlie Company.

SP/4 GLENN HINDLEY: Well, right now I'm in a mortar platoon. I'm sort of a bystander. I sit back and watch most of the stuff, because we don't really get involved. We just sit back and we never use a gun or anything, so that makes it nice. Right now I'm in a gun squad; I'm a gun squad leader, and I think I'll make it a rule that we don't have to fire the gun. Well, I haven't shot anybody yet. I don't plan on it. I haven't fired my gun since I been here, and I like it that way.

LAURENCE: How can you get away with that?

HINDLEY: Just don't fire it. I plan to go across—across country when I get back, because I'll see the people I knew over here plus I'll be able to talk to a lot of other people, maybe convince them that killing for peace just doesn't make sense.

LAURENCE: Charlie Company has suffered a casualty. The point man, exhausted from pushing all day against the thick jungle bush, has collapsed from the heat. The convulsions have stopped, now, but he must be medivacked.

PFC. STEPHEN PUGET: Just can't walk through that kind of stuff all day. Just can't do it.

LAURENCE: What does it do to you?

PUGET: Well, try to name something it doesn't do to you. It—my partner, Marsh, walked into that right—it's littered out there. Just can't hack that stuff all day.

LAURENCE: Puget, the point man, will be able to rest for a day or two, but for a hundred other men in Charlie Company, the long, exhausting days of pushing through War Zone C, the physically punishing work, and always the eventuality of combat and killing will continue.

One April day, the brigade commander, Colonel William Ochs, banned further news coverage of Charlie Company. He did not charge that there was anything wrong with the coverage. He simply said that any additional Laurence reports would not be in the best interests of the company.

As a fitting, if involuntary, *envoi*, Laurence reported on an aspect of service life familiar to any man under arms, anywhere, any time, in any war:

JOHN LAURENCE: Mail call. Once every four days, along with a fresh supply of food and water, Charlie Company gets letters from home. Mail call means more to a soldier spending part of his life in an Asian jungle on orders to kill and be killed by other men —mail call means more than anything else, except perhaps that he is still alive, and four days shorter—four days closer to what the military vocabulary calls zero, the day a man gets out of Vietnam, what the line troops call going back to the real world.

PFC. ROBERT TESCHKER: Letter from my fiancée.

LAURENCE: Good news?

TESCHKER: Well, yeah. There's some things I don't like to hear, but mostly it's good. Always cheers me up. It's one day I always look forward to.

LAURENCE: What's the news?

TESCHKER: Oh, well, she's got a brother who is in the service, too, but he's back in the States, and just writing about him coming home, and things she's been doing. She got a raise at work, so she's kind of happy about that. And clothes she's buying for the summer coming up. Mainly, I guess she wishes I was there with her.

LAURENCE: What do you wish?

TESCHKER: Oh, I wish the same thing, but I'm getting along, I'm used to the idea, so mainly I just keep writing and hoping that she keeps writing to me. I don't care about the hot meals, and getting more food and things like that. It's mainly the mail. That's what I always look forward to. Well, it's really—it just keeps my morale high all the time.

LAURENCE: How you feeling now?

TESCHKER: Oh, I feel pretty good. You get four letters in one day, you can't help but feel good, and you save the best ones for the last anyways.

LAURENCE: Pfc. Lee Boling decided to clean his rifle while his friends in Second Squad read their letters. He received none. No mail?

PFC. LEE BOLING: No, I didn't get any mail today.

LAURENCE: Does that ever bother you?

BOLING: Yeah, it is, it really is, you know. Can't wait, you know, for some word from home, you know. But it ain't the first time, don't guess it'll be the last time, either. I'll get some next time for sure.

LAURENCE: How's it happen?

BOLING: Pardon?

LAURENCE: How does it happen?

BOLING: Oh, well, it's usually just a hang-up in the rear somewhere, didn't get it sorted, or something. But there'll be some next time.

LAURENCE: Pfc. George Rivera got six letters, the most ever at one time in the ten and a half months he's been in the field in Vietnam. He figures it's because he's getting so short, so close to going home, and his family knows he's been badly wounded once and that he's really worried now about surviving the final days.

You made quite a haul?

PFC. GEORGE RIVERA: I sure did. It's been a long time.

LAURENCE: Any news?

RIVERA: Nothing out of the ordinary, just everything's fine, take care of yourself.

LAURENCE: It won't be too long before you'll be going back home, will it?

RIVERA: God willing, I hope to be home May 15.

LAURENCE: You told me you were a little

worried about making it the last couple of months.

RIVERA: Yeah. When you get short like that you kind of get—start to worry about —you—you worry about when you're walking down the bush, you worry about getting hit. For me, I worry about getting hit again. I don't intend for that to happen again, but you can never tell. You feel that there's somebody after you, specifically, just you, because you're short. They don't want nobody else, they just want you, and it gets pretty scary. It's very dangerous to—you know—to be like that, in that position, very dangerous. Usually, when you're not worried about going home, you just hear a shot and you hit the ground immediately, but when you start thinking about it and looking around, you're not thinking about getting down. Well, it's pretty dangerous.

LAURENCE: Spooky.

RIVERA: Spooky. It's really something.

Charlie Company could no longer be reported on camera. High military officials had decided that the reports were no longer believed to be in the best interests of the company or its commander.

But, in an ironic accident of war, correspondent Laurence ran across Charlie Company again—as more than 25,000 U.S. and South Vietnamese troops drove into Cambodia, following President Nixon's announcement:

JOHN LAURENCE: Charlie Company made a combat assault deep into Cambodian territory today, part of the massive task force of American and South Vietnamese soldiers trying to encircle the North Vietnamese command headquarters. The helicopters flew for miles, mostly at treetop level, over the flat, quiet countryside that exploded this morning.

The first American troops in the assault force crossed the Cambodian border within minutes after President Nixon announced the operation to the nation. Charlie Company landed in an open farmyard and moved into the neat rows of rubber trees in a nearby plantation. There was no immediate opposition. Most of the men had no idea they were going across the border until this morning. Some were apprehensive and uncertain. Captain Rice, the company commander, was efficient, confident, and completely in command.

CAPTAIN AL RICE: Azure two nine. [Indistinct] Okay with the ground to air about two hundred mikes. Let's hear a echo. Okay, you see where all the people are down here? Tell them towards me. Tell them to the left.

LAURENCE: The men moved quickly on orders now. They are in a strange and mysterious new war zone, behind enemy lines, in Charlie country, as they call it. They are certain they will soon be fighting. Some, like Sergeant Dunnuck, are looking forward to the action, intrigued by a military offensive designed to destroy the North Vietnamese headquarters, if it is still in the area.

Another nation. But it was the same war. And it was still Charlie Company, a unit rescued only momentarily and accidentally from the anonymity of the official dispatches and the casualty reports.

History Under Pressure

war is measured in blood and dollars. a common casualty is truth. by its nature, the free press, meaning all the news media, is as much the enemy of the military command, which sees war in concepts of strategy and victory, as it is of politicians, who see the world in the same limited terms. under the pressure of logistics and time, sometimes because of inadequacy, rarely for more sinister reasons, the media may misreport an event, particularly under conditions of war and particularly under the odd conditions of the undeclared war in Indochina. this is not an apology—through the ages, the record of the press as instant history is better than that of victorious generals or statesmen. Caesar the journalist endures through the ages, as opposed to monuments won by Caesar the politician, Caesar the general. the easiest way to challenge a story that is not the story you would tell is to charge misrepresentation. given the choice, the public often accepts the official version, and that is a sad comment, partly on press performance, perhaps, but mostly on the citizen unaware that the press is not the real loser when the First Amendment is challenged. the fettered press still profits; the citizen whose news is managed ceases to be a free man, whether or not he knows it. what follows is a classic example of an attempt to discredit an unpleasant story, an inside view of the moral dilemmas faced by men whose job is to report the war, and, most tragically, the price paid for reports from the battlefield.

Weeks before President Nixon announced the incursion into Cambodia, correspondents in the field were digging at the story. As South Vietnamese troops flocked into Cambodia in spite of U.S. appeals not to do so, Saigon denied the incursions and allied soldiers on the border barred correspondents from telling the story.

For years the border crossing had been sealed off by barbed wire and barricades. The fact that it was now open proved to be one of the more significant developments in the war. A few days earlier President Thieu said he hoped that Cambodia and South Vietnam could cooperate in ridding the region of Communist forces. Officially or unofficially, that cooperation began without the presence of the press. Months later the story—or the "no story"—was to be repeated in Laos.

Excuses for exclusion of the press are unacceptable. From the beginning of the Vietnamese war, civilian newsmen reported cases of atrocities committed by allied troops —despite threats, censorship, and suppression.

Both the United States and South Vietnam signed the 1949 Geneva Conventions governing treatment of war prisoners. Article 17 states: "No physical or mental torture, nor any other form of coercion, may be inflicted on prisoners of war to secure from them any information of any kind whatsoever." In specific reference to undeclared or civil wars, the articles prohibit "violence to life and person, in particular murder of all kinds, mutilation, cruel treatment, and torture."

What occurred following a report broadcast on the CBS Evening News in November, 1969, could have happened to any magazine, newspaper, or television or radio network.

A film story, from Vietnam, showed an atrocity by South Vietnamese soldiers, in the presence of Americans. For reasons not entirely clear, the White House engaged in an undercover campaign to discredit the story by charging it was faked. The campaign involved the prompting of receptive reporters and columnists to publish White House suspicions about the authenticity of the report.

Clark Mollenhoff, then Special Counsel to the President, and a prizewinning investigative reporter, confirmed that he had investigated the story but refused to say who had authorized the investigation. Syndicated columnists Richard Wilson and Jack Anderson repeated the substance of the charges. They suggested that CBS News authenticate the report, Anderson arguing there can be no defense for faking the news.

The fact is that after the original broadcast, CBS News had furnished the text to the Pentagon, which had made its own videotape recording of the story. But, in keeping with its policy in such cases, CBS News declined a request for outtakes—that is, film which was not broadcast—and refused to name the Vietnamese cameraman who shot it on grounds his life could be gravely endangered by reprisals, further believing that the Army had ample resources to investigate the incident without reliance on an independent news agency as its informer. The Pentagon's response was the campaign to discredit the report.

The documentary had told something about the nature of the war in Vietnam. The flack it created told something about the government and its relations with news media that carry stories the government doesn't like:

CORRESPONDENT: . . . Sergeant Mot stabbed the prisoner a second time, when the prisoner did not appear to be resisting or threatening his captors. We do not know if he was alive at that time. And, after the stabbing, a picture we did not show before. The body of the prisoner was slit open. We do not know why.

It has been suggested the advisers were Australians, not Americans. That is untrue. It has been suggested the combat assault was really a training exercise. That is untrue.

It has been suggested the enemy was dead when he was stabbed. But the man who stabbed him concedes the prisoner was alive when knifed for the first time, before our film scene began. Sergeant Mot claims self-defense. That may be true, although we did not know of that possibility when we first broadcast the story last fall, and the Pentagon, despite its own investigation, has not alleged that as a fact. It is clear the prisoner was stabbed a second time and his body then was mutilated.

The Pentagon may wish to believe this story never happened. But it did.

White House Press Secretary Ronald Ziegler asserted, "Neither the President, nor my office, nor [Director of Communications] Herbert Klein's office, nor anyone else at the White House to our knowledge ever authorized any investigation . . . nor has any involvement by questioning or talking to reporters about it been authorized." As to the identification of Mollenhoff as the source of the charges, Ziegler said Mollenhoff's responsibilities did not involve investigating news media.

It is frequently argued that the news media emphasize or even report only those atrocities committed by American or allied troops. Apart from the obvious fact that reporters and cameras alike seldom travel with the other side in wartime, this is a misconception. Atrocities are committed by both sides, and no newsman in Vietnam sees enemy forces as the forces of light. Generally, however, the Vietcong terrorist tactics are more selective, if only because they depend on villagers for food and shelter. Generally, but not always.

Communist forces attempted to disrupt South Vietnam's Senate elections with a terrorist raid outside Da Nang:

CORRESPONDENT: The targets of the enemy attacks were children. In the middle of the night mortar shells began falling on an orphanage run by Buddhist monks. After fifty hits in and around the orphanage and nearby hospital buildings, some thirty men attacked. The orphanage was undefended. No soldiers, no barbed wire, no trenches slowed the enemy. Uniformed, helmeted soldiers, thought to be North Vietnamese, simply walked in and began throwing grenades at the children and the staff. Automatic rifles and machine guns sprayed bullets in the rooms. Of the nine persons killed, five were children. Of the forty wounded, two-thirds were children.

A young man wept at the coffins of his mother and, atop it, his baby sister. Survivors said that during the raid the chief Buddhist monk was dragged into a courtyard, his hands bound, and shot. Also hit was a nurses' residence, where three more died. The enemy had come from nearby hills, where South Vietnamese marines went the next morning, in search of the attackers.

The Vietnamese and the Vietcong have promised terrorism, children no exception.

The free citizen expresses his opinions freely; the journalist is free to express them only in his off-hours, of which there are few

if he is doing his job. Whether it is exposing a scandal at city hall or the horror behind the casualties of war, he has learned to compartmentalize his opinions, unless he is writing an editorial. He may be cynical about the masthead slogan proclaiming that people, given the facts, will find truth, but he is obligated to the unwritten law that his interest is disinterest. Few choose to be typewriter warriors.

It is no more pleasant for a correspondent to look on death and tragedy than it is for any other citizen. It is, however, part of his job. The emotions behind the coverage are a different matter, and they take an emotional toll. Peter Arnett is a New Zealander who reported for the Associated Press from Vietnam for eight years with high distinction, including a Pulitzer Prize. In July he was reassigned to New York, feeling that covering the war is a young man's game. "I'm too old," he said. He was thirty-five at the time. He was interviewed by Morley Safer:

PETER ARNETT: As a reporter, I've often found the one way to make a telling point— the real way to make a telling point is to get a dramatic incident or get a dramatic quote from someone. So after the Tet offensive I was one of a group of newsmen who went down to Binh Tri, in the delta, and I had the fortunate—I was fortunate that I'd been there a week before the Tet offensive.

I knew all the Americans there. And one American major said to me in a moment of revelation, he said, "Well, we had to destroy the town to save it." The place was blown apart, 450 civilians killed. So I used that in my story, and it's been widely quoted since, but there have been charges that I made up the quote, that it was unfair.

But I don't think it was unfair. I think that incident and that quote characterized a view of the war that—or a policy that was prevalent in 1968. I don't say that policy is prevalent now. I think that that quote possibly helped to alter policy. Now they don't blow away towns in Vietnam. They do in Cambodia, but not in Vietnam. The rules are tighter here, and I think that's how we can make a contribution.

A big criticism of television is that they're looking for blood on the moon every night, because they—a lot of the time they want war and they want blood and guts. Well, I don't think there's anything particularly wrong with it, because for every incident, there are hundreds that they aren't photographing.

And even right now, say a relatively quiet week in the Vietnam war, there's probably two or three thousand people dying violently out there, being killed, killing each other. And so . . . to somehow pretend that—that it's not important or it's being overdone is not true. I think pacification's important, but I think the most important aspect of Vietnam has been the killing and the war. That has been the overriding factor. It's not the politics or the pacification; it's the killing. It's the people who are getting gunned down, of both sides, that's the—to me, the important factor. And that's what I have concentrated my reporting on.

QUESTION: Do you think, looking at Cambodia, that—across the border to Cambodia, that, you know, my God, I've seen it all before. There it is, it's—it's happening again. We've gone full circle.

ARNETT: Yeah, well, I must say that when President Nixon made the dramatic announcement of the Cambodian incursions, I had the same sinking feeling in the pit of my stomach as I had when President Johnson announced that U.S. marines were landing at Da Nang. And it . . . to me it opened a whole new epoch of the war. And that means I can just see another decade of it, the killing around here.

QUESTION: . . . People ask—have asked of me, and I know of other reporters . . . with all the killing, do you become so hardened to it that you just don't notice it anymore? Has that happened to you?

ARNETT: No, well, I probably was a reverse case. As I said, I took a hardboiled approach to . . . covering the Vietnam war from the very beginning. I'd seen dead bodies on the police beat back in Sydney that, up here, the—the dead that I saw, it just—I just didn't let it really register within me, and I saw dead—I've seen as many as 120 dead Americans on a battlefield at the Nhatrang Valley, and I've seen 200 at a time North Vietnamese just chopped to pieces by artillery, and I've always tried to look past that, and I've sort of written about it, but somehow, maybe it's because I'm leaving that I start to—I just—I just—it's starting to sicken me now, but the—the slaughter is sickening me.

. . . I went across with the troops into Cambodia early in May in the little rubber plantation town of Snoul [that] had been hit and the North Vietnamese had dug in, and there was a battle for the town. We went in on the tanks next morning and the enemy had fled. Left in the marketplace were five bodies, a woman, looked like three kids, and a man, had sort of been all fused together with napalm. And I thought . . . I just don't want to see any more bodies.

That may be one of the reasons that I'm sort of—that I have fewer regrets at leaving. Somehow, the slaughter is catching up with me. Because now I know that I can see that it's just going to be a continuing slaughter, you know, and it's just going to go on.

I figure that I've had enough of it for the time being. I need to go to a decompression chamber somewhere.

At least 30 newsmen have died on Indochina battlefields. Seventeen are missing in 1970.

Two of those killed were CBS News correspondent George Syvertsen and reporter-producer Gerald Miller. They died May 31, thirty-four miles south of Pnompenh, when the jeep they were riding in on a peaceful-looking highway either struck a mine or was hit by enemy fire. The jeep was gutted by flames. Their bodies were found in shallow graves near the roadside.

Syvertsen was thirty-eight, a Columbia College graduate, a linguist, married. Gerald Miller was forty-two, a native of St. Louis, educated at George Washington University there and the Sorbonne in Paris. He was married, had two daughters, eleven and ten, was a World War II and Korea veteran.

Syvertsen and Miller knew the danger of their assignment, for the news media one of the most hazardous operations yet. Syvertsen and Miller didn't have to be on that dangerous road where they met their deaths. No one ordered them to go. There was little personal glory in store; they had both established their courage and their ability long ago. There were no financial bonuses waiting for them at the end of that road. They went because they were reporters and they believed there was something there that the American people ought to know. That was their job. They dedicated their lives to it.

In the midst of the Cambodian incursion, John Gunther, perhaps the century's most famous exponent of journalism as history under pressure, died in New York. The events, separated by thousands of miles, were nonetheless related, as Eric Sevareid saw them:

> The President will argue tomorrow night that the Cambodian exercise has shortened the war. Maybe. It may also have cut short the lives of a dozen or more broadcast and newspaper reporters and cameramen, some from this office. Three or four are, or were, prominent persons in this trade.

A few years ago the Metropolitan Life Insurance Company did a little actuarial study about those known as prominent people. It found that prominent people lived longer than the average; among them scientists, clergymen, educators, and military men lived the longest. Executives, judges, and lawyers the next longest. Those prominent persons with the shortest life expectancy are writers, editors, correspondents.

This morning here in New York some friends gathered in a church out of respect for John Gunther. He was not only a prominent journalist; at one time he was probably the most famous American reporter of them all. He almost made it to the biblical three score and ten, and managed to die in bed. Neither he nor his innumerable friends around the world would have thought that likely. He consumed life voraciously, and in all logic life should have consumed him long ago.

He was one of the inventors of a kind of literary form, the book-length reportage, which brought distant, wispy realities to life and colored them bright, enthralling millions of readers and inspiring hundreds of young men and women to wish to go forth and do likewise. Very probably including some of those now missing somewhere in the Cambodian forests.

Gunther was a leader in that original, extraordinary band of American journalists, some with midwest hayseed still in their hair, some, like the Sheehans and Mowrers, scholars and linguists, who rampaged through Europe in the twenties and thirties, and somehow ended up on first-name terms with kings and bartenders. More than diplomats or politicians, it was they who told America what was happening and what was going to happen to the civilization of the West.

A Feeling of Déjà Vu

*at the opening of the decade of the seventies Cambodia occupied roughly
the same amount of American concern as Vietnam had a decade
earlier: a faint knowledge that it was there, like a nervous headache.
the United States was under no commitment to aid Cambodia, the latter
having rejected protection from SEATO, the South-East Asia Treaty
Organization established under the Eisenhower presidency and
functioning in the new decade as a collapsed umbrella. diplomatic
relations between the United States and Cambodia had been resumed
only in June of 1969, after a four-year lapse when Cambodia called things
off following a border incident. officially neutral, Cambodia served as
sanctuary and supply source of men and munitions to Vietcong and
North Vietnamese forces in South Vietnam. about the size of the state of
Missouri, with a population of less than seven million, Cambodia was a
constitutional monarchy, all the seats being held by members of the
Sangkum party, founded by Prince Norodom Sihanouk in 1953 after he
had abdicated his throne in favor of his parents. not surprisingly,
he was elected chief of state by the Assembly in 1960.*

Cambodian neutrality existed more in the breach than in the observance, of course. If the Sihanouk regime tolerated the Communist presence, its objections to Allied incursions during the Vietnam war were channeled diplomatically. Americans claimed "the inherent right of self-defense" by firing into Cambodian territory whenever U.S. or South Vietnamese troops were shot at across the border.

When American firepower killed or wounded Cambodians or damaged their property, the Cambodian government lodged protests, demanding compensation. An instance: On February 20, 1970, the United States formally apologized, paying $11,400 for thirty-five Cambodians killed or wounded in air attacks against Vietcong artillery positions in Cambodia over a two-day period the previous November. This averaged out to something over $325 per Cambodian national involved and was accompanied by a note asking the government to prevent the use of its territory by enemy forces.

The tenuous relationship between the two nations was illustrated by the *Columbia Eagle* incident. That 7,500-ton U.S. freighter, bound for Thailand with air force ammunition and napalm, was seized March 14 in a two-man mutiny.

The pair, after commandeering the vessel, used a phony bomb scare to force twenty-four crewmen into lifeboats. The crewmen later were rescued. The armed men forced Captain Donald Swann and the remaining thirteen crewmen to take the ship to an island off the Cambodian port of Sihanoukville. Clyde W. McKay, Jr., and Alvin Glatkowski would later say that their act was only "the first of a series of mutinies" designed to impede the Vietnam war. They called themselves supporters, although not members, of the Students for a Democratic Society. After the captain filed mutiny charges, they were described as "pot-smoking hippies."

While a coast guard cutter trailed the ship into Cambodian waters and five U.S. naval vessels stood by for "contingency assistance," the Cambodian government announced it would not return the ship, fearing a "risk of misunderstanding."

"So," said the government, "we are just going to leave it there."

This was the statement of an early-seanon skater testing the ice. For there was a new, rightist Cambodian government involved. Not until April 8 was the ship released.

In January, Prince Sihanouk had left the country for treatment in a French clinic to lose weight, thus unbalancing hefty affairs of international moment. Plans called for him to visit Moscow and Peking—the fat cure was revealed only later—even before he learned of anti-Communist demonstrations in Pnompenh, the Cambodian capital. An estimated twenty thousand demonstrators attacked both the North Vietnamese and Vietcong embassies there, protesting the presence of forty thousand Communist troops in the country.

It may be that he was too attentive to counting calories and party loyalty, but Sihanouk left the country in charge of Premier Lon Nol and Deputy Premier Sirik Matak, his most outspoken opponent and a critic of government controls and "corruptions." Both men also opposed Sihanouk's tolerance of Communist troops in the nation.

Sihanouk flew to Moscow to warn Soviet leaders that his government would fall to "conservatives" unless the Communists withdrew. Back home, diplomatic letters went off to North Vietnam and the Vietcong demanding withdrawal of all their troops within days.

Communist embassies were sacked in Pnompenh, Communist negotiators asking for compensation. While Sihanouk made no apparent progress in persuading the Soviets to use their influence with Hanoi and the guerrillas, Cambodia's military leaders turned to the South Vietnamese for assistance in shelling Cambodia-Vietnam border camps.

The new governmental dramatics toward a posture of neutrality were quickly reflected by Communist troop action along the South Vietnamese border.

Sihanouk was formally deposed in a bloodless coup March 18, the last day of his mission to Moscow. But before he left, the popular, erratic prince indicated that he knew the difficulty of his position and, in the light of later charges that the United States was involved, offered an interesting comment:

> They do not need to make a coup against me. You know, I'm not very attached to power. So, you know, if I see one day that the people and the army wanted to go to the right, I will—I will certainly help them go to the right. Everything is possible, but I do not want to accuse the United States. I have not any proof about it, but I can say that some officers in our army and many deputies and many members of the government . . . they want to be your allies in order to have dollars, your dollars. They do not care—they don't think about the destiny and the fate of our homeland. They don't mind about it. They are more patriots toward dollars than toward Cambodia.

American officials expressed surprise over Sihanouk's ouster, but few counted him out of Cambodian politics. Some suspected, in the beginning, that Sihanouk had instituted the coup as a desperate, dramatic way to shed his nation of the Communists. Senate Majority Leader Mike Mansfield, an admirer of Sihanouk, saw "disintegration, chaos, and additional difficulties ahead":

> When you think of that country, you have to think of Sihanouk at the same time. They're just like that, and one will not get by without the other for very long. . . . Sihanouk is one man who, no matter how you interpret him, always knew what he was doing, always had his objective in mind, and always was able to accomplish it . . . the one man in all of his kingdom who can keep the kingdom together.

The new government moved quickly to crush any attempt by Sihanouk to regain power, declaring what amounted to martial law, suspending most constitutional rights for six months. Asian observers believed that the Communist forces in Cambodia would fight for his comeback. In Saigon, Vice President Ky said a Cambodian civil war could lead to a take-over by North Vietnam. "The Cambodians," he said, "would be vulnerable because they're not as hardy as the Vietnamese."

Even as Sihanouk broadcast from Peking urging his people to rise and overthrow the people who had overthrown him, the new government achieved at least outward signs that it had the situation under control in the capital if not the countryside:

> GARY SHEPARD: The city itself is quiet. Shops and business establishments are keeping their normal hours and hotels are once again doing a brisk tourist trade. Journalists are officially not permitted to enter Cambodia, but . . . the government has been looking the other way when newsmen enter the country with tourist visas.
>
> An official "state of emergency" which was declared by the National Assembly last week is still in effect. That gives Prime Minister Nol the authority to suspend the freedoms of speech, press, assembly, and private correspondence. In recent days, there has been a rapid move to erase visible reminders of the Sihanouk government. Here, on Sihanouk Street, huge photographs of the prince have been removed, and even his name has been taken off the signposts at every street corner. . . .
>
> Rumors are everywhere in this city that Prince Sihanouk will attempt to return and reestablish his government here. General Lon Nol has made it clear that if Sihanouk tries to do that, he will be stopped by whatever means are necessary. Still unclear is how the new government will attempt to back up its demand that the North Vietnamese and Vietcong forces leave Cambodian soil. At the moment, North Vietnamese forces inside Cambodia alone outnumber the entire Cambodian army.

Those numbers were discouraging: a 35,000-man army, backed by light tanks, medium and light antiaircraft and field guns, and a few 105-millimeter howitzers; a 1,500-man navy operating with 18 patrol boats; and an air force with 45 combat aircraft.

On March 26, the United States command in Saigon disclosed that for the first time American planes had bombed Communist positions inside Cambodia. Simultaneously, the North Vietnamese and Vietcong announced that they were closing their embassies in Pnompenh. They said the action did not represent a diplomatic break with the new regime, only a suspension of relations.

South Vietnamese troops, backed by jets, attacked Communist units two miles inside Cambodia the following day, announcing a body count of fifty-three Vietcong. While the thrust appeared to have been carried out at Cambodia's request, a State Department spokesman in Washington said the United States opposed an extension of the war into Cambodia.

In spite of the diplomatic niceties, it was clear that Cambodia was becoming another battle area in Southeast Asia, even as U.S. ground forces remained in Vietnam:

RICHARD THRELKELD: It's dawn, and Alpha Troop One Nine is commuting to war, twenty-one GIs bound for a jungle clearing a mile from the Cambodian border, American soldiers hiking their way through the sweating jungles of South Vietnam, searching for an elusive enemy. The temperature is almost one hundred degrees and the jungle stifles even the tiniest breeze. The going is slow. There could be a North Vietnamese regiment hiding a few yards away and no one would see it. Nobody talks, so you start thinking.

Specialist Four Duane Moore is thinking he is going to meet his fiancée in Honolulu in two weeks, and he will show her the Silver Star the general pinned on him yesterday. Devalier is the lone medic in the platoon. He's scared—scared from the moment he gets out of the chopper to the moment it picks him up, scared that someday he's going to get killed picking up a wounded buddy. Jorgensen just became a sergeant, but he doesn't like it—he'd rather be up walking point where the action is. He's already got three Purple Hearts, so everybody calls him "Hero."

Then there's Lieutenant Hubley. Everybody calls him "Blue"—that's his radio call. Blue didn't want to come to Vietnam. He'd much rather be a businessman than a soldier, but right now he's in charge of the lives of twenty-one men. Somewhere in this jungle there are several hundred North Vietnamese soldiers who could wipe out this little American unit to the last man in an unguarded moment. Today, though, it's quiet, a few bunkers uncovered, then a quick lunch and back down the trail to the pickup zone. Just a peaceful walk in the sun.

MAN ON RADIO: Okay. Okay, would you roll in now, at two seven zero. From the smoke approximately one zero zero meters away from me now, judging from here.

DEVALIER: All right, who's wounded? All right, give me some cover. Get him back here. Get him back here if you can. Can you move him? Can—can you move him? Okay,

bring—try to bring him back here. Remember to stop the bleeding.

CORRESPONDENT: And Devalier, the medic, having survived another rescue mission, brings back a wounded man. Who is it, who is it, the question spreads down the line. Oh, Christ, it's Hero, the sergeant who likes to walk point. How bad is it? A couple of leg wounds.

SGT. CRAIG JORGENSEN: We were walking down the trail. I was walking point, and I noticed a side trail, it was one of the side trails we came down. It had more use on it than when we first came down it. So I looked up and spotted, it was an NVA, he had on a green uniform, and an AK, and it was like a, you know, quick, the whole thing, I opened up on him and he opened up on me. Yeah, I'm afraid it looks that way. But he's lying up there on the trail. I got hit in both legs, but that's about it. Well I've got seven months in the country now, three Purple Hearts. I don't need a fourth.

CORRESPONDENT: The enemy soldier who shot Jorgensen cannot be found. He may have survived or dragged himself off to die. Most of the time you never really know. The problem now is to get Hero out of here, so Blue calls in the Medivac helicopter and sets up a perimeter to protect him. Hero has stopped making brave jokes now. The shock has worn off and the pain has begun. The helicopter hovers over the jungle and in the midst of the fire fight his buddies put Hero on the rescue chopper and he's pulled up a hundred feet—a hundred feet to a hospital bed and a one-way ticket out of the Vietnam war. And then it's quiet again, Alpha Troop One Nine, less one man, gingerly making its way back through the heat and the smell of gunpowder, back to the pickup zone.

Tomorrow the military communiqué will read one American was wounded in an engagement with an unknown size enemy force. Enemy casualties are unknown.

Sergeant Jorgensen was released from the hospital, with another Purple Heart, while in Cambodia itself there were violent demonstrations in support of the ousted Sihanouk.

Government forces sealed off the provincial capital city of Kompong Cham after two members of the National Assembly were chopped to death with knives and axes attempting to halt a crowd of Sihanouk supporters who had set fire to the local courthouse. When the demonstrators refused to disperse, army troops opened fire, killing twenty-seven, wounding sixty-two, many of them women and children.

The killing, in the words of a British tobacco buyer, "was fairly indiscriminate, a twelve-year-old child and a woman, one or two women and young men."

The government appealed to the United Nations Security Council to pressure for the removal of Communist troops, saying that if the international body did not feel the situation was serious enough, it would ask for U.S. military aid "but not troops."

You did not have to be a cynic, then, to believe you had already seen the movie. This, as Eric Sevareid noted, "has often enough been the prelude to requests for American military personnel. Altogether, the Vietnamese war is once again revealed for what it implicitly always was, the centerpiece of a general Indochinese revolution and civil war encompassing all three countries.

"The official notion of several years ago that American intervention would stabilize Southeast Asia now has more of a dreamlike quality to it than ever. The official notion of the past few months that we could neatly extract our own troops while the South Vietnamese neatly expand their power until the enemy withers down to impotence—this is acquiring the quality of a dream, at least to more and more observers."

Dreamlike, the Cambodian government denied that American forces had the right to pursue Communist troops into Cambodian territory and a day later, declaring that "calm has been restored," released more than four hundred political prisoners jailed by Sihanouk. Trinh Hoanh, secretary-general of the revolutionary committee, told the prisoners, "You were branded pariahs and criminals because you were compelled by your conscience to oppose despotism." But the civil war between pro- and anti-government forces flared, with the victor in doubt. The fact of civil war was no longer in doubt.

Although the argument would be advanced, as it had been in Vietnam, that Cambodia was an invaded nation rather than a country ripped by civil war, some elements of civil war surfaced clearly. An estimated 400,000 Vietnamese lived in Cambodia and the Nol regime, whipping up anti-Vietnamese sentiment against the invading Communists, used phrases like "the time has come to save our country, the Cambodian race, and our religion." Some one hundred Vietnamese civilians, detained as possible Vietcong, were killed by gunfire in their barbed-wire compound. The Cambodian commander said men, women, and children had been caught in the cross fire between Cambodian and Vietcong troops, but eyewitnesses described it as "massacre," saying Vietnamese survivors were told by government troops to run and were then fired upon.

As Cambodia asked for arms to combat Communist troops, Senator Mansfield urged fellow senators to oppose any form of military aid, charging Cambodian leaders with moving toward mass slaughter of Vietnamese civilians living under their rule. And a body count at the Mekong River seemed to bear out the charge:

BERT QUINT: The war, and its human flotsam and jetsam, has come floating down the Mekong. Face down they come, rigid arms outstretched as though grasping at some seaweed that would stop their drift, singly and in groups, the pattern varying as it varies with live humans strolling down a dirt road.

How many are there? In the ten minutes or so it takes to cross the river on the Highway One ferry at Neak Luong, I didn't have the speed of eye or discipline of will to turn the bodies I saw into numbers, but there must have been fifty.

Who are they? It's hard to be sure, but they seem all to be men, and because they are wearing the shorts of a Vietnamese farmer rather than Cambodian sarongs, it is safe to say that they are Vietnamese.

Government officials say that they are Vietcong killed in battle. Maybe. But it's no secret that a lot of Vietnamese civilians living in this country in villages along the river have been killed for suspected collaboration with Communist troops and in retaliation for the beating Cambodian soldiers have been taking in clashes with the Communists.

This seemed to be the high tide of floating bodies, but for hours after this ferryload of living debarked, the dead kept floating by.

In spite of the earlier claims that "calm has been restored," the government regime was openly asking for outside arms aid. Nol did not specify any country, but his appeal apparently was directed to the United States.

South Vietnam denied that its troops had moved into Cambodia to slow Communist domination of the countryside and, officially, Washington appealed to the South Vietnamese to forgo their forays, but U.S. support bases sprang up within a few hundred yards of the Cambodian border and Allied soldiers barred foreign newsmen from following the action.

On April 20, 1970, President Nixon announced troop withdrawals of fifty thousand men over a period of months from Vietnam. But by then, the slow stride of events since the turn of the year made it clear that the Cambodian combats were complicating the Viet-

namization program, while battles snarled just nineteen miles from the capital city:

BERNARD KALB: This is the closest the war has yet struck to Pnompenh. It's the latest evidence of the Vietcong advance, and the latest evidence of the limited capability of the Cambodian forces. The Vietcong are just down the road a few hundred yards. Nobody knows how many Vietcong are there; the guess is a couple of hundred. But they took the town of Saang about twenty-four hours ago some three miles down the road.

The colonel in command is career army. He says that he's got four battalions on his side, but that a couple of them aren't much use—brand-new recruits. The colonel wants to save lives. Instead of ordering a ground attack, he called for an air strike. It takes time, communications are not the best, but finally T-28s appear, strafing runs on Vietcong positions. But the strafing gets the Vietcong to pull their own triggers, and war breaks out. . . .

That's what they call "incoming"—some Vietcong mortars coming in our direction. Lots of small-arms fire all over the place. Turns out that the enemy had also infiltrated into the other side of this river, so there's a cross fire hitting this command point. But after a while it's quiet, as though there had never been a war.

The strangest things happen. Just before the shooting broke out, even before the air strikes, when no one was moving down this road, which had Vietcong at the other end, these two Buddhist monks suddenly appeared as though they were tourists, just like that. They reported that the VC were down the road, and then the monks left some water. The water becomes holy; everyone tried to get a little of it.

Meantime, the colonel was saying, "We're hoping Americans will help us with arms . . . because we are fighting the Communists. It's a race against time . . . between us and the Vietcong. The Vietcong are hurrying to get the most Cambodian territory while we Cambodians are waiting for military aid."

And back down the road for a mile or so, there were Cambodian reinforcements, waiting, waiting in all kinds of trucks to join the war, this war that keeps getting closer and closer to Pnompenh.

". . . closer and closer to Pnompenh." Like the Paris after which French colonizers modeled it, Pnompenh seemed the soul of its nation; strategically, rivers, agricultural areas, infiltration routes are vital. But to the great world, a capital represents a nation in more than a strategic or even political sense; strategy is second to circumstances—Washington the symbol rather than the Pittsburgh mills or the midwestern breadbasket; London rather than Birmingham or Devon.

And so it tells something of the nature of this war to jump ahead, remarking the almost separate "battle of Pnompenh." For if much of the rest of the nation was conceded to enemy troops—and it was—the capital and the highway connecting it with the nation's only deep-sea port, Kompong Som, clearly were areas to be held at all costs. Through spring, summer, fall, and winter, the tides of war eddied around the capital, casualties a dozen here, a hundred there, at crossroads towns for which there is no glossary.

The fluidity of the war, a concept of win one, lose one, with the few staked battles symbolized by the capital, made claims proffered by either side equally serious, equally foolish, and nearly impossible to judge in terms of conventional war. Everyone was learning, and thousands died. Cambodia seemed in the language of its colonizers a grim reflection of *plus ça change*—"the more things change, the more they remain the same."

The Communists fought a frustrating hit-and-run war. Government forces, not strong enough to wage full-scale combat, destroyed their own villages to make sure nothing was left behind for the enemy.

There was a growing suspicion that the Cambodians were "only slightly better disciplined and trained than your average Boy Scout troop." On April 17 the United States announced it would offer Cambodia some Russian-made AK-47 automatic rifles captured in South Vietnam. Senator Mansfield objected: "I am opposed to military aid to Cambodia in any way, shape, or form."

The consensus held that President Nixon was adamant about not sending U.S. advisers deep into Cambodia. He was reported hopeful that interior fighting would be backed by advisers and arms from Thailand, Korea, Indonesia, and other Asian countries. Carefully, there were few comments about the border areas. The Senate Foreign Relations Committee announced on April 22 it was sending investigators on the trail of American military involvement in Cambodia.

The small arms shipment pointed up, as Eric Sevareid noted, that Cambodia's "war is becoming an integral part of the general fighting in Indochina, in which we are so deeply involved that this government doesn't yet know just how to get out of it, or when, in spite of hearty official assurances to the contrary. . . . Hawks look at events in Cambodia as an opportunity to distract and surround the Communist units and bases. Doves look on them as offering only an extension of the general quicksand for America to flounder in."

The administration used much the same terminology in characterizing the Cambodian conflict that previous administrations had in describing the Vietnam war. The White House said that the fighting in Cambodia could not be considered a civil war but rather resulted from a foreign invasion. "It is an obvious fact," said White House News Secretary Ronald Ziegler, "that forty thousand Communist troops in Cambodia are clearly an invasion by a foreign country and could in no sense be considered a civil war." The reports were that there would be "no direct intervention by U.S. troops." American involvement was to be limited to supplying Cambodian troops with U.S. arms and equipment.

South Vietnamese troops continued to sweep into Cambodia as the Soviet Union accused the United States of "military provocations" that could have "the most serious consequences."

President Nixon on April 29 authorized American advisers and support units to assist South Vietnamese troops in strikes against Cambodian sanctuaries. In Washington, angry senators of both parties charged the administration with expanding the war.

Even the hawks were muted and limited in their support. As a political sidelight, the decision almost instantly unified the dispirited Democratic party, while Senator George Aiken of Vermont commented, "Whatever chance we had of winning the Congress is out the window."

For the moment, so were political considerations as the world awaited a presidential address on Cambodia.

On April 30 the Senate Foreign Relations Committee issued a statement calling the Allied operation "a grave development" and demanding that the administration answer "important questions" concerning Indochina policy. Great Britain, which had backed U.S. moves in Vietnam, withheld support for the Cambodian feint. The Soviet Union accused the allies of a gross violation of the 1954 Geneva agreements on Indochina. Congressional broadsides emphasizing disagreement and confusion over the move placed President Nixon on a momentary political defensive.

On the front itself, the big surprise was not that South Vietnamese troops were in Cambodia, which had been known for more than a week, but that they had penetrated so deeply into Cambodian territory. South Vietnamese Lieutenant General Do Cao Tri emphasized the extent of American involvement:

> Well, it's normal, and because we are working together and closely since many years. Everywhere we operate, we have—we have always the support of U.S. airmen. . . . I consider the enemy as a common enemy, where they are. If they are inside our territory, we destroy them. Now, if they are in Cambodian territory, we fight them also.

The Cambodian government, which had been informed about the allied sweep into its territory but not consulted, said it would protest "in principle."

In a nationally televised address on April 30, President Nixon announced that a major U.S. troop offensive was under way in Cambodia. He said it was "not an attack on Cambodia," since the areas involved "were completely occupied and controlled by North Vietnamese forces."

The President said, "We take this action not for the purpose of expanding the war into Cambodia, but for the purpose of ending the war in Vietnam."

The attack, he said, concentrated on "the key control center" and "headquarters for the entire Communist military operation in South Vietnam." Faced with the possibility that Cambodia could "become a vast enemy staging area and springboard for attacks on South Vietnam," the President said he was faced with three options:

- To "do nothing," thus imperiling U.S. forces in Vietnam and confronting the allies with "an untenable military position."
- To offer massive military aid to Cambodia, which "could not be rapidly and effectively utilized" by the Cambodian army.
- "To go to the heart of the trouble . . .

[which] means cleaning out major North Vietnamese and Vietcong-occupied territories" that serve as sanctuaries for attacks in Cambodia and on South Vietnam.

Speaking of "intolerable" intransigence by the enemy at the conference table, the President said, "We will not react to this threat to American lives merely by plaintive diplomatic protests. If we did, credibility of the United States would be destroyed in every area of the world where only the power of the United States deters aggression."

Speaking of an "age of anarchy" when great institutions at home and abroad are under attack, the President continued, "If, when the chips are down, the world's most powerful nation . . . acts like a pitiful, helpless giant, the forces of totalitarianism and anarchy will threaten free institutions throughout the world. . . .

"If we fail to meet this challenge, all other nations will be on notice that despite its overwhelming power the United States when a real crisis comes will be found wanting."

He ended with a reference to Senator Aiken's comment that the Cambodian actions ended chances for the Republicans to gain control of Congress. "I would rather be a one-term president and do what I think was right than to be a two-term president at the cost of seeing America become a second-rate power and to see this nation accept the first defeat in its proud 190-year history."

In Boston the following day, Senator Edward Kennedy hit hard at the President's speech in phrases that would be repeated, expanded on, by other critics in coming months:

Last evening we heard the same words and implications again, the same words that we have heard for the past five years of nightmare. Logistics, sanctuaries, combat support, cleaning out of areas, freedom-loving defenseless people, the one more chance to hit the enemy hard. They flow, these words, on the smooth surface of phrases about avoiding humiliation, no defeat, supporting our boys, and the like. They flow, but they can no longer lull. For now we know what they mean. They mean sorrow, they mean death, they mean increasing air strikes, Thursday's casualty figures, and perhaps some new Hamburger Hill, and in some new country for some new reason that we dare not question.

This is madness, and it must be said. It is also demeaning to a great nation to attempt to justify it in the name of patriotism and honor and glory.

On Capitol Hill, as through the nation, the presidential announcement provoked anguished criticism, hawkish praise, and a good deal of old-fashioned soul-searching. For the first time since 1919 and President Wilson, the Senate Foreign Relations Committee called for a meeting with the President. Aiken said it didn't seem too much to have a meeting with the President once every fifty years.

Allies in the Far East endorsed the President's decision and, it goes without saying, the Communist nations reacted with political blasts. France, which had lost out in Indochina, deplored the move, saying it could only escalate the fighting; Canada expressed "regret" over the action and Britain was rebuffed in an effort to talk Russia into reviving the Geneva conference that was supposed to have brought peace to Southeast Asia.

The Foreign Relations Committee, in a report recommending the repeal of the Tonkin Gulf Resolution, charged that the executive branch was conducting a "constitutionally unauthorized presidential war in Indochina," ignoring the war and treaty-making powers of Congress.

As critics talked about cutting the presidential purse strings on the war or questioned his legal authority to act in Cambodia, the general concern was whether President Nixon's actions were forcing a constitutional crisis between Capitol Hill and the White House. The presidential meeting on May 5, 1970, with the Foreign Relations Committee, its House counterpart, and two other committees was overshadowed by the deaths of four Kent State University students and campus disturbances across the nation protesting the shooting of the Kent students and the Cambodian incursion. The meeting produced no change in the divisions among those present.

Meanwhile, more than 25,000 American and South Vietnamese troops were driving into Cambodian territory, making little contact with the enemy and beginning their search for the Communist headquarters which was an announced major allied objective.

Alpha Company, Third Battalion, Twenty-second Infantry Regiment, was moved without explanation to a forward staging area at Tin Ngon in Vietnam, five miles from the Cambodian border. The men were told only that they would be moving out and to take enough C rations to last three days. Then they learned they would be airlifted by helicopter into Cambodia as part of a task force attempting to wipe out a major base camp on the other side:

> FIRST SOLDIER: I don't know. I'll tell you what. If I [indistinct], I'd just say I'm just going—I'm going—I'm going with them. I ain't going out. If they got about eight people staying I'm going to stay back, too, 'cause it ain't worth it.

> GARY SHEPARD: You realize what can happen to you?

> FIRST SOLDIER: I don't care. I never even [indistinct]. Dishonorable, bad conduct, undesirable discharge—that don't mean that

much to me. It means a whole lot to my father and my mother, see. This is why I'm here now.

CORRESPONDENT: Are you scared?

FIRST SOLDIER: [Indistinct] I was scared when I got my draft notice. Being scared ain't [indistinct]. Yeah, I'm scared. Who ain't?

CORRESPONDENT: Time grew short. Other men of Alpha Company began to speak out as well, and it became apparent that there were few of them who really wanted to go.

SECOND SOLDIER: Most of us got very few ammo, and we're not really prepared. Just overnight notice for us, really. We're just really not prepared.

CORRESPONDENT: When those choppers come in here in a little while and load you guys up and take you in there, are you going to get aboard, or are you going to stay here?

SECOND SOLDIER: Well, it really depends on my buddies. I'm all for what they—if they go, I'll have to go. It really don't do any good for just a few of us to stay. Got to get a lot of us.

CORRESPONDENT: How many of the men here do you think really want to go in there today?

SECOND SOLDIER: Very few. But there's not enough—very many of them willing to stand up for what we know is right, but I don't know, if they'll [indistinct] about going into it.

CORRESPONDENT: You say the morale's pretty low here in Alpha Company?

SECOND SOLDIER: Definitely. Very low.

CORRESPONDENT: Why?

SECOND SOLDIER: Well, the way we've been getting pushed around. We don't get supplied like we're supposed to. They don't tell us what's going on or what we're going to do or anything. So it's definitely very low.

THIRD SOLDIER: We went on missions where the ARVN refused to go out, into their country. They refused to go out and fight, but yet still we fight. What makes a—a hero? Courage? What makes a coward? Like, going to Cambodia, would that make us heroes? They don't want us there. If it was, that would be a different thing. Now, we're supposed to go through some village—village which—you can ask any officer around here—they don't even know where we going. If they do they're not telling us.

CORRESPONDENT: When the helicopters arrived to carry Alpha Company to the new war in Cambodia, there was some hesitation, but no one stayed behind. Each man moved out when he was given the signal, wondering, perhaps, what he would face when he jumped out of the helicopter across the border, wondering too whether he would ever make it back.

As demonstrators gathered in Washington to protest "Cambodia and Kent State," President Nixon defended the incursion, saying that history would show it "served the cause of a just peace in Vietnam." The President accepted full responsibility for the move—"I believe it will work out. If it doesn't then I am to blame."

From frontline communiqués to back-home debate and testimony, the war was confusion. The Pentagon announced that U.S. troops had captured a major base complex in Cambodia that could be COSVN, the North Vietnamese military headquarters for South Vietnam. But White House News Secretary Ziegler said this was not confirmed, that it was his understanding that COSVN actually was "a group of men who moved from place to place." The find was the biggest base uncovered so far, in terms of construction and communication facilities.

By mid-May, President Nixon was saying that Cambodia was "an enormous success," with more than 50,000 enemy killed and more ammunition captured "than the enemy expended in Vietnam over the last five

or six months." There was, of course, a price for this: U.S. weekly casualties hit a high for the year—123 Americans killed, 997 wounded; 450 South Vietnamese reported dead.

But COSVN, despite the high priority given to its discovery, proved to be as elusive as a halfback.

At the end of it all, after U.S. troops had withdrawn, COSVN and the furore attending it proved to be like so much of the Indochina war: a definite arrival at no conclusion. No one claimed the allies had found the headquarters, no one claimed they had not, and, finally, no one claimed it had ever really existed.

In spite of military successes, Cambodia raised long-term questions amounting to a gamble, as Eric Sevareid noted:

All this begs the great questions, of course, of the constitutionality of the President's action, the international repercussions, the profound domestic division, and one can only guess at the situation a few months from now if and when the enemy readjusts to these blows. But the President will not be devoid of arguments and facts on the military level. There is a fairly widespread conviction among his critics here that he is really seeking to end this war by final military victory. If he isn't, he very much wants a military success, dramatic in nature, and this may turn out to be it.

He has on his mind, after all, not only the students and other antiwar forces, but powerful right-wing forces ready to explode in their turn at anything resembling a military humiliation. Should that happen, he would really lose control of American opinion, so Cambodia remains what it was—an immense gamble.

And it was over the question of this gamble that the debate centered, Secretary Laird affirming that "every single public pronouncement, every single timetable has been met. And I can assure you that the

President of the United States continues meeting those timetables, those deadlines that have been stated publicly. . . . And his program to end this war and to bring peace in Southeast Asia is the most credible program that has been presented at any time to the American people since we became involved in Southeast Asia."

Clouded by debating, the fighting continued.

The ironies of war are always present. Even with the best intentions, civilian and soldier view the days of battle differently. The GI in a "popular" war knows that it is hell in a different sense than anyone else who proclaims the sentiment. When there is division both on the front and at home, the collision of experiences becomes something deeper than a vignette.

A U.S. unit fought inside the Cambodian border for an area as meaningless to the people back home as most Oriental place-names. But, along with events immediately following, it demonstrated the different lenses through which the war is viewed by civilians —even politicians of power—and by the men who do the fighting:

GARY SHEPARD: Bravo Company's mission is to take Hill 423, a seemingly insignificant piece of terrain ten miles inside Cambodia. Little did the men realize when they moved out that when they made it to the top they would have another name for Hill 423.

The enemy was waiting when Bravo Company and a reconnaissance platoon from Echo Company began the assault, and it wasn't long before the men were in the midst of bitter fighting. The battle raged on for nearly four hours, and before it was over, six members of Bravo Company had been wounded. While the rest of the company pressed on to the top of the hill, the wounded were carried to a small jungle clearing where a helicopter would carry them to hospital beds in South Vietnam.

Specialist Four Chris Kepolose of Albuquerque, New Mexico, was killed in action during the battle. When the company finally made it to the top of Hill 423, the men decided to name it after him. From then on, it would be known as Shakey's Hill.

SP/4 JOHN SHIRING: Well, he kind of had a speech impediment and he always stuttered so, like on the LZ one night we all got drunk, and that's how he picked it up, Shakey. So they started calling him Shakey all the time 'cause he stuttered so much. . . .

He was only nineteen years old. Well, more or less everybody kind of looked after him, because, say, he was the baby of the platoon, you know. . . .

CORRESPONDENT: Shakey's Hill turned out to be a major Communist supply depot, everything from Chinese Communist AK-47 rifles to machine gun bullets and medical supplies. . . . Just how large a cache is it?

LIEUTENANT BOB LEWIS OF MIAMI, FLORIDA: Well, it's—I feel it's going to be one of the largest ever found, including Vietnam or Cambodia, the reason being we found, let's see, twenty-nine bunkers, and you can see what comes out of one bunker—It scares you, because it could actually—this could—this could be enough ammo for another Tet offensive, I believe—I mean, plenty of it to supply many, many, many troops. I've never seen anything like it before in my life.

CORRESPONDENT: In a few days helicopters will fly in here and take Bravo Company to some other part of the war zone, but the men who fought for Shakey's Hill will never forget this place.

In June, as President Nixon addressed the nation on the Cambodian campaign, a hastily assembled delegation of congressmen, governors, and administration officials left on a four-day fact-finding mission through the war zone. The guest list was heavily sprinkled with supporters of the President's Asian policy, an exception being a New Hampshire Democrat, Senator Thomas McIntyre.

One of the stop-off points was Shakey's Hill, where the military went to some lengths in preparation for the fact finders:

JOHN LAURENCE: The top of Shakey's Hill was a mudhole in the hours before the arrival of the President's fact-finding delegation. It had rained all night on the troops of the Ninth Infantry Division, who relieved the battered men of Bravo Company. . . .

The order of this day was: look professional; that meant clean and orderly. The garbage of war which normally litters such places was carefully cleaned up. Captured enemy weapons were polished. Clean white linen was placed on the tables that were especially lifted to Shakey's Hill for the inspection of the captured arms.

The military exercise in showmanship went as far as haircuts for the soldiers, three barbers having been flown into the fire base. Some of the men were given clean fatigues and combat boots, which they normally get less often. The officers gave careful instructions to the troops about their behavior.

OFFICER: Okay, now, they'll be in here at ten fifteen, so let's get going on it. Everybody get changed. Everybody got a haircut now? What about you, Ralph? Let's get a haircut. Everybody shave. Who hasn't shaved around here?

CORRESPONDENT: Most of the GIs were not at all impressed by the sudden shift in their normal routine.

PFC. GLENN BOLLMER: This is a crummy place. It's a mudhole. You just, you know, you sit around in the mud and you sleep in the mud and get dirty.

SOLDIER: Just like animals.

BOLLMER: Not today. We're going to play games, and that's about it.

PFC. DENNIS BRENN: They don't want them to go home and say, you know, and tell all their voters, "Boy, your kids really got it hard over there." Say, naw, they got clean clothes and good living conditions—all kinds of good stuff.

CORRESPONDENT: Is that true?

BRENN: Oh, yeah. No, we don't have anything. We live like animals until somebody comes. Sleep in the mud, rain. Now we get all dressed up, you know.

CORRESPONDENT: The delegation arrived in four helicopters, minus the most skeptical member of the fact-finding team, New Hampshire's Senator Thomas McIntyre. All the rest were there: Governors Shafer, Love, and McNair, Senators Tower, Murphy, and Cannon, Congressmen Price, Bray, Whitehurst, and Fisher. They were immediately led into a tent for a long account of the action in Cambodia, the fight for Shakey's Hill, and the cumulative results of the arsenal of captured weapons. As a souvenir, each member of the delegation was given a North Vietnamese web belt. The delegation inspected the carefully prepared display of captured enemy weapons. Each of the visitors was invited to talk to troops from his home state. Each soldier was carefully chosen, dressed, shaved, and briefed beforehand.

CORRESPONDENT: Throughout the tour of Shakey's Hill, the Air Force ran close-up air strikes. It was a spectacular sight, napalm at two hundred yards, low-flying jets streaking across the tops of trees blasting their guns, dropping their bombs.

Finally the visitors were led down a jungle path that had been carefully chosen for them to inspect two of the bunkers that had held some of the captured weapons. A few of the elderly legislators climbed down a rickety ladder to inspect the cache site. They were not told that the weapons they were looking at down in the hole had been put there, having once been removed, to give them the impression of reality. Senator Tower of Texas said afterward: "You could question the political effects of the offensive into Cambodia, but you could not question the military achievement."

And Senator Tower saw nothing out of order in the special preparations for the visit:

This is what they ordinarily do when anybody in government visits them. They say they clean up. I did it when I was in the Navy in World War II. When a top-ranking officer came on board, we shaved and we put on clean clothes. That's in the nature of things; that's the way—that's the way the military works.

The task force, reporting to the President, found little to criticize in his handling of the war, saying the move into Cambodia had proved successful and productive of immediate dividends.

American bombings of Cambodia, first officially confined to stockpiles and interdiction, stepped up almost in the ratio of U.S. aid—from $30 million to $250 million.

President Nixon called the just-concluded invasion a military success; the Senate vote, after almost two months of debate, told him, in effect, not to do it again without congressional approval:

MORLEY SAFER: If you isolate the guns and ammunition and rice as simple statistics, the sheer tonnage of what was taken in Cambodia is impressive. The figures issued by the military here, which include the results of both American and Vietnamese operations, the box score, as it's called, do not include any estimate of how many arms and men were in the sanctuaries before the intervention, so it's impossible to estimate just how badly the enemy was hurt. One of our most important officials in Saigon admits that our intelligence in Cambodia is, quote, "abominable."

Herewith the joint U.S.-Vietnamese battle claims. They say 11,285 enemy were killed, 2,024 captured. Weapons: 19,303 rifles, enough to equip 55 enemy battalions; 2,514 larger weapons, mortars and rockets, enough to equip 33 battalions. Rice: 6,900 tons, enough to feed more than 25,000 men for a year. Ammunition: 1,777 tons of it. That includes 59,000 grenades, 10 million machine gun rounds, plus 1,800 rockets, and a hundred thousand rounds of large-caliber mortar and rocket ammunition. Enough, say the military, to launch almost 19,000 attacks by fire, an average of eight rounds per attack. Plus 55 tons of medical supplies and 432 vehicles. That does not include bicycles.

Losses suffered by American and Vietnamese were 339 Americans killed, 1,501 wounded; Vietnamese, 800 killed, 3,410 wounded.

Incidentally, we do not announce our own losses in matériel. It's known that many tracked vehicles, tanks and personnel carriers, were destroyed in Cambodia.

The favorite term of military briefers, the kill ratio, has been maintained at ten enemy to every one friendly, precisely the ratio the Saigon computer, for the past five years, has been saying will win the war.

Officers back in Vietnam are officially elated with the box scores, but privately frustrated by the results of the Cambodian offensive. They had sought a major battle that would break the back of enemy operations in Cambodia and Vietnam, but they encountered only small security units guarding arms caches, which makes the claim of 13,000 dead and imprisoned enemy slightly questionable. And, of course, COSVN, the main objective of the operation, managed to slip away.

As U.S. planes moved to fly support for allied troops, and Communist forces seized large sections of the nation, Eric Sevareid saw a grim future:

"We are not deeply involved, militarily, in Cambodia, but our political, economic, and advisory commitments to that embattled government have surely deepened. There are plenty of verbal assurances to be had around here that Cambodia is not and will not become another Tar Baby, but the doubts are growing, not diminishing."

"Kind of a Miniature Vietnam"

it is in Laos, population three million, touching on both North and South Vietnam, Cambodia, Thailand, and China, that the United States' Indochina involvement most deeply reflects the mysterious West. through three administrations, there have been official denials of varying vigor that Washington was much involved in the small but strategic land whose neutrality was guaranteed under the Geneva accord of 1962, to which the United States and Hanoi were both signatories. but Hanoi maintains a sizable army in Laos to aid the Communist Pathet Lao rebels against the neutralist government of Premier Souvanna Phouma. officially, there are no U.S. ground troops in Laos, no more than the number of military "advisers" there were in Vietnam in 1961, but the heavy bombing of Laos' Ho Chi Minh Trail was acknowledged, if not spelled out, under pressure. just how sizable a commitment in Laos and what form does it take?

In the fall of 1969, a Senate Foreign Relations subcommittee, headed by Senator Stuart Symington of Missouri, held a closed-door probe of U.S. military commitments around the world.

The testimony would not be released for five months, fatefully on the very day that President Nixon announced the Cambodian incursion. Although Cambodia overshadowed the heavily censored report on Laos, Symington made clear he had found the Laotian entanglement serious enough to hope it would serve as a warning against American involvement elsewhere in Indochina.

In response to pressure by enemy forces threatening the Laotian government and infiltrating men and supplies into South Vietnam, the testimony indicated, the United States was waging a growing clandestine war. Secrecy was needed to avoid jeopardizing the neutrality of the government, but U.S. bombing attacks increased along with the enemy troops.

When, on November 1, 1968, President Johnson ordered an end to the bombing of North Vietnam, the targets were simply switched to the Ho Chi Minh supply route. A change in American administrations changed nothing in this case. In 1969, according to military testimony before the Symington subcommittee, those raids tripled, at an estimated cost of $3,190 per mission—or, as Senator Mike Mansfield figured it, something like $600 million a year. Added to this was an estimated $150 million yearly for Central Intelligence Agency personnel reportedly acting as advisers to government troops.

At this time, the matter of human casualties was left conveniently vague. So heavily was the testimony censored that the official transcript did not even show that CIA Director Richard Helms had testified, let alone report any of his testimony, although his appearance ranked high on that lengthy list of "worst-kept secrets in Washington."

Early in 1970, United Press International reported that the United States was losing planes at the rate of five a week over the Ho Chi Minh Trail. This added up to about 300 planes and 150 pilots lost over Laos since the bombing halt in North Vietnam. And in spite of official disclaimers as to the extent of U.S. involvement, it was clear to newsmen on the scene:

BILL McLAUGHLIN: Indochina's forgotten war, the on-again, off-again, but bloody and bitter struggle in Laos, has just produced a new crop of war refugees. The famed Plain of Jars is being cleared of all its people. Not for the first time, they are in the way, this time in the way of a new Communist offensive and United States Air Force bombers waiting to strike the Communists.

For the time being the Royal Laotian Army and the U.S. Military Assistance Command have a shaky control over the plain, but only for the time being. Two new North Vietnamese divisions have reportedly moved into Laos. Together with their local Communist allies, the Pathet Lao, they have begun an offensive to take the plain, one of the most fertile farming areas of Laos. The feeling here is they stand a good chance of succeeding. These people want out and away, away from the Communists and away from the inevitable U.S. bombing runs.

Fifteen thousand Laotians are being airlifted out of the Plain of Jars. The job is being done with a speed and dispatch rare to this tiny kingdom. Almost three thousand refugees a day are being carried off the plain in C-130 cargo planes.

The planes, incidentally, fit well into the patchwork pattern of this strange war. They belong to the no-name airline. Actually, they and their crews have been provided by the United States Air Force. For the emergency Plain of Jars airlift, they are on loan to the Central Intelligence Agency's private airline, Air America. Laos hasn't the men or equipment to do the job, and the United States, keeping its profile low, would just as soon avoid publicity. The planes are flying question marks. They carry no markings, no identification.

The air journey ends some thirty-five miles to the south, at Vientiane Airport. Laotian police cadets are on hand to help the dazed refugees past the plane's slipstream and into waiting trucks. There is no time to ask questions about where they are going and what the new land is like. The trucks will take them thirty miles to the east, to unpopulated territory that, for the moment at least, is well outside the combat zone.

These people have been promised by the U.S. and Royal Laotian governments new homes, new land, and enough food to eat. But no one has promised them that they won't have to move yet again. You don't make that kind of promise in Indochina.

The situation quickly deteriorated. A week later, six North Vietnamese battalions were reported massing for attack in the Plain of Jars; three days later, on February 16, 1970, four hundred U.S. airplanes failed to stop a ground attack; two days later, on the eighteenth, B-52 bombers, apparently diverted from Vietnam in an escalation of U.S. efforts, flew in direct support of Laotian ground operations for the first time. Previously—or so the military claimed—U.S. air strikes had been confined to the Ho Chi Minh Trail.

A day later, Idaho's Senator Frank Church denounced U.S. military operations as being conducted in Laos without treaty or congressional authorization. He said the attacks, hundreds of miles from the Ho Chi Minh Trail, had nothing to do with the war in Vietnam. In Vientiane, sources said the B-52 raids helped blunt the enemy offensive; Premier Souvanna Phouma claimed he knew nothing of any B-52 attacks.

Whether or not he had heard of them, the raids reportedly were continuing to inflict heavy casualties. But the North Vietnam buildup continued, with some estimates putting the troop numbers at fifteen thousand in an offensive sweeping to within miles of the highway linking the nation's two capitals, Vientiane and Luang Prabang. And the premier called for an emergency meeting of the fourteen nations that had signed the Geneva agreements guaranteeing Laotian neutrality.

Republican Charles Mathias of Maryland told the Senate on February 25 the storm signals were flying, with the U.S. engagement in Laos violating congressional directives and threatening to repeat the "mistakes" of our Vietnam involvement. But Secretary of Defense Melvin Laird, acknowledging that there had been U.S. air strikes in Laos, told reporters that there had been no basic change in American policy:

> The President has made it clear that we have used American air power to protect American forces in connection with the Vietnam war. He has also made it clear that there are no American military forces engaged in ground combat in Vietnam, that we have a military assistance mission there. . . .

CORRESPONDENT: You mean in Laos?

LAIRD: . . . in Laos. We have a military assistance program there, but there are no ground forces of the United States military involved in combat operations in the—in Laos.

Senator J. W. Fulbright was not reassured:

> The press reports are very disturbing. They do not report that ground combat units are there, but they report, as you know, very extensive bombing by the B-52s, and one report said they—they thought these were former Green Berets in civilian clothes that are armed. There's a group of them. One report, news report reported them at one of the airfields, and then there was a—well, there were extensive reports about the bombing by the B-52s, in the Plain of Jars.

CORRESPONDENT: Well, who are we to believe?

FULBRIGHT: Well, judging by past experience going back six or eight years, the press reports have turned out to be much more accurate than the official statements with regard to Vietnam. We know that.

More than mere accuracy seemed to be at stake in Laos, as Eric Sevareid noted:

> Next door to Vietnam, in the geographical expression of Laos, the United States and North Vietnam are fighting an auxiliary war, in spite of those Geneva agreements supposedly neutralizing Laos. This has been going on for years. The American people know something about it only because of the press and in spite of the government.
>
> A growing group of senators are persuaded we do not know enough about it, and are determined to break down the wall of official secrecy. They want to know, for one thing, why, after years of American efforts at training and supply, the Communists have been able to push the Laotian army out of the Plain of Jars with such apparent ease.
>
> Today, ranking officials here said again that we are in Laos only to protect our position in Vietnam—we bomb the enemy supply trails there but have no ground combat forces there. If we did, that would be a violation of congressional directives.
>
> The senators are not satisfied with these generalized assurances. They are beginning to get eyewitness testimony to the effect that the American servicemen working at various functions in support of the Laotian forces, but masquerading as civilians, run to many hundreds, perhaps thousands. Neither the public nor Congress has had a breakdown of the costs of our operations in Laos. By one report the Central Intelligence Agency alone spends around a hundred million a year in that country.
>
> And we have economic aid operations, millions spent dropping food, clothing, and farm implements to Laotian peasants. Much of this is done through private, American-run airlines, paid by the number of flights and flying times. Documented claims of widespread waste—unnecessary flights deliberately laid on, hundreds of tons of material dumped at

random in the jungles to collect the fees—these stories are now reaching the congressmen concerned.

We are in Laos to protect our position in Vietnam; we are in Thailand to protect our positions in Laos and Vietnam. Asia is a large place. We fight a war of attrition in Vietnam, a body count war, and the premise seems to be that Asia will run out of Asians.

It was in Laos that the confusions and conflicts of the whole Indochina picture seemed most sharply in focus:

BILL McLAUGHLIN: The most important thing about San Thong, a dot on the map just south of the Plain of Jars, is its airstrip. It may not look it, but this is one of the busiest little airports in the world. Every day there are more than three hundred takeoffs and landings at San Thong, considerably more traffic than many domestic U.S. airports ever see.

Most of the planes and helicopters are piloted by Americans working for Air America, or directly employed by the U.S. Central Intelligence Agency. They bring in food, arms, and ammunition for General Van Pao's secret army, which is now bearing the brunt of the fighting in Laos against the North Vietnamese.

The people around here mostly belong to what appears to be a vanishing race. They are Montagnards, Meo tribesmen, culturally and ethnically different from both Laotians and Vietnamese. Now they're being used by both sides, by the Laotians, the Americans, and the North Vietnamese, as a kind of human no-man's-land, a buffer zone between the U.S.-backed Laotian government and the North Vietnamese and their Laotian Communist allies.

The Meo were once supposed to be a happy-go-lucky people. That was ten years ago, before the current war for Laos got under way. Since then, the 350,000 Meo people on the government side have lost 20 percent of their tribe, and over 40 percent of their men.

San Thong is also a hospital for the Meo guerrillas. The situation here has gotten so desperate that many of the wounded are thir-teen, fourteen, and fifteen-year-old draftees. They hardly seem big enough to carry a rifle. As soon as they get patched up they are sent out again to the front lines.

The San Thong hospital also has a VIP prisoner, Nguyen Van Tho, a medic from the Twenty-seventh North Vietnamese Battalion, who was captured in one of the battles on the Plain of Jars two weeks ago. Tho knows why he is in Laos. He says he's here to help the Laotian people get rid of the American imperialist aggressors. It is a difficult struggle, says Tho, but in the end Vietnam will win.

"If the military seesaw goes down in Vietnam, only to rise in Laos," said Senator Mansfield, "our situation will not have improved; it will have worsened." He saw the United States and North Vietnam involved in Laos "up to their necks." As pressure on the administration increased for a fuller report card on Laos, Secretary Laird found himself clashing with Senator George McGovern of South Dakota:

SECRETARY MELVIN LAIRD: The military assistance program, provisions for it, of course were made in the Geneva accords of 1962, and we are operating in accordance with the Geneva accords of 1962, but I can categorically state that there has been no buildup of individuals, whether civilians or military, on the ground in Laos or within the country. I cannot tell you where Senator McGovern gets other information.

SENATOR GEORGE McGOVERN: I think he's giving us a misleading picture. What the secretary has said about the actual number of American forces in Laos may be true. It may be that there has been no significant buildup there, but that raises the question: how many American forces have we had in there all along? There are a number of people who are highly informed on this area who believe that we are hitting Laos now with a heavier daily bombardment than we were North Vietnam even at the heaviest period of the bombing of North Vietnam, and based on what I've been able to piece together, that's what I believe.

The debate developed a new wrinkle when Senator Abraham Ribicoff of Connecticut charged that thousands of U.S. dollars from a fund set up to stabilize the currency of Laos had turned up in a New York City bank. Ribicoff, something of an authority on black-market operations in Southeast Asia, said that American commercial pilots were smuggling $400,000 a week from Saigon to black-market money dealers in Bangkok, Thailand.

What was billed as "the first full accounting given by any President to the American people about the secret war in Laos" was offered by President Nixon on March 6. He said there were 1,040 Americans in Laos, 616 directly employed by the United States, 424 more working under special contracts. Only 320 of those Americans, the President said, were engaged in military advisory or training jobs. No American stationed in Laos had ever been killed in ground combat operations.

Americans dead in the air war over Laos: 393, the President said, and he said there had been only one B-52 raid on the Plain of Jars, that is, away from the regularly bombed supply route. The President did not say the United States would never commit ground troops to Laos. What seemed more realistic, and what was being talked about, was that if Laos fell, U.S. troops would go to neighboring Thailand, as they had in 1961 when President Kennedy sent them, in part to head off a Communist takeover and in part to calm the nervous Thais.

The Nixon statement only temporarily muted senatorial criticism. The report itself quickly came under fire when the President's statement that there had been no U.S. combat deaths in Laos was acknowledged as error; twenty-six men had died there. Then, a day later, the figure was upped to "less than fifty" with a promise that henceforth a weekly list of U.S. forces killed in Laos would be issued.

And the Laotian government called for more American air support, in what, after years of clandestine activity, was clearly "a kind of miniature Vietnam." Premier Souvanna Phouma said that the Pathet Lao and North Vietnamese were stepping up their attacks, attempting to recapture the rice bowl region to replenish stock seized by the allied forces in Cambodia. Whatever the reason for the offensive, Americans were clearly needed to blunt it:

BILL McLAUGHLIN: This is the village of Ban Nag Boua, a Catholic village destroyed last month. It wasn't destroyed by the North Vietnamese; they attacked and American war planes were called in from their bases in Thailand. U.S. aircraft also hit a neighboring village, destroying the school and a number of houses.

This patrol, a company of the Royal Laotian Army supported by two armored personnel carriers, is setting out in support of Ban Na Son village. During the night, the village and its army outpost were under attack by an estimated four companies of North Vietnamese belonging to the Da Cong, a kind of North Vietnamese Special Forces. There is much evidence of Communist military activity in the area, an abandoned camp where the North Vietnamese or Pathet Lao left behind a few traces of their passing, socks and medical equipment.

The commander of this rescue and reinforcement operation, Colonel Atsaphong Thong, gives the orders to move out from his command car. Information here is scarce, but the unit knows the North Vietnamese are near, so it moves cautiously. The enemy did not go far. Firing breaks out from the surrounding forest just as the patrol arrives at the outpost.

There have been many tales, few of them flattering, about the fighting ability of the Laotian army. This unit apparently has not heard them. It attacks, charging across the rice fields into the North Vietnamese positions in the forest. The two armored personnel carriers move in to cover their advance, opening up with machine gun fire.

This is where American support for the Laotian army is crucial. A light U.S. observation plane flies in, probably from its base a few miles south in Thailand. The plane is unmarked, but the pilot is clearly an American who knows his job. While he spots the North Vietnamese positions with smoke grenades, he talks to the Laotians in the outpost below and calls in more air support.

The American forward air controller directs the incoming T-28s, ancient prop trainers turned fighter-bombers, against the North Vietnamese positions. Thanks to the air support, the enemy drifts away. Without it, the fight for Ban Na Son might have ended differently.

As in Vietnam, a helicopter flies in to take away the dead and wounded. The Laotians have lost two dead and at least twelve wounded, including civilians. It is impossible to estimate the enemy losses, but there are three Vietnamese bodies on the ground, and fifteen automatic weapons have been left behind.

On April 1, the government rejected Communist proposals for peace talks, largely because foremost among the enemy demands was the unconditional halt of all American air raids in Laos prior to negotiations.

The pattern was familiar: tentative offers of peace talks by both sides, collapsing over minor points, and major demands for the impossible, and the weekly battle count—this time less of deaths than crewmen and aircraft missing: three planes one week, no crew; two crewmen missing the next, two more planes; then four deaths in a helicopter. The low casualties that attract almost no notice . . . and the clashes of temperament and philosophy that do: Senator Fulbright revealing secret testimony from Secretary of State William Rogers saying that the United States would not commit ground troops to

Laos even if it were overrun; Rogers's reaction, "angry and disappointed," and a denial he ever made such a flat statement.

There was the ebb of battle and the flow characteristic of the Indochina war: that unheard-of U.S.-operated support base at Sam Thong, seventy-five miles north of Vientiane, reported in danger of falling, then falling—with all twenty Americans reported out safely—then, in two weeks, a government announcement that its troops had recaptured it. And, still later, that characteristic comment on the Indochina war—report of looting; civilian employees at the base saying the victorious Royal Laotian troops who reoccupied the base had "proceeded to steal or destroy whatever they could find—drugs, medical supplies, beds, and other furniture."

Laos remained a battleground between the Nixon administration and its critics. Typical of the differences, a midsummer confrontation between U.S. Ambassador to Laos Gordon Godley and the Senate Foreign Relations subcommittee:

MARVIN KALB: To Senator Symington and other members of this Foreign Relations subcommittee, Ambassador Godley is the American proconsul in Laos, not only a diplomat running a vast, expensive CIA operation, but also a general directing U.S. air attacks against Communist forces. In part for this reason, the White House ordered Godley to say nothing on the record, in fact, to destroy all tapes and transcripts of his testimony, an unprecedented order.

At year's end, in spite of the lights of publicity first cast upon it, Laos remained the most mysterious and enigmatic phase of the mysterious and enigmatic American involvement in Southeast Asia, the proverbial puzzle within a mystery.

The sense of mystery quickened at year's end with stories that U.S. B-52 bombers based in Thailand were flying an average of nine hundred missions a month, striking at the Ho Chi Minh Trail in Laos. While a mission planner called the air strikes "entirely effective," there were growing indications that the Laotian hills threatened deeper involvements. If the Pentagon believed that the bombings alone stemmed the flow of Communist supplies, skeptics remained unconvinced.

Scenes from exclusive CBS News film showing atrocity in Vietnam which U.S. government sought to discredit.

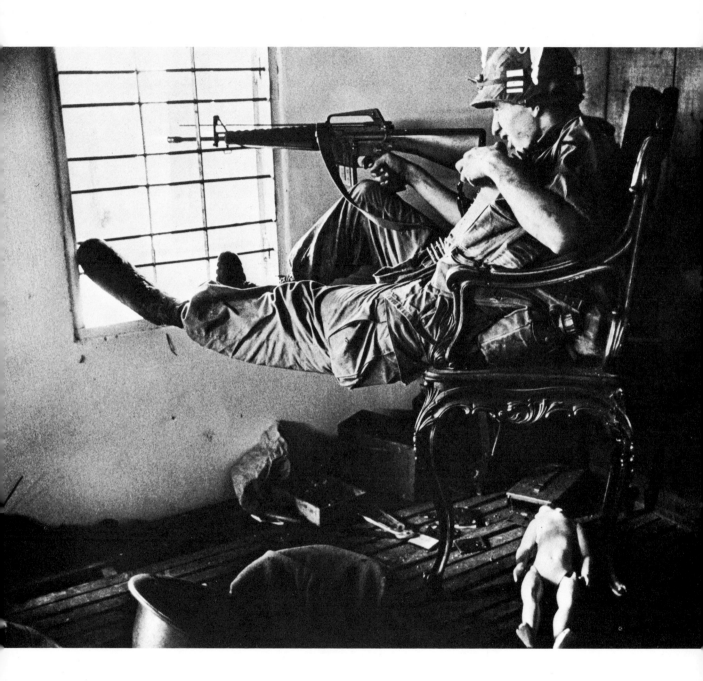

The State of the Nation

the President set the tone for government concern in his State of the Union address, emphasizing as second only to the environment "the war against crime." there seemed a sense of powerlessness not only against the mugger but against climbing prices, climbing unemployment. authority figures like the policeman and the schoolteacher joined industrial employees on strike. death removed major figures with little indication that policies would be affected. The United Auto Workers' Walter Reuther, a labor giant for thirty years, died in a plane crash; his successor, Leonard Woodcock, quickly proved to the auto industry that he could be just as tough at the bargaining table, leading a costly eight-week strike against General Motors. South Carolina's L. Mendel Rivers, who had overseen much of the three trillion defense dollars spent by the nation since 1946, died, to be succeeded by Louisiana's F. Edward Hébert, equally a partisan of the Pentagon. and, in accelerating pace, American youth seemed to gallop from parental premises.

Former Attorney General Ramsey Clark has said that "crime reflects the character of a people." In that respect, the nation in the first year of the new decade demonstrated a character disorder: campuses of the most widely schooled youth in American history burst into flames, both literally and figuratively; the FBI's annual report, issued in June, 1970, noted a record increase in bank robberies and a 13 percent rise in other serious crimes.

But, more important, the gross national product dropped for the first time in twelve years. Inflation and unemployment coincided, an economic equivalent of suffering from chills and fever.

The final 1970 census figures show an increase of 13.3 percent over 1960, the lowest growth rate since the depression years of the 1930s. There are, by official count, 204,765,770 Americans. For the first time more of them live in the suburbs than in cities, carting their problems along with them.

And national sanctities—from breakfast food to the automobile—have been assailed:

CORRESPONDENT: Every year, cereal manufacturers spend millions of dollars to convince children their breakfast products not only taste good, but are good for them, packed with vitamins and energy.

ANNOUNCERS ON COMMERCIAL: Surprise. [Indistinct] the colorful cereal circles, sparkling with sugar crystals. Surprise . . . Try Kellogg's vitamin-powered Sugar Smacks, honeyed, sugared puffs of wheat, now vitamin powered . . . Kellogg's Rice Krispies, the nutritious rice cereal . . .

CORRESPONDENT: A Senate Commerce subcommittee viewed eighteen minutes of such commercials today and heard testimony that most cereral advertising is grossly misleading. Robert Choate, a consultant to the White House Conference on Food, Nutrition, and Health, said a comparison of sixty common breakfast cereals, based on information obtained from the manufacturers, showed forty offer practically no nutritional value. He rated Kellogg's Product 19 and General Mills' Kaboom and Total as most nourishing, and Quaker and Nabisco Shredded Wheat as least. Choate accused cereal manufacturers of trading on a nutritional illiteracy, offering flavorings and prizes instead of proteins and vitamins.

ROBERT CHOATE: Big on Saturday morning kiddie cartoons are General Mills' Cheerios, Coco Puffs, and Trix. General Foods touts Raisin Bran. I notice in analyzing some other Saturday mornings that General Foods had a bigger television component than we saw that day. Quaker Oats shouts Quake, Quips, and Captain Crunch. Each has a TV budget over half a million dollars a year. None are in the top nine nutritionally. All contain sugar. I might parenthetically note that General Mills' Wheaties, not seen on this—these Saturday mornings, is a major advertiser with a budget of $1.1 million. Nutritionally it rates twenty-ninth out of the sixty. "The Breakfast of Champions" is right in the middle of the pack.

Our children are deliberately being sold

the cereal sponsors' less nutritious products over television. I believe our children are being programmed to demand sugar and sweetness in every food. I believe our children are being countereducated away from nutrition knowledge.

CORRESPONDENT: General Foods and Kellogg issued statements claiming cereals are a good nutritional buy and, besides, breakfast foods must taste good before children will eat them. Subcommittee chairman Frank Moss said, however, he found Choate's testimony "powerful" and vowed to work toward stiffer federal scrutiny of food products. . . .

Even the most serious problems need not require solemn answers. As great auto corporations searched for ways to get the lead out of their gasoline, an Englishman offered a barnyard approach to a great urban dilemma:

MORLEY SAFER: This is Harold Bate's manure extractor. He runs his car—believe it or not—on chicken manure, and he's been doing it for an awfully long time.

Mr. Bate, how long have you been operating your car on manure gas?

HAROLD BATE: Oh, about fifteen years.

CORRESPONDENT: Does it run as well as on ordinary gasoline?

BATE: Better.

CORRESPONDENT: The process works this way. Mr. Bate adds a chemical compound to the raw material. He puts the mixture into a pressure chamber and the resulting bacterial action produces cheap, odorless methane gas.

What about the performance of the car itself? Do you get pretty good performance from—

BATE: Oh, yes, yes. The car—performance is, I should think, about 25 percent above the top grades of petrol. Of course, all gases, propanes and methanes, are about 103 octane. They're completely antiknock. You can shove the compression up to about twenty to one and it won't knock.

CORRESPONDENT: It's a pretty battered old car you have there, and yet—

BATE: 1955, Hillman.

CORRESPONDENT: Do you get a fair speed out of it on—

BATE: About 75 to 80.

CORRESPONDENT: Mr. Bate says that with chicken power it would be as if you were paying one cent per gallon of gasoline, and you would be getting about thirty miles to the gallon. But even more important, the natural gas gives off no harmful fumes, harmless carbon dioxide instead of carbon monoxide that can kill people and destroy plant life.

BATE: There's your exhaust from—

CORRESPONDENT: From our car.

BATE: From your car, and there's the exhaust from mine.

CORRESPONDENT: And what's coming out of the exhaust on yours right now?

BATE: Just carbon dioxide, more or less water.

CORRESPONDENT: No lead?

BATE: No.

CORRESPONDENT: Nothing. It's remarkable.

BATE: It is, yeah. Clean air for America. That's what Mr. Nixon's looking for, now, isn't it?

CORRESPONDENT: And all of this, he says, can be cured with a cheap, simple device, the Harold Bate chicken manure gas converter. Mr. Bate's old Hillman chugs away down the byways of the English west country, laughing at the unsightly gas stations that blaspheme on nature's beauty. He has no need of them and, if you believe Mr. Bate, they live in fear of him.

So perhaps we've heard the last of all those chicken jokes. Clearly, the reason the chicken now crosses the road is to offer you trouble-free motoring, and we await the television commercials offering to put a chicken in your tank. But, most important of all, we can forget the oil-rich sheikdoms of the Persian Gulf. It's the chicken-rich countries we must now turn our attention to.

A Lithuanian seaman jumped ship from a Soviet vessel to a U.S. Coast Guard ship and, after a confused and bloody battle, was returned. The repercussions reached the White House, resulting in the dismissal of high-ranking Coast Guard officers. Furious political and editorial comment followed, with White House guarantees that it would never happen again. (In the last three years of the 1960s, 657 bills were introduced in the Senate to avoid deportation of Oriental ship jumpers. Eighty percent of them, according to a Senate Ethics Committee report, came from four New York lawyers and nine Washington lobbyists, at fees up to $750 per illegal immigrant.)

It remains increasingly difficult, however, even for the native-born to get around. Strikes bother the troubled air, the troubled railroads, the troubled automobile industry. American women of all races denounce what they see as servitude; the spastic economy reflects doubts of the national future; millions of dollars have been conceded lost in federal funding of transportation, while Congress has haggled over food programs for children.

Intellectuals have turned to youth in a way that would not have been possible in 1960 or 1950 or 1940, when wise men shook heads over "this younger generation."

Symptoms have spread to the Congress, where the seniority system has come under serious attack.

The nation, something over 50 percent of it under twenty-six, confronts as never before the idealism of youth, and youth's confusions, while elders fumble around in the tradition of the ages, somehow making things work, some way.

The Wheels of Government

elected by 43.4 percent of the voters, Richard Nixon entered office with a Congress dominated by the opposition party, the first president-elect in a century facing that problem. a third of the way through his term, he reportedly saw himself "reestablishing public confidence in the office of the presidency." on the other hand, Democratic opponents charged the President "lacks a vision, a set of fundamental beliefs, about where this country should be headed." somewhere between those partisan political viewpoints lies the hard truth.

The Nixon Doctrine of 1969 was pushed by events and the Congress perhaps a little further than even the President would have wished in the first year of the new decade. That doctrine, arguing against America's role as moral policeman for the world, spelled out an emotion felt by many voters and, more importantly, by the voters' natural constituents—the politicians. Thus Congress passed the Cooper-Church legislation barring ground troop intervention in Cambodia, seriously debated the Hatfield-McGovern act that would have codified a time limit for United States withdrawal from Indochina, and repudiated the Tonkin Gulf resolution of 1964. This last was most important, for it showed how dramatically American thinking had changed since passage of the legislation used by President Johnson to step up the Vietnam war:

BRUCE MORTON: The vote was historic, confusing, and lopsided—81 to 10. Confusing because pro-administration hard-liners voted for repeal; repeal's leading advocate, J. William Fulbright, voted against it. Fulbright voted no because he objected to the procedure—a bill from his committee swiped by Republican Robert Dole and offered as an amendment to something else. Stealing a man's bill, Fulbright said, is a little like stealing his cow. Dole answered that this was National Dairy Month, and nobody would want to steal a cow then. Like everything else in this Indochina debate, senators disagree over what repeal meant.

SENATOR ROBERT DOLE: I think the symbolism was that there's been a great erosion, of course, in the Senate over the past six years with reference to support of the Vietnam war, plus there's a recognition, I think, particularly on the Republican side, and many on the Democrat side, that President Nixon is in a period of de-escalation, not a period of escalation, and therefore the Gulf of Tonkin resolution, which was an instrument of escalation, is no longer necessary. It was referred to as the "get-in" resolution. We're now getting out.

SENATOR J. WILLIAM FULBRIGHT: I think it removes any constitutional authority for the continuation of the war. It does not remove the President's authority, and his—his legitimate, constitutional authority to protect the troops while they're there, to bring them home safe and sound. It would certainly remove any authority, I think, to expand the war into China, into Thailand, or elsewhere, or even—even back into—into Cambodia, assuming he gets out of there.

But if America has turned inward, there is no clear movement away from a posture of defense that is close to belligerency. The Senate rejected a move that would have cut defense spending from $71.2 billion to $66 billion. President Nixon pushed the Safeguard antiballistic missile system, called the ABM, as a bargaining chip in arms control talks with the Soviets. Congress bought the message, voting for expansion of ABM sites. Humming "Let's Give Peace a Chance," the nation continues traditional support of the military, even as it moves toward a closer scrutiny of its operations:

BOB SCHIEFFER: This man does not always wear a uniform, but he is a military officer on active duty. He is one soldier in a small army whose mission is to look after the needs of Congress, and to foster good relations between Capitol Hill and the Pentagon. It is, in effect, an army of lobbyists, over three hundred of them. They don't like to be called that; they say they are "legislative liaison." But the little army's duties range from conventional lobbying activities to helping congressmen answer their mail.

They operate from a series of offices on Capitol Hill, and from other suites at the Pentagon. They are assigned to congressional committees, they draft proposed legislation, they collect information for and about Congress, they plan congressional junkets overseas, and they help when Congress holds investigations into the military. Still, Assistant to the Secretary of Defense Richard Capen says their mission is often misunderstood.

RICHARD CAPEN: Well, I think it's—it's very unfair to refer to the professional people in the Department of Defense as lobbyists. I would feel that it's much more important to describe our operation as a service organization, serving the members of Congress, and I think that if we were to cut down on our operation that the congressmen and senators would be the first to protest.

CORRESPONDENT: *Congressional Quarterly* says that 269 special interest groups registered as lobbyists last year. All of them together reported spending a total of $5.1 million on lobbying activities. In contrast, and by its own count, the Pentagon, which registers no lobbyists, reported spending just over $3 million on legislative liaison. That is ten times more than the amount spent by the highest-spending civilian lobby group, the National Association of Letter Carriers, which headed the drive for a postal pay raise. It is, in fact, a total greater than the amount reported spent by the top twenty-five civilian lobby groups. . . .

The liaison men claim their job is service, to give advice when requested, to furnish facts in an impartial way. But Rear Admiral Means Johnson, the Navy's top liaison man, says the job sometimes entails more than that.

REAR ADMIRAL MEANS JOHNSON: Well, the project officer is interested in anything affecting his project, and it could be just a remark at lunch that such and such didn't look too—didn't look too promising, and then we would be able to immediately get the information over to the staff member and try to allay his fears, his doubts about that particular component.

CORRESPONDENT: Congressman William Moorhead, among others, questions just how impartial the Pentagon is when it responds to congressional requests.

CONGRESSMAN WILLIAM MOORHEAD: When they find that a member of Congress is on the other side of the fence, when they suspect that he is trying to check up on misuse or negligence in handling the taxpayers'

money, they're very, very close chested, they play the cards close to the chest. I don't say that we don't ultimately get the information, but it's just human nature—you naturally give better service to your friends than you do to those that you think are your enemies.

CORRESPONDENT: Oregon's Republican Senator Mark Hatfield is also a strong critic of defense spending, and the Pentagon's growing influence, but he does not place all of the blame on the Pentagon.

SENATOR MARK HATFIELD: I do not fault the Pentagon. I fault the Congress, for too many years automatically accepting all evaluations that have come from the Pentagon in terms of budgetary requests, new weapons requests, and therefore if anyone is at fault for the inordinate imbalance between the—the Congress and the Pentagon, it is the fault of the Congress, not the Pentagon.

And yet good money continues to follow bad in defense spending, even as congressional and other critics zero in on waste. Not long after Ernest Fitzgerald, an Air Force auditor, revealed that the service had spent $2 billion over its original estimate in developing the C-5A cargo plane, his position was abolished. He was subsequently hired by a congressional committee charged with watching Pentagon spending, but the Merry-Andrew spending habits of the military are more easily acquired than quitted:

CORRESPONDENT: A Congressman charged today that a navy unmanned helicopter program has been a $250 million failure, with 411 of the first 740 of them having crashed. Representative Sidney Yates, an Illinois Democrat, called it a classic example of ordering production while research was still going on. The drone helicopters had been planned for an antisubmarine program called Dash. In addition to the ones that crashed, Yates said, others have been put into storage, in his words, "probably for good". . . .

A Senate subcommittee ended an eight-year investigation with a conclusion that already was generally accepted: the F-111 swing-wing jet, originally started as the TFX, was a multibillion-dollar fiasco. However, the report did level some sharp criticism at former Defense Secretary McNamara and other former top Defense officials, particularly Deputy Secretary Roswell Gilpatric. It accused Gilpatric of conflict of interest by having served earlier as a counselor to the TFX builder. It asserted he deliberately tried to hide the nature of that relationship from the Senate. In reply, Gilpatric said his counselor role never involved military matters and that the Justice Department had looked into the matter and cleared him.

Administration shifts and firings reflect a chief executive who, loving football, believes in team play as a lesson of life. Secretary of Health, Education, and Welfare Robert Finch, faced with mutinies in his department, moved himself out of office; U.S. Office of Education Commissioner Dr. James Allen was fired after he criticized administration Indochina policy; and Interior Secretary Walter Hickel, after repeated reassurances that his critiques were acceptable if not yearned for, found himself out of work.

The White House privately argued that Hickel had been a poor administrator who handled badly his letter criticizing the presidential approach to youth. The officially stated reason was mutual lack of confidence. Hickel, reportedly under pressure to resign, said that "if I go away, I'm going away with an arrow in my heart and not a bullet in my back."

But he subsequently was reported to be disturbed over the manner in which he had been fired. Hickel had been summoned to a meeting with other officials at the Executive Office Building on a pretext and, only after arriving there, was told the President wanted to see him. He presumed that the maneuver was intended to keep him from advising the press in advance of the meeting. Hickel told friends he was disappointed the President "did not have the guts" to tell him to come over and get fired.

The departure of Finch, a close political ally of the President, was more traumatic:

DANIEL SCHORR: When you're the youngest member of the Cabinet, and the first to go, and you're leaving a divided department, you have to put up a pretty brave front at your final reception.

Bob Finch knows of the widespread impression that he's leaving in defeat, and he resents that. He knows that many of those saying good-bye to him, though fond of him, believe he was not strong enough in fighting this department's battle at the White House. He frankly says that those who considered him a liberal standard-bearer misjudged him.

For the staff of Health, Education, and Welfare, farewells to the boss, and to the boss' wife, are no novelty. They have seen eight secretaries in the department's seventeen years—the highest turnover of any Cabinet department. But Finch's departure after only eighteen months is, for them, particularly unsettling. They have long felt that they were the agency with major problems and minor power, representing the uninfluential, the sick, the poor, and the young, and many employees feel that if Bob Finch, the President's friend, couldn't make it, then the department can't.

But Finch, because he is the President's friend, was in the worst position to fight this department's battles, and friends like Assistant Secretary James Farmer know that Finch had to be tolerant about policies rejected, nominees he couldn't get aboard, and some thrown overboard. And though he says that he'd have liked another six months to leave on a more upbeat note, there's no question he's glad to leave behind this $60 billion administrative monster.

Geographically, he's not going far—a few blocks to the White House, where he'll be sworn in as counselor next Wednesday—in spirit he's taking a long, long journey.

But the departure of Commissioner Allen caused even more controversy since, in spite of charges of "administrative inefficiency," he seemed clearly a target because of his criticisms of the administration. Allen himself said that Finch gave him no reasons for his ouster:

I was simply told by him that—that he had been asked to seek my resignation. My position on some matters that were very crucial today in our society, such as desegregation, bringing about integrated education in our country, which I have long strongly fought for and believed in, the statement that I made about the impact of the decision to go into Cambodia on the educational system, were probably things that were not in line with the thinking in the White House, and I believe that those were the things that were foremost in the reason—in asking for my— one of the reasons for my—the request for my—my dismissal.

The touchy matter of education will continue to be a central issue of the seventies, and no subject of debate has been more booted about, on aspects ranging from the busing of students to desegregation.

A northern liberal, former governor of his state, onetime head of the Department of Health, Education, and Welfare, came out in support of southern arguments that change in school integration has unquestionably been greater in the South than in the North since 1954. Connecticut's Abraham Ribicoff stunned and confused Senate colleagues when he took to the floor to endorse a southern-sponsored amendment to the education bill:

What we have is a racist society. Schools are segregated because we have a segregated society. The housing patterns are segregated and the children go to segregated schools, and as a consequence we have had a fantastic deterioration of education all across America. The time has come for all of us to be very realistic about our problems, recognize that our nation and our educational system is in danger, and we're never going to do this as long as we think the problems are only southern problems and not northern problems.

We are so hypocritical, and we should face up to the fact, when the blacks move in, the whites move out. And what is bothering me is this whole semantic puzzle, this—just the talk that all of us indulge in, and nobody faces up to the problem. Until the North feels the pinch the same way the South feels the pinch—until that time comes we are not going to face up to the basic problem that's bedeviling this nation of ours.

The Nixon administration itself turned to lawsuits, rather than the cut-off of federal funds for school districts failing to meet desegregation guidelines, prompting angry reactions from some civil rights groups and a revolt in the Civil Rights division of the Justice Department. But the battles between the President and some Congressional foes were not confined to matters of desegregation. In a dramatic television appearance President Nixon vetoed an appropriations bill for the Departments of Labor, Health, Education and Welfare that was $1.1 billion more than he requested, setting the tone for legislative and administrative war over domestic priorities that foreshadowed more to come.

Like Kissing Your Sister

*seldom has there been an off-year election like 1970's. the President,
living up to his reputation as the most political of men, staked his name
on working toward a Congress he could live with comfortably. not since
Franklin Roosevelt in 1938 had a chief executive taken a more active role
in an election that did not directly involve his office. more money was
spent, more words spoken, than in any nonpresidential year in memory.
the voters stayed away in droves and produced a result many found
encouraging, demonstrating a concern in voting for the man, not the
party. both parties claimed ideological victories; viewing it with what
objectivity is possible, the result seemed more like a tie game in football.
a tie game, according to coaches, is about as exciting as kissing your sister.*

Vice-President Agnew kicked off the campaign in September, acting rather as the Nixon of the Nixon administration. Serving as Vice-President to Dwight Eisenhower, Richard Nixon had been called on to hit the road for congressional elections; now he asked Spiro Agnew to do the same for him.

There were no indications the Vice-President found the job onerous. He immediately stressed the two major administration campaign issues: the so-called southern strategy and the emphasis on crime. He told a Memphis audience that there was a "rather blatant discrimination against the South" in school desegregation, and that until the Nixon administration could restore "even balance" to the Supreme Court it could not get the clarifying decisions it sought. On the matter of crime, the Vice-President outlined a major campaign theme:

> There's a new deadlock of democracy today, between a progressive President carrying out his mandate for reform and a reactionary Congress in the grip of bitter men who've forfeited that mandate. Nowhere has this Congress been more derelict than in its ho-hum, business-as-usual attitude to the President's program to control and reduce the crime and filth in our society. Sixteen months ago the President proposed the toughest bill in the nation's history to uproot the corrupting influence of organized crime. The bill still sits there, languishing in Congress. Fourteen months ago the President asked unprecedented power for the Justice Department to crack down on the narcotics merchants who are growing rich destroying the lives of thousands of our young people. That bill, too, just sits there, languishing in Congress. How many children, my friends, must we pick out of the gutters and alleys of our great cities, dead of overdoses of heroin, before Congress finally decides that maybe it's time to act?

The Vice-President also added a phrase to the political dictionary with attacks on what he called "an awful liberal-radical coalition," including some Republicans, that "stimulates the type of leadership which encourages the dissident element in our society." Among his more obvious targets was New York Senator Charles Goodell, whose prompt reaction—"I am confident that the people of New York State will not allow Spiro Agnew to pull the lever for them in November"—

proved to be misplaced. An added fillip to the campaign resulted with publication of the report of the President's Commission on Pornography, repudiated by both the President and Vice-President:

GEORGE HERMAN: The basic finding of the commission was that an analysis of all available studies shows no correlation between the availability of such sex-oriented materials and the rate of sex crimes of sexual pathology. Says the report, the patrons of such places may be characterized as "predominantly white, middle-class, middle-aged, married males dressed in business suits or neat casual attire."

The commission found a majority of Americans behind the idea that any adult who wants this kind of stuff should be allowed to get it, but that children are a different matter. Therefore it makes these major recommendations to Congress and the American people: All federal, state, and local laws forbidding pornography to adults who want it should be repealed. But there must be safeguards to keep pornography away from children and adults who don't want it. A massive program on sex education is proposed, especially for parents, teachers, and counselors of children. And, finally, continuing research, perhaps the most likely of all the recommendations to be implemented.

Chairman William Lockhart, dean of the Minnesota Law School, is unperturbed by the dissents within the commission and the controversy outside of it.

DEAN WILLIAM LOCKHART: I knew what kind of a job this would be, and I knew the kind of things that would happen no matter what position we took; there would be many who emotionally were—were bothered by the recommendations of the commission. I felt this needed to be done. I felt this needed to be done by an unbiased group. I knew that whatever recommendations we made would be controversial. And you've got to have controversy, you've got to have disagreement, and we expect it. But I think it will—our legislative policy making will be increasingly based on informed knowledge of the facts rather than the assumptions and the guesses and the fears on which such legislation has been based in the past.

CORRESPONDENT: Dissenter Charles Keating, the only Nixon appointee on the commission, opposes the repeal of antiobscenity laws.

CHARLES KEATING: I think the same thing would happen here that has happened in Denmark, namely that we would become a society pagan, animalistic, and given over to all of the baser vices. I think the good common sense and the basic morality of the American people, particularly in the Congress, will cause the report to be basically ignored.

But it was the President himself who drew the most attention as he took to the campaign road. He identified the "attitude of permissiveness" with the Johnson administration, calling on "the silent majority" to answer "radicals and dissidents" and those engaging in obscenities.

"If a candidate has condoned violence, lawlessness, and permissiveness," he said, "then you know what to do. . . . The four-letter word that is the most powerful of any in the world is 'vote.'" His freewheeling comments about crime in America had already involved him in controversy even before the campaign season started. In an unscheduled, hastily arranged news conference in Denver, he had asserted that Charles Manson, charged in the slaying of eight persons and at the time on trial for his life, was guilty:

I noted, for example, the coverage of the Charles Manson case when I was in Los Angeles—front page every day in the papers, it usually got a couple of minutes on the evening news. Here is a man who is guilty, directly or indirectly, of eight murders without reason. Here's a man yet who, as far as the coverage was concerned, appeared to be a rather glamorous figure.

CORRESPONDENT: Reporters were stunned that President Nixon, a lawyer, would make such a statement. When bulletins began moving on news wire services, Press Secretary Ronald Ziegler tried to issue what he called a clarification. Ziegler at first declined to say the President had misspoken, but did say the President had failed to use the word "alleged" in calling Manson guilty. When asked if he was retracting the President's statement, Ziegler finally replied: "I think I've done that."

Another controversy was sparked by an attack on a presidential motorcade in San Jose, California, just five days before the election:

CORRESPONDENT: The unfriendly crowd quickly turned into an unruly mob, and the election may have been turned around. Since then President Nixon has taken every opportunity to remind voters that the Republicans are the party of law and order, and that the Democrats are the party of permissiveness. There could be some risks in this strategy. It could backfire. But Richard Nixon, always a tough political opponent, obviously believes the gamble is worth taking.

The worth of that gamble was challenged by the election results. Of thirty-five Senate seats at stake, ten Republican and twenty-five Democratic, the Republicans won eleven, the Democrats twenty-two, and conservative independents two. The best-known casualties included such selected Nixon-Agnew targets as Democrats Albert Gore of Tennessee and Joseph Tydings of Maryland and Republican Goodell. But the road show did not help administration favorites like George Murphy of California and Ralph Smith of Illinois.

In the 435 House races, Republicans held their losses to about a third of the normal for such elections, the Democrats gaining only eleven seats. But this could be partly explained by the fact that the President was elected with a Democratic Congress, and the customary midterm turnover was therefore ruled out.

The Democrats won big in the thirty-five gubernatorial races, taking twenty-two statehouses. Perhaps the most interesting immediate aspect of the election involved the Democratic gains in the Republican stronghold of the Midwest and Rocky Mountain areas, while the GOP fared well in the Northeast, long anathema to conservatives.

But if the verdict was a split decision, it offered a longer view toward the changing concepts of American politics. Harry Truman used to carry a sign on his office desk noting that "the buck stops here." Perhaps more than in any previous national election, the American voter of 1970 demonstrated a disenchantment with party politics and a tendency to argue that the buck stops on the state and local levels. Eric Sevareid interpreted the meaning of the vote:

Once more the American people proved they are overwhelmingly allergic to extremes of either right or left as well as to extreme pressures of slick money or rhetoric. And they still like fresh, youngish faces if the accompanying minds are moderate.

The job of governor is now like the job of mayor—impossible. The gap between demands and the resources to fill them is too wide; and high-speed communications have shortened patience. The short, unhappy tenures of mayors and governors can extend to presidents. He must struggle to bridge the same awful gap.

The campaign war is over and the people want a little political peace. But this capital of Washington will stay hot. The Democrats think they smell blood, think their quarry is wounded.

If the President changes any long-range strategy, it will be his economic strategy. The calm statistical assurances of his economic advisers will meet a blistering cross fire from Republican political and business leaders around the country. What the President seems to need is an economic high command, including some men from the Congress, not a collection of individual advisers. He never did lay out a tax policy for Congress, which promptly followed its own instincts and lowered taxes in a period of gathering inflation.

Economics will provide the central battleground for the war between the White House and Congress, more than defense or foreign policy, which the President has talked so much about. There is rather little disagreement over his Vietnam schedule or his lowered-profile philosophy of foreign policy in general.

The disagreement is over how that policy is to be conducted—just what is the role of Congress in the making and unmaking of wars—like the one in Cambodia. This will be a continuing public argument, especially so if Hubert Humphrey replaces Mr. Gore on the Foreign Relations Committee, which seems logical, since Humphrey served there for some thirteen years.

And the fascinating personality play will go on, with the critics in the aisle seats noting down every nuance in the apparently altered roles and influence of key men like Agnew and Muskie.

Politics, like the weather, never goes away.

And neither do the questions of employment and inflation seem likely to disappear with stage-center roles to play in the nation's political future.

"We've Got a Problem"... 200,000 Miles from Earth... "A Pretty Large Bang"

the surprise is not that man fumbles around with outer space. it is that he is there at all, this adventurous tinkerer, the only living being between his mother ship and the next stop, the earth's moon. he only dreamed about it for a thousand thousand millennia or so, and then it took just twelve years from the first artificial earth satellite—Russia's sputnik—to the first lunar walk, July 20, 1969. the decade of the seventies opened with spatial events such as the increasingly sophisticated unmanned probes, the growing concentration on space platforms and shuttles, the emphasis on more cooperation between the two outer space powers, but the most dramatic stories, as always, involved men; in this case, three brave men who almost didn't make it back alive.

161

The fact that the skies still held more mysteries than answers seemed all but forgotten. In addition, the on-the-nose success of the world's first two moon landings, by United States astronauts, took the edge off the pre-flight drama for Apollo 13. If there was recollection that three men scheduled to fly the first Apollo mission had died in a launch pad fire, well, that had been three years before. Since then, there had been nothing but success, and the near-misses that are a part of most attempts to scale outer space were forgotten in arguments about the cost of the space program itself and its place in terms of national priorities.

That changed with the flight of Apollo 13. It seemed vaguely troubled from the start —from the moment, numerologists might argue, that it was assigned an unlucky number, instead of, say, Apollo 12A. And yet it provided a cliff-hanging quality unlike any other of the space flights, a three-day-plus drama as what was estimated as the largest television audience in history watched three men, victims of human error, limp home through space on what seemed little more than a shoeshine and a smile.

The jinxed enterprise was threatened first by what was almost a joke—a childhood disease ordinarily of no consequence to adult males. Dr. Charles Berry, the space program's director of medical operations, reported that the three "13" astronauts had been exposed to German measles through Charles Duke, a member of the backup crew. Blood tests indicated that two members of the prime crew had adequate immunity, but that a third—Lieutenant Commander Thomas K. Mattingly, Jr., did not. "The evidence is very substantial," the National Aeronautics and Space Agency said, "that about the time we would be conducting lunar operations, Lieutenant Commander Mattingly would be coming down with symptoms such that his capacity for successfully carrying out . . . operations would be called into question."

"The only way doctors could guarantee that he would not get sick during the flight," it was reported, "would be if he got sick before and recovered. For the past two days, everyone has been watching Mattingly closely, hoping he would get sick, but so far he's refused to cooperate."

The question then was this—whether to postpone the flight back to May 9, with the difficulty of keeping the complex Saturn Apollo ready to fly (at a cost of about half a million dollars to the taxpayer), or to replace Mattingly with backup astronaut John Swigert, Jr., despite reluctance to break up a crew that had been working together. The lengthy delay would be required to bring the moon in the right relation to the earth with proper lighting on the proposed landing site at the Fra Mauro Hills, believed to contain some of the oldest material on the moon.

Wally Schirra, a former astronaut who is now a member of the CBS News space team, minimized the problems involved if Mattingly should be replaced:

We had all sorts of agonies in the older days. You recall we said we couldn't break up the team, we couldn't put a new man in at the last minute. And we meant it. We had launch schedules that were every two months. But we have a case now where we have six months. Swigert's been working for one long time. He worked with me in the support crew role with Apollo 7, which was way back in '68. The other thing is that the command module pilot is really a loner. He has the task of minding the store while the other two are off doing very close teamwork with the LM, landing on the moon. . . .

And so, after four days of indecision, the space agency decided to go with Swigert after he passed a battery of last-minute tests to see if he could team with the already chosen astronauts. One was Commander James A. Lovell, Jr., who headed the trio, and already had flown three flights and spent more hours in outer space (572) than any other man in history. The third, Fred W. Haise, thirty-six, was, like Swigert, a civilian and a space rookie.

Now the mission itself, no longer overshadowed by excitement over the crew and a case of German measles, took stage center. Unlike its predecessors, which had touched down on level terrain, Apollo 13 was aimed for the rugged lunar highland and a thirty-three-hour stay, during which there would be long moon walks by Lovell and Haise and, it was hoped, the first color television pictures back to earth.

Vice-President Spiro Agnew and West German Chancellor Willy Brandt were among the spectators at the lift-off on April 11. For the first two and a half days and 200,000 miles, there were only minor problems. There was more than the customary joshing between the men in the spacecraft and Mission Control in Houston, Texas. Swigert at one point recalled he had forgotten to file his income tax return. He was told that an extension would be worked out. The flight was proceeding so close to perfection that a scheduled midcourse correction was canceled.

Describing it as "a nice, easy flight," the astronauts sent back a television program to prove it, Haise demonstrating the hammock he would sleep in on the moon, Swigert volunteering for the by-now-familiar-to-the-point-of-being-obligatory free-floating demonstration, Lovell showing the way through the connecting tunnel between the lunar and command modules, christened *Aquarius* and *Odyssey* by Lovell. That was late in the day of April 13.

And then at 10:07 P.M. Lovell radioed to the Manned Spacecraft Center officials in Houston, "We've got a problem."

Haise reported, "We've had a pretty large bang."

Swigert reported loss of power in an electric line hooked into a fuel cell that used oxygen from tanks located in the service module, and Lovell said, on looking out the window, "We're venting something out into space. It's a gas of some sort."

As the oxygen and power dropped toward zero, Lovell told ground control what it was about to advise him—that "we're going to have to go to a LM lifeboat." This meant that they would rely on the oxygen and power of *Aquarius* to keep them alive and return them home.

Reaction on earth was instantaneous, as described in Washington by Eric Sevareid:

Life and work go on here in the capital, as everywhere else, while the three imperiled young men circle the moon and aim their crippled spaceship toward the earth and life, but the quiet tension is felt everywhere, and few can address their work with full attention. The accident has come at a bad time for this government and the people in it; too much has been happening here these last two weeks or so, too much of it adverse, painful, and acrimonious. Everyone is thinking of the three men, first of all, but there is a kind of subknowledge that if a tragedy occurs, it will be one of the most dramatic and dramatized of all time, and could only deepen the spiritual miasma that already weighs upon this national capital.

In those moments, the routine became high drama. "It is not likely," went one report, ". . . that any three men have ever waged such a dramatic battle so fully in the attention of the world. A foreign newspaper said, 'The concern they create is as great as the work undertaken. It creates a human solidarity.' "

The men had suddenly become mankind,

the world "the good earth" indeed, and the lunar module, designed to land the two moon walkers on the lunar surface and return them to the command module, a lifeboat. For with the command ship all but dead after the accident, they would rely on the engines of the fragile lunar vehicle to return them to safety, with questionable supplies of oxygen, power, and coolant water. As for the accident, flight director Glynn Lunney said the following morning:

> I don't think anyone understands it, but it appears that something gave way, causing the problem with the fuel cell—something in the cryogenic tanking system gave way, causing them a problem with the fuel cell—probably a physical impact of some kind. . . .
> VOICE: Are the astronauts safe, I think, is . . .
> LUNNEY: Well, they're . . . they're safe in the sense that we have the situation stabilized now, we think. I think our only concern about safety is that we're now about seventy hours from home, and we have to keep the situation that way, and bring them on home.

Seventy hours from home. And, we noted, " a lot of imponderables left." A need to jettison, first, the service module, and —as the men neared earth—the lunar module, their lifeboat, and, most immediate and most important, a firing up of the LM's engine in a change of configuration that would carry them around the moon and whip them on their return flight.

President Nixon, notified of the harrowing turn of events as soon as they happened, ting a briefing, awakened at three in the stayed up past midnight the first night getting morning for an updated report, and drove to the Goddard Space Center in Greenbelt, Maryland, the next day for an extensive briefing. He held a state dinner as planned that night but canceled the entertainment portion of the evening.

At Mission Control in Houston, "atmosphere was businesslike . . . but for now, it all seems to go well. . . .

"Throughout the day, a steady stream of friends came to the houses of astronauts Lovell and Haise. Some of the tension had eased . . . but the crisis remained. . . . The wives say they will remain secluded until their husbands have returned safely. They have refused to talk to newsmen."

Even after successful burns that got the ship back on a free return to earth and accelerated it, there remained a crucial burn to put it on target. Uncorrected, their course would take the men 104 miles away from earth, to perish in space.

As far as hitting the envelope of atmosphere around the earth, it was like the forward pass in football—three things could happen and only one of them was good. That would be an arrival less than one degree off the projected entry angle. If the ship hit the earth's atmosphere too steeply, it would be crushed; too shallow, and it would bounce back, irretrievably, into space.

With that most critical of burns approaching, ten thousand joined the Pope in prayer at the Vatican, special prayers were said at the Wailing Wall in Jerusalem. The Soviet Union, Great Britain, and France led other nations in sending ships to alternate splashdown sites. The cosmonauts sent a message to the astronauts saying, "We are following your flight with great attention and anxiety. We wish wholeheartedly your safe return to our mother earth."

Only 48,000 miles from earth, the burn was as successful as the most optimistic could have hoped for, and the astronauts spent their final full day in space on course for splashdown 555 miles southeast of Samoa. With the heat turned down to save power—

and conversation with earth held to a minimum for the same reason—temperatures in the command module were at forty-five degrees. This made eating and drinking unpleasant and when they were able, the crew slept huddled together in the warmer, but smaller, lunar module. The safest thing to say was that "each moment that ticks away is another in which nothing has gone wrong to endanger their lives."

Zeroing in on Target Earth, the astronauts jettisoned the service module, where the explosion had taken place, photographing it as they moved away. Lovell reported, "There's one whole side of the spacecraft missing. . . . It's really a mess." The three men, now in the command module, jettisoned their lifeboat just an hour before they reentered the earth's atmosphere at 24,680 miles per hour, a speed the atmosphere quickly reduced. At 1:07 P.M., their odyssey ended just nine hundred yards from the point it was aimed for after its hairbreadth journey.

From ticker tape showers in Wall Street to witch doctors' incantations in Africa, the whole world seemed to celebrate. Live pictures via satellite carried the safe return through Britain to the Soviet Union and twenty-two other nations on the Continent and in North Africa. President Nixon proclaimed a day of prayer and announced that he would fly with members of the astronauts' families to Hawaii to present the crew with Medals of Freedom. Secretary-General U Thant of the United Nations said, "All men will marvel at the unmatched combination of skill, courage, and spirit."

And in Spain they even canceled the bullfights.

A space agency official said he felt twenty years younger. But the greatest relief was expressed by the astronauts' families. After thanking the men at Mission Control for returning her husband and his crew safely, Marilyn Lovell said, "I have never experienced anything like this in my life, and I don't care ever to experience it **again**." Mary Haise, after speaking to her husband: "Oh, it was kind of wild. . . . We were all kind of shouting back and forth. But he looked so great, and we were so thankful." And the third astronaut's father, Dr. J. Leonard Swigert, summed it up: "It was a wonderful beginning, a beautiful ending, but I wouldn't give you two hoots for the interim."

The story did not end on that happy note.

"Had this happened during the first moon landing attempt," as Eric Sevareid commented, "efforts would probably have been redoubled. But Americans have twice walked the moon already, and the public mood has changed. Moon exploration still excites the scientific world for valid scientific reasons, but not many others outside their ranks. That very difficult question may be raised on a national scale—when is enough enough?—as it has long since been raised concerning both nuclear weapons and the Vietnam war."

There was still the missing ingredient necessary to all high drama: why did it happen that way? NASA Administrator Thomas O. Paine appointed a six-man board to investigate the cause of the misadventure. By this time, it was known that one of two oxygen tanks had exploded, tanks that powered the command module through three fuel cells in the service module.

The review board, headed by Edgar M. Cortright, director of NASA's Research Center at Hampton, Virginia, later released its findings. It blistered NASA and two contractors, finding "the accident was not the result of a chance malfunction . . . but, rather, resulted from an unusual combination of mistakes, coupled with a somewhat deficient design":

CORRESPONDENT: It was partly because no one thought this could happen, a short circuit igniting the Teflon insulation on a wire inside the oxygen tank. But afterward, this test and more than one hundred others proved it could. The fire caused pressure to build inside the tank. Finally it ruptured, the explosion blowing out the side panels just below the Apollo spacecraft. But, according to the review board chairman, Edgar Cortright, it could have been even more serious if it had happened on the launch pad.

EDGAR CORTRIGHT: Well, I think it's impossible to say with certainty what would have happened, but the potential was there for a major conflagration on the pad. If the oxygen when dumped into bay four had ignited with the insulation and with the aluminum structure, then the service module propellants and the adjacent bays could have been ignited, and the entire launch vehicle perhaps destroyed. I don't think it's practical to relocate these tanks, or necessary. The correct fix in the view of the board was to modify these tanks so combustion is not possible, or destructive combustion, at least, is not possible within them. In other words, tanks should not fail in this manner, and that's the way it should be corrected.

CORRESPONDENT: Much of the investigation—and this report is more than a thousand pages long—seems a replay of the aftermath of the 1967 fire which killed three astronauts. In both cases the fire hazard was unrecognized. In both cases there was criticism of NASA management and North American Rockwell. Today's report said there was a serious oversight in which all parties share, NASA, North American, and Beech Aircraft. But despite the board's finding of an unforgiving basic design, it recommended no major modifications of the spacecraft, just improving the warning alarm system and removing combustible material. The board did, however, recommend adding emergency supplies to the lunar module, the lifeboat.

The recommended changes pushed back the flight of Apollo 14 at an estimated cost of $15 million. But much was learned from the flight of Apollo 13, and part of it, perhaps, was expressed by the President:

I thought the most exciting day in my life was the day I was elected President of the United States. And then I thought perhaps next to that was the day Apollo 11 completed its flight, and I met it when it came down in the sea in the Pacific. But there's no question in my mind that for me, personally, this is the most exciting, the most meaningful day I have ever experienced. I feel that what these men have done has been a great inspiration to all of us. . . . How men react in adversity determines their true greatness.

Paying More for Less

"I am now a Keynesian," said the President after a postelection television interview. the reference, of course, was to the late economist John Maynard Keynes, whose economic theory of heavy government investment in the public sector, as opposed to the traditional concept of the balanced federal budget, was a prime target of fiscal conservatives for years. not the least of such critics had been Richard Nixon. the elections seemed a clear demonstration of governmental economic policy, since there was little substantial disagreement over the conduct of foreign affairs and a division of minorities over domestic concern outside the dollars-and-cents realm. an eye on the next presidential election and the intervening well-being of the nation, Mr. Nixon has seemed clearly intent on moving to strengthen an economy that is deeply in trouble.

This was not the White House view when President Nixon had predicted that 1970 would be "a good year" economically, with signs that the economy was responding to "our fight against inflation." At the same time he had predicted an increase in the gross national product, reflecting the views of his Council of Economic Advisers.

Instead, along with the first drop in the GNP since 1958, unemployment closed out 1970 at its highest level in seven and a half years. This combination of events forced an announced reversal of administration economic strategy. For two years the President had argued the conventional Republican view that a balanced budget was an absolute need. By December of 1970 he was saying a budget deficit was a necessity. For two years he had refused to "jawbone"—using presidential pressure against big business and big labor. By December he was attacking oil companies and construction unions to bring down price and wage demands.

The President continued to argue that his economic program had succeeded in stop-ping inflation without recession, although not as well as he had hoped. But the figures at year's end showed 5.8 percent of the American labor force was out of work, 4.6 million people—1.9 million more than the year before. Earlier arguments that the depressing economic figures reflected the strike at General Motors, the nation's largest private employer, were dented by the statistics at the end of the year.

It seemed, over the first year of the new decade, that the oldest means of transportation available—shanks' mare—was the only trustworthy one. It made no difference whether you were transporting yourself, a carton of oranges, or a letter. There was difficulty in moving the product from one place to another. A strike of teamsters, riddled by violence, lockouts, and wildcat actions, hit hard at trucking industry operations. There were two major rail strikes—four unions representing 500,000 rail workers demanded a 40 percent pay increase over a three-year period to match the kind of settlement achieved by the teamsters.

the times involved the nation's air controllers, yonder for more than two weeks, charging who took off into a ground-bound wild blue

Perhaps the strike most significant of excessive work loads as travelers found themselves jammed up at air terminals. A psychiatrist testified in court that 50 to 60 percent of the men whose duty is to oversee the safe departure and arrival of airplanes need psychiatric care, largely because of overwork. A not unsimilar conclusion was reached by a panel study of blue-collar workers headed by former Labor Secretary George Shultz. It warned that blue-collar workers, comprising 40 percent of American families and earning between $5,000 and $10,000 a year, live in anxiety over class status, a "feeling of being forgotten."

A strike of letter carriers that started in New York City spread to the West Coast before it was settled with a pay raise. The only way to get your mail was to send someone with a letter of authorization to pick it up at the post office, where supervisors attempted to cope with a desperate public:

DAVID CULHANE: A lot of people are going to have a pretty good alibi for not paying a few bills. Most companies apparently haven't considered the problem, but most will probably allow some leeway.

The strike started at midnight. Several thousand night workers went out immediately, and eventually there were some 36,000 postal workers either striking or honoring picket lines. The issue is simple enough. The mail carriers want more money.

The men in the picket lines say their annual pay of $6,100 to about $8,400 after twenty years is not enough. They want wages ranging from $8,500 a year to $11,700, plus some new benefits.

The New York system handles an average of about 35 million pieces of mail a day. If the letter carriers stayed off the job for any length of time, the effect would clearly be near chaos. There are about 3,300 super-

visory personnel, and they simply could not handle the flood. Even under normal conditions it takes a remarkable amount of time for one piece of mail to cross Manhattan.

And if you thought I was going to quote that line about the snow and the rain and the carriers and the swift completion of their appointed rounds, you're wrong. And besides, the line doesn't say anything about strikes.

Before the strike was ended, and for the first time in the nation's history, a President called on the military to take over the job of moving the United States mail. Before the strike had started, the President proposed reorganization of the chronically bankrupt post office into a non-Cabinet department run by a board of governors. After the strike, that reorganization was authorized by Congress.

The troubled economic situation affected more than the union worker living on his wages. Wall Street, the stock barometer of national health, witnessed the collapse of major brokerage houses and the confidence of some investors:

MIKE STANLEY: It's the small investor, the man who is encouraged by Wall Street to "buy a share in America," who is most distressed.

IRVING WEISS: I have quite a bit of margin. I'm about to be sold out. I always had a dream that some day I can retire and enjoy the fruit of happiness like any human being. It's unfortunate that this thing had to take, I mean, had to happen.

CORRESPONDENT: New York Stock Exchange President Robert Haack labels as exaggerated rumors reports that several brokerage houses are on the verge of collapse, but concedes the seventeen-month decline hasn't helped investor confidence.

ROBERT HAACK: There was a significant decline in the price level of stocks, and there is nothing that will impede morale or work to the detriment of confidence more than a significant decline, and the decline that we've had here is probably the most significant that we've seen in some forty years.

CORRESPONDENT: The stock market slump hits many in the pocketbook, but many professionals remain optimistic.

FIRST MAN: Another six months from now people will say look at those . . .

SECOND MAN: Why didn't I buy stocks?

FIRST MAN: . . . prices. Look at the prices we could have got it at.

CORRESPONDENT: Still, for waiters in Wall Street restaurants and unemployed brokerage house employees the situation is bleak.

NAT GLICK: There's fellows that used to come in that eat steaks. They're eating a little less now. They're not eating steaks like they used to.

CORRESPONDENT: Mr. Glick, what about your tips? Have they changed?

GLICK: Oh, tips have gone down, too, 15 to 20 percent.

CORRESPONDENT: Is your specialty readily adaptable to any other career field?

SHELLY KANOFF: Absolutely not. My own personality and capabilities are the only things that I can fall back upon.

CORRESPONDENT: So you are then locked into the securities industry?

KANOFF: Locked in and possibly very shortly locked out.

CORRESPONDENT: The growing feeling in the securities industry is that when the slumping bear market does finally come to an end, a return to the roaring bull market of the sixties is not in prospect. Rather, chastened go-go fund managers and more cautious individual investors are expected to make for a more conservative, less speculative marketplace.

The market reflects the fever, not the disease. But in the first year of the new decade, Wall Street's shakes were reflected by other economic ills as noted, including strikes by fractions of the total population seeking marginal gains through what Eric Sevareid called "masked conspiracies against people . . . forced to pay the costs in higher prices and higher rates. It requires no sagacity to know that this cannot and will not go on indefinitely."

The Great Chicago Trial—Water and the Fish

*the Chicago conspiracy trial, more properly United States of America,
plaintiff, versus David T. Dellinger et el., No. 69, Crim. 180, originated
in the antiriot provisions of the 1968 Civil Rights Act. the defendants
were charged on two counts, stemming from disorders at the Democratic
National Convention: conspiracy to incite riot and crossing state lines
to incite riot. (two charges involving incendiary weapons became side
issues.) the case shaped up as a classic test of constitutional
questions. and then the participants took over and, to the lay eye,
substantive issues dimmed as rhetorical rockets burst in the air. by the
time the trial ended, four and a half months after it started, some
two hundred witnesses had testified and the transcript ran
twenty-two thousand pages. at least fifteen books resulted, five of them—
at last count—by the defendants.*

Surely, by now, the outlines of the trial are familiar. Television and the press recorded the daily goings-on in Chicago's Federal District Courthouse from the beginning, September 26, 1969, to the end, February 18, 1970.

By that time, the names of the leading participants were as familiar as characters in a long-run television program, which, in a sense, the trial had become: David Dellinger, Rennie Davis, Tom Hayden, Abbie Hoffman, Jerry Rubin, along with two less flamboyant figures, Lee Weiner and John Froines. (The case of an eighth defendant, Bobby Seale, the Black Panther leader, was severed from the rest in November, 1969, when he was sentenced to four years in prison for contempt of court. Interestingly, his abbreviated presence—bound and gagged to prevent his outbursts—remains to some the single most impressive picture in the matter, almost a symbol. The chief prosecutor said afterward that Seale had "more guts and more charisma"—such is the language of the seventies—than the others.)

There was the trial judge, the Honorable Julius J. Hoffman; the prosecuting team led by United States Attorney Thomas A. Foran; and the defense counsel, William Kunstler and Leonard Weinglass. And, centrally, the defendants, hippie-haired, some of them, and love-beaded.

The legal issues were blurred by exchanges of wisecracks, arguments over which bathroom the defendants could use, an impromptu birthday celebration. Witnesses brought their own star quality: poet Allen Ginsberg; journalist-novelist Norman Mailer; folk singers Judy Collins and Arlo Guthrie, who were not allowed to perform; Georgia legislator Julian Bond and former Attorney General Ramsey Clark, who was not allowed to testify.

But behind the facade of high drama and high jinks, there boiled the same forces that brought violence to the Chicago streets in

August, 1968. This flared during several courtroom disruptions, most classically on January 6, 1970, when Chicago Mayor Richard Daley took the stand:

JOHN LAURENCE: The courtroom buzzed with electric tension unmatched since the shackling of Bobby Seale and, within minutes after the mayor took the witness stand, exploded. Twenty-three worried-looking lawmen guarded the courtroom with intense determination, contrasting the looser lifestyles of the defendants and their friends. The spectators' gallery was packed, some of them young people who waited all night outside the courthouse in subzero weather; others, wives and friends of the government and the mayor, who received special attention.

A simple question and answer sparked the violence. Defense attorney William Kunstler: "Mayor Daley, what is your relationship with Thomas Foran, the U.S. attorney who's in the courtroom today?"

"I think he is one of the greatest attorneys in this country and the finest man I have ever met in private and public life."

Hissing was heard from the gallery. The deputy U.S. marshals, encouraged by the judge to take care of the rear row, began to take spectators out of the courtroom. People fell down, women screamed, one man was punched in the face repeatedly by a burly marshal. Four members of the defense legal staff, including two women, were dragged out of the courtroom. Two were arrested.

Mayor Daley spent two and a half hours on the witness stand, carefully shielded from the bitter accusations of the defense by the objections of . . . Foran. Judge Hoffman sustained nearly ninety government objections, to such questions as: "Mayor Daley, do you hold any position with the Democratic National Committee?" "Objection." "Sustained." "Did you not order your police department to shoot and kill or shoot to maim black people in the city of Chicago?" "Objection." "Sustained." "Mayor Daley, on the twenty-eighth of August, 1968, did you say to Senator Ribicoff, 'Obscenity, you Jew, obscenity, you lousy obsenity, go home'?"

Foran: "I object to that kind of conduct in a courtroom, of all the improper, foolish questions."

"That is not a made-up question. We can prove it. There was a lip-reader."

The judge refused to allow an answer, ruling it a leading question. He also refused defense attempts to have Daley declared a hostile witness. In fact, the mayor smiled most of the time, not to be provoked by hostile questions. In that way, the defense was prevented from asking even tougher ones. Only at the end did Daley frown as he listened to a stinging indictment of himself, Daley described by the defense as part of a conspiracy to prevent or crush any significant demonstrations against the war, poverty, racism, in support of alternative cultures at the 1968 Democratic National Convention.

If the trial, then, was not the farce some recall—thinking, perhaps, of the day the defendants wore mock judicial robes—it raised some honest fears that higher courts might rule on a sideshow, or peripheral, rather than a constitutional issue. Some defendants freely admitted they saw it as a forum. One commentator noted that the New Left might paraphrase Chairman Mao: "The mass media are to the revolutionary as the water is to fish."

After a suspenseful wait, the jury returned its verdict:

CORRESPONDENT: The seven defendants were brought to the courtroom from their jail cells, unshaven and unaware that the jury had reached a verdict. The wives, families, and friends of the defendants were ordered out of the courtroom by Judge Julius Hoffman, who agreed with the prosecution that they had created disturbances in the past, and he wanted no interruptions today. The girl friend of Abbie Hoffman was carried out screaming, "These men will be avenged on your grave, Julie, and the grave of your pig empire!" The fact that the jury, believed to be deadlocked for four days, had reached a verdict came as a surprise. Several of the jurors appeared to be visibly shaken waiting for the verdict to be read. Mrs. Jean Fritz, thought to be one of the three holdouts for acquittal, seemed to be the most disturbed.

Judge Hoffman asked the jury, "Have you reached a verdict?" The jury foreman handed the verdict to a federal marshal to be delivered by the clerk of the court. On the charge of conspiracy, all seven defendants not guilty. On the charge of crossing state lines with the intent to incite a riot, David Dellinger, Rennie Davis, Tom Hayden, Abbie Hoffman, and Jerry Rubin, guilty. On the charge of teaching the use of incendiary devices, against John Froines and Lee Weiner, not guilty. There was applause from the defense table because of the acquittals. Dellinger hugged Lee Weiner, who was acquitted of all the charges, along with John Froines, who put his head in his hands and began to cry because the five others were found guilty.

The five guilty verdicts came under the 1968 antiriot law, which in the course of the trial had become confused with the older conspiracy law. Each defendant had been charged on separate counts of conspiracy first, and inciting a riot, or, in the case of Froines and Weiner, of teaching the use of incendiary weapons in the second count. The five found guilty face prison terms of five years apiece.

After the verdict, some of the major participants in the trial expressed their reactions.

U.S. ATTORNEY THOMAS FORAN: Well, I think that the verdict proves the very thing that has been under substantial attack in this case—it proved that the judicial system works. I think it just proves that the very thing these men don't like works wonderfully.

ASSISTANT U.S. ATTORNEY RICHARD SCHULTZ: And I think that by continuing through this prosecution, going to verdict, and having the verdict that we have, we have established, as best that we could, that they simply could not do, in the courtroom in the last four and a half months, what they— what they did and attempted to do in one week during the Democratic National Convention in Chicago.

FORAN: To prove the system, the trial had to finish and had to go to the jury, and it did.

CORRESPONDENT: But it—but if they would have acquitted them, you would have considered that a . . .

FORAN: No, sir, that's a victory. How could these guys complain about the system, if they found—they were found not guilty? How could the ones who were found not guilty complain about it? The system works.

MAYOR RICHARD DALEY: The jury proved very clearly, and in their findings have said what we have said all along—that some people did come to our city for no other purpose than to riot and to create violence.

DEFENSE ATTORNEY WILLIAM KUNSTLER: It's really what is called a compromise verdict. That jury had people on it who believed in the innocence of those defendants on every count. They held out till the last minute, and then they were overwhelmed by the other jurors and were forced to accept a compromise.

CORRESPONDENT: Defense attorney Kunstler plans an appeal of the five convictions. The defendants were led back to jail, still defiant of the judicial system they had challenged consistently for the past months.

Checking reports that the convictions had resulted from a compromise reached during a late-night conference at the jurors' hotel, a reporter spoke with Mrs. Ruth Petersen:

CORRESPONDENT: Mrs. Petersen, was there some kind of deal made in the verdict that the jury reached?

MRS. RUTH PETERSEN: A deal? No, not really.

CORRESPONDENT: Was there some trading back and forth?

MRS. PETERSEN: Oh, yeah.

CORRESPONDENT: Guilty and innocent? Mrs. Petersen, how many of you felt that way, that they were guilty of conspiracy?

MRS. PETERSEN: Better than half of us.

CORRESPONDENT: Well, how come the jury didn't convict?

MRS. PETERSEN: Well, in order to get these here three they were—didn't want to convict them—they—that's why we compromised a bit.

CORRESPONDENT: So the compromise was made on the conspiracy charge.

MRS. PETERSEN: Uh-huh. Yeah.

CORRESPONDENT: How did you—how long did you have to negotiate with the three holdouts?

MRS. PETERSEN: Oh, gee, we went around and around and around, and we done a lot of praying in order to hope that they'd see our point of view, too.

CORRESPONDENT: Do you think that the jurors were influenced, any of your fellow jurors, by the way that the defendants dressed and wore their hair?

MRS. PETERSEN: No, I don't think so.

CORRESPONDENT: It was a little unusual, you must admit.

MRS. PETERSEN: It was, yes, and that— they all said they need a good bath or good hair—hair wash and comb. After all, everybody's got their own rights to dress and look the way they want to.

CORRESPONDENT: There was a big issue made all during the trial, of course, and you probably couldn't help but be aware of it, that—about the outbursts in the courtroom.

MRS. PETERSEN: Yeah. That was really something. We didn't get to see too many of them, you know, but what we did were—it shook us up sometimes—I know with me it did.

CORRESPONDENT: Do you feel as though you've done a service?

MRS. PETERSEN: I sure did. I served my country and I done my duty, I think, and I hope it's for the best.

On February 20, Judge Hoffman im-posed maximum five-year sentences on those convicted of crossing state lines with intent to incite riot. He also fined them $5,000 each, half the maximum, and ordered them to pay the cost of the trial. The sentencing mixed drama, comedy, and the stern realities of law in unequal proportions:

CORRESPONDENT: One by one, the defendants made their final statements before sentencing, in the most serious and eloquent session of the trial. In contrast to his usual stern demeanor, Judge Hoffman actually laughed, for the first time trial observers could recall. The five defendants were unusually somber, unshaven, and seemingly depressed by their confinement at the Cook County Jail.

David Dellinger, the fifty-four-year-old pacifist and accused architect of the conspiracy the government could not prove, spoke first. "We came to Chicago believing in democracy," he said, "and we learned that the present two-party system is not democratic, and should be returned to the people." Addressing the judge, Dellinger said, "I keep thinking of you as King George III. You're trying to hold back the second American revolution, but there's an awakening in the country. People will die in the streets and die in prison, but the awakening will not be denied."

Rennie Davis, the twenty-nine-year-old son of a former White House official, spoke briefly. "It is not a time for words," he declared. "It is a time for action. My jury will be in the streets tomorrow, and their verdict will keep coming in. My only hope is that I'll be out of jail by 1976, and then the American people are not going to recount history; they are going to relive it." Speaking to U.S. Attorney Thomas Foran, who had accused Davis of acting, for the jury, like the boy next door, Davis declared, "When I get out I'm going to move next door to Tom Foran, and organize his kids for the revolution. We're going to turn the sons and daughters of the ruling class into Vietcong."

"I think the verdict is a tragedy," said Tom Hayden, the founder of SDS, "but the fact that four jurors thought we were innocent is testimony to the ability of people to wake up—wake up to the nightmare of American life. But they don't know how to hold out, how to fight to the end."

Abbie Hoffman, the Greenwich Village psychologist who became a cultural revolutionary, appeared confused. "I feel like Alice in Wonderland," he said, "only it's 1984. I'm still waiting for the permits for Lincoln Park. I still think Lyndon Johnson is president. I haven't eaten in six days. . . . I'm not on a hunger strike, but I can't eat the lousy food in prison. It's not the right place for a nice Jewish boy with a college education." And Judge Hoffman, who is Jewish himself, could not contain his laughter. Hoffman the defendant concluded, "When people go from one state of mind to another state of mind in the future, I only hope they go youth fare."

Jerry Rubin was the most agitated of all. "The machines of the government are sending the human beings to jail," he cried. "We're on trial because we're trying to wake America up by shouting and screaming and standing on our heads. We're on trial for being ourselves, and we refuse to change ourselves to win this case." And, holding up a copy of his new book, Rubin walked around the courtroom showing the picture of himself as a twenty-one-year-old. "You're jailing your youth, America, for the crime of dreaming, and our idealism."

Protests, some violent, dotted the land—in Chicago, Madison, Wisconsin, Boston, and other communities. The case will not be resolved until higher courts rule on the verdicts, which are under appeal, and perhaps not even then. The defendants—out on bail, along with their attorneys, who were sentenced for contempt along with all the defendants—remain much in the public eye, addressing rallies, writing books and articles, plowing substantial royalties into various causes.

But most of the unresolved issues were brought out immediately after the jury handed down its verdict:

JERRY RUBIN: If I'm put in jail next week for ten years, I know damn well that the people in this group are going to break down the bars and free me.

CORRESPONDENT: Jerry Rubin did go to jail, and although his followers did not free him, they have reacted violently. In Seattle, some fifteen hundred protesters assaulted the federal courthouse, smashing down the door, throwing rocks, breaking windows, and firing a tear gas grenade. They moved on to a window-breaking rampage in the downtown section. Police arrested seventy-nine. Similar, although less serious, demonstrations took place in Berkeley, California, and New York City as several thousand radicals violently protested the severe contempt sentences handed down to the Chicago Seven and their defense attorneys, William Kunstler and Leonard Weinglass.

Could there have been a passive trial, a quieter trial, under different conditions?

LEONARD WEINGLASS: That's hard to say. I—under different conditions I assume you mean a different judge, different prosecutor. Given the nature of the defendants, I don't think so. I think Abbie Hoffman is Abbie Hoffman, Jerry Rubin's Jerry Rubin.

CORRESPONDENT: Rubin and fellow Yippie Abbie Hoffman wore robes into the courtroom once. It was among their milder actions. With David Dellinger and Rennie Davis, they called the prosecution witnesses liars. They shouted profanities at the judge. They called him a fascist, a racist, a tyrant and sadist. They fought with the federal marshals. In fact, they were so insulting the ten men of the defense drew contempt of court sentences totaling more than nineteen years in prison and alienated a large part of the public.

How far can the challenge to jurisprudence go in common sense?

WILLIAM KUNSTLER: Well, it can go as far as the Panthers in New York are carrying it, or as far as the Chicago Seven have carried it, or farther, because I think it's a vulnerable part of the system. It's the old question whether you just do peaceful picketing or whether you go one or two or three steps farther. I think that's been transferred into the courtroom now.

PROFESSOR FRED INBAU: If we can't, by the lawful processes, discourage this kind of conduct, if we can't bring people to trial and have the trial proceed in an orderly fashion, I think we're going to have a mood developing in this country, and I see some evidence of it already, to the effect that if you can't try people in the courtroom, individuals, groups of this type, then we'd better let the police try them on the streets. And that would be a most unfortunate consequence.

TOM HAYDEN: If they continue to bring people in the courts for their views, for their ideas, then the—the court system is not going to be able to manage it. They're going to have to start putting us in glass boxes or in other rooms and bringing in videotape for us to watch people accusing us, because you can't preserve order in the courtroom while you're suppressing the right of people to give their political defense.

PROFESSOR PHILIP KURLAND: I hate the thought of—of this notion of preventive detention, which is now entertaining so many people in Washington, would be extended so that these people would not be brought to trial, but simply held until such time as they might be shown to be able to behave in a courtroom. That I regard as a horrific possibility.

CORRESPONDENT: The legal debate about the effects of disruption on the judicial system does not concern the Chicago Seven. Their audience throughout the trial has been the young, especially the long-haired hippies who waited all night outside the Federal Building to get into the courtroom. They singled out Judge Julius Hoffman for scorn. His age—seventy-four. His raspy voice, short stature, and strict judicial manner became the target for the defendants' invective.

They discussed their strategy shortly before being sent to jail.

RUBIN: And it's like he says what's in every judge's head, and—but he just says it out loud. And he's every judge, he's every parent, he's every teacher, he's every [indistinct]—he's authority in America, and he's right out there and up front, and to that extent he's a right-wing Yippie, and it's—it becomes a clear—theatrically clear conflict between life-styles.

That's why I think Julius Hoffman is the main issue in the trial—is Julius and the fact that the goal from the beginning of the trial has been to give him a heart attack.

ABBIE HOFFMAN: I mean it was a tactical military blunder, probably one of the greatest since Waterloo, you know, or Dien Bien Phu, to drive us out of Lincoln Park in Chicago in August of 1968. It was a second tactical military blunder to hold this trial.

RUBIN: We don't respect the Democratic party, and so we went to the streets to oppose it. We don't respect the court system, and so we break every rule that the court system has. And I'm sure that in every living room across the country there's a battle about the trial, with parents saying, well, there, you know, you have to have laws, and there should be a test of the laws, and so forth, and they, and you can't have riots, and the kids rooting for us as if we were baseball players.

CORRESPONDENT: If the kids were rooting for the Chicago Seven, they were able to watch a play-by-play on network television news broadcasts. And that became another element in the legal debate, as expressed by the president of the Illinois State Bar Association.

HENRY PITTS: And I just state that I think that a concerted effort has been made —it appeared to me—to try this case in the —take the case to the public, as they're saying it. They weren't trying to try it in the courtroom.

RUBIN: I don't feel guilty at all in saying that my [indistinct] is to get this thing on television. I think that the government wants to put us away quietly, nobody knows about

it, eight men convicted. And what we're trying to do is let everybody know about it.
We're screaming and yelling, the whole world
is watching.

On March 31, in an unrelated case, the
Supreme Court ruled that a trial judge could
expel a disruptive defendant from the courtroom, cite him for contempt, or shackle and
gag him. Deeper questions about the Chicago
trial, of course, remain.

Angela, the Panthers, and Cesar

*the United States, it has been cruelly observed, was founded by white men
two of whose beliefs were the slaughter of the red race and the
enslavement of the black. the matter of racial prejudice, however, has
caused more self-debasement than any other in the national past,
a preoccupation seldom equaled elsewhere. it can be argued that we have
more to feel guilty about on this score than other countries; the record
does not entirely bear the statement out. but in a nation committed to the
arguments of its founding fathers for equality, freedom, and the
judgment of the individual on the basis of his own merits, the awful
racial divisions in the United States clearly have caused anguish and
passions unknown in countries where circumstances of birth are accepted
as part of life. the traditional view of America, as stated if not lived,
has been the melting pot concept. it faced its strongest challenges and
most outspoken advocacies in the 1960s. in the early years of that decade,
resolution of racial differences seemed so close—after all, we were even
joking about it on television, chortling compassionately over racial and
ethnic gags on late-night talk shows. and then, the mood somehow
soured—the murders of a president, a senator, a black minister all
identified with integration were somehow symbolic of the rebirth of a
national distrust. integration was a concept that would save our soul
in 1960; in 1970 it was regarded by some spokesmen for both black and
white as suspicious. worse, by 1970, there seemed no clear way to identify
anyone as a spokesman for any race. Martin Luther King was dead;
George Wallace was again governor of Alabama.*

Angela Davis bears all the credentials of
the certified martyr, a kind of Joan of Arc
for her race, symbolically punished by
"whitey" for a fearlessness in speaking out.

A brilliant and beautiful student whose
achievements were marked by scholarships

176

to universities in the United States, France, and Germany, she was hired as an acting assistant professor of philosophy by the University of California at Los Angeles. When she announced a proud belief in communism, the state's Board of Regents, led by Governor Ronald Reagan, moved to dismiss her. A California court ruled against the dismissal.

But early in 1970 she was fired—not for her political affiliation, according to the regents, but for off-campus activities in support of radicals and challenges to American society. Her obvious physical attraction and stated refusals to calm her rhetoric made her an apparently attractive symbol to liberals. Then, the incident at the Marin County Courthouse in San Rafael, California, on August 7, 1970, reported by David Monsees of KPIX-TV:

CORRESPONDENT: Judge Harold Haley was hearing the case of a San Quentin inmate accused of knifing a prison guard when an unidentified man armed with dynamite and an automatic weapon entered the courtroom. The defendant, along with two other inmates testifying for him, reportedly joined with the unidentified man in rounding up the judge, a deputy district attorney, and three woman jurors. A deputy sheriff who was in the courtroom at the time described his experience.

JAMES LAYNE: The suspect that was on the stand got up, walked over to one of the San Quentin guards—by this time we're all lying on the ground—

CORRESPONDENT: How many of the guards were there?

LAYNE: There were five.

CORRESPONDENT: Five guards in the room?

LAYNE: Yeah. And he told one of them to get up—I think the suspect's name was McKenna, or the one that was testifying was McKenna, and he said you've held me in San Quentin for X number of years, I was

unjustly accused, now for the love of God take these cuffs off of me, I want to be a free man.

CORRESPONDENT: Once outside the courtroom, all nine people moved to a panel truck. As it pulled away, two county cars blocked its path and the shooting began. Gunfire came from automatic rifles, shotguns, and pistols. When it was over Judge Haley was dead, the deputy district attorney had been critically wounded in the back, one woman juror was wounded in the arm, two of the inmates were dead, as was the unidentified man. He had fallen over the truck's steering wheel, with at least two sticks of dynamite in his pockets. Whether the escapees, or police and guards returning their fire, killed the judge won't be positively known until the coroner's inquest.

A few days later it was charged that Miss Davis had obtained the weapons used by the convicts to kill Judge Haley. She was identified as a close friend of teen-aged Jonathan Jackson, who allegedly had carried the guns into the courtroom.

She disappeared, reportedly fled to Algeria or Cuba. But police picked her up in a New York City motor lodge, along with a male companion, and eventually returned her to California to face murder charges. Under the law in that state, an accomplice who furnishes the murder weapon is as guilty as the perpetrator of the crime.

And so her case exposes a good many of the raw nerve ends in American life. Her youth, her blackness, her revolutionary views all raise serious questions. The president of Yale University expressed public doubt in connection with another case that a Black Panther could receive a fair trial in the United States; Angela stood for the Panthers' revolutionary rhetoric. Russian scientists charged she was being victimized by American jurisprudence.

In Chicago, a grand jury found that

police were justified in the shoot-out death of Black Panther Fred Hampton; subsequently, another jury charged police brutality and destruction of evidence. But there has remained a conviction that race war is a national plot rather than local stupidity. Eric Sevareid commented on its irrationality:

> Historians have a phrase to describe the collective human chemistry that fueled the mass tragedies in much of Europe and Asia over the last couple of generations. The politics of hysteria, they call it. Save for rather short bursts, limited in extent and effect, America has been spared this plague in this century, but it is never totally absent, and seems to be increasing.

The passions of the new decade turned to growing numbers over wide locations of police killings, many of them by blacks. In Cleveland, it was as simple a matter as a black walking up to a parked patrol car, announcing to a white policeman, "I've got a message for you, whitey," and murdering him, and then dashing away. The shootings were not only by blacks; patterns of anti-police violence were apparent in many communities. Even more irrationally, the slaughters were patently aided by the nation's gun control laws, permissive to a point that makes some intellectuals doubt the American sanity.

Racial grievances flash over the nation like heat lightning. Blacks arming themselves, bullets traveling both ways. It often seems as though part of the stubborn streak frequently hailed as ingrained in the national character amounts to obdurate determination to avoid facts.

But racial divisions in general have begun to attract attention from the White House to the street corner. President Nixon, declaring an end to "suffocating paternalism," called on Congress to help "the most deprived and isolated minority group in our nation"—American Indians. Shortly before his dismissal, Interior Secretary Walter Hickel testified for support of proposals to improve legal protection for Indians against threats to their natural interests. He said that there was more truth than poetry in the Indian complaint that "white man speaks with forked tongue."

By way of publicizing their plight—after decades of largely quiet acceptance—American Indians occupied Alcatraz Island—an abandoned federal prison—in San Francisco Bay, demanding that it be given them to develop as a native American cultural and educational center, and tried similar action on Ellis Island in New York Harbor, a continent away.

To many, however, the most appealing of the minority leaders was Cesar Chavez, the thirty-five-year-old Mexican-American who represented a constituency not only of his compatriots but of perhaps the most badly treated group in the nation. Three doctors testified before a Senate subcommittee on the life of the migrant farm worker today:

DR. HENRY LIPSCOMB: These people are hungry for care, and these people are dying for want of it.

DR. RAYMOND WHEELER: Children die. Even worse, most of them live, numbed by hunger and sickness, motivated only by an instinct for survival.

DR. GORDON HARPER: It is a hard journey through a land where money and profit move men's hearts more than does human misery.

CORRESPONDENT: Three Field Foundation physicians who studied health and other migrant labor problems, mainly in Florida, Texas, and Michigan. The Senate subcommittee hearing their testimony wants to find out who is responsible for the living conditions of migrant families.

DR. WHEELER: We saw housing and living conditions horrible and dehumanizing almost to the point of disbelief. In Florida and in Texas, we visited housing projects, built with public funds, which defy description. The migrant and the seasonal farm worker live shorter lives, have more illnesses and accidents, lose more babies, and suffer more than the rest of us.

DR. HARPER: "Babies die all the time," says one grower, when asked about a notorious case of a nine-month-old who died last year of diarrhea and dehydration after being refused admission to a hospital in southwest Michigan. "Why should they get so excited," the grower asks, "when a baby dies here?"

SENATOR WALTER MONDALE: I would like to come away from this hearing with a sense of hope that things are going to happen. As you make this case of outrageous and immoral treatment of human beings, the truth of it is that hearings like this, and public presentations like this, have occurred time and time again. The capacity of our society to mangle people who lack the power to stand up for their own rights is virtually limitless.

Employers of the migrant workers, given their day in court to testify, did not fare well. "Generations of abuse and neglect cannot be rooted out in weeks, or even months," said president J. Paul Austin of Coca-Cola, which employs thirteen hundred migrant workers in its Minute Maid orange groves. He pledged continuing, if recently awakened, company efforts to "solve this problem."

Senator Mondale argued acerbically that "unless we join together to change the problem of powerlessness, I think there will be instances such as those which you are undertaking, in which a few farm workers and migrants may have a somewhat better life, but the condition of the migrant and the farm worker will continue to be one of this nation's greatest scandals."

George Wedgworth, of the Florida Fruit and Vegetable Association, denied conditions were as bad as depicted, questioned the motives of the critics, noted that America's food industry is better than Russia's. His main complaint was against a recent NBC documentary.

GEORGE WEDGWORTH: To take what little dignity a person has away by categorizing him as a bum, which was done in the film "Migrant," I don't think is good.

SENATOR MONDALE: Will you yield there?

WEDGWORTH: Yes.

SENATOR MONDALE: Wasn't this the young child who said of himself that he felt he was a bum?

WEDGWORTH: That's true, but—

SENATOR MONDALE: Now, what kind of system produces that kind of tragedy? That's what we're at here today.

WEDGWORTH: Well, I—I—

SENATOR MONDALE: That wasn't editorializing. That was a child whose life has been ruined, and I'd like to see some expression of concern out of you. These people are being mangled and destroyed, and we hear nothing of this.

WEDGWORTH: Senator, you have not heard my remarks. I am concerned. But to take the very poor and say that's typical—typical of all migrant children is just not fair. If I have not convinced you with our sincerity and concern over this—this program, then I have failed.

CORRESPONDENT: What the Florida growers have been saying is that there are deplorable conditions, but that they are improving—not fast enough for this Senate committee.

In July, 1970, came the culmination of a bitter labor battle likely to affect the future of agriculture and agricultural workers. The vineyards of California underwent a systematic organization after ten years of struggle and sometimes striking, being unionized after a war few thought could be won. The man responsible was leader of the United Farm Workers Union, Cesar Chavez, whose union stamp, the eagle, became a symbol of victory.

"It's something that we had an idea that we'd like to see it happen, but never dreamt that it could be in—in such a—well, the way it's happening," said Chavez. "It's becoming a pretty, pretty very popular bird."

The contracts won by Chavez called for annual wage increases, paid vacations, insurance, and a medical plan—all barely dreamed of a few years earlier by most of the pickers, most of whom are Spanish-speaking.

In spite of the bitterness of the battle, the Chavez group moved to incorporate agricultural workers other than grape pickers under the eagle symbol. Chavez, leader of a group that was a minority both in its racial origins and its profession, pushed relentlessly his policy of nonviolence—emerging from jail, where he'd been sent for boycotting a lettuce grower whose workers he was attempting to organize, on Christmas Eve:

> In the long run, no one wins—no one really wins in this long struggle. We're not, contrary to public opinion, crazy about boycotting and striking. We'd much rather negotiate, and so we're inviting the grower community, in the spirit and peace of this holiday, to sit with us, and to do it right away.

But the vast challenge of reconciliation among American racial and ethnic groups remains—optimism even harder to come by now than during the decade past.

The President in a lighter mood.

President Nixon and Vice-President Agnew confer.

Republican Charles Goodell during his unsuccessful campaign for reelection to the Senate from New York.

Richard Ottinger of N.Y., flanked by fellow Democratic Senator Edmund Muskie (Maine) and Arthur Goldberg.

James F. Buckley, Jr., the first Conservative party candidate elected to the U.S. Senate from New York State.

Defendants, "The Chicago Seven."

Artist Howard Brodie's on-the-scene crayon impressions, as well as all other drawings in this book, were made for Walter Cronkite's TV news coverage.

Abbie Hoffman wearing boxing
gloves in court.

Abbie Hoffman and U.S. marshal in tug of war for Vietcong flag during trial.

Black Panther Bobby Seale, bound and gagged, during Chicago conspiracy trial.

Bobby Seale telling Panthers in court to "cool it."

Defense Attorney William Kunstler and Judge Julius Hoffman arguing.

Spectators at Chicago trial.

Chicago conspiracy trial jury.

Judge Julius Hoffman.

Angela Davis, believed by many to be a victim of "establishment" persecution because of her radical political convictions.

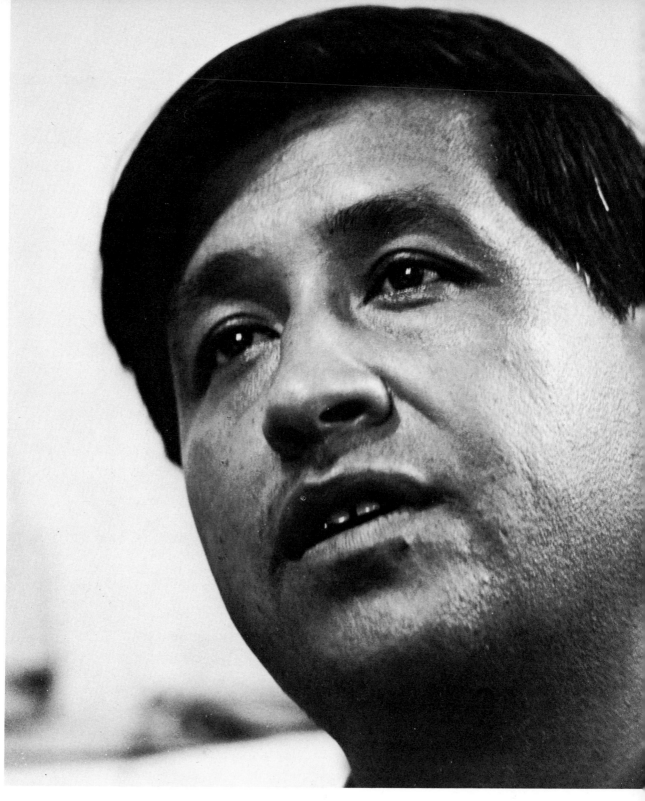

Cesar Chavez, relentless leader of the United Farm Workers Union, has brought new hope to Spanish-speaking migrant workers.

Paying More for Less

THEN

196

Paying More for Less

NOW

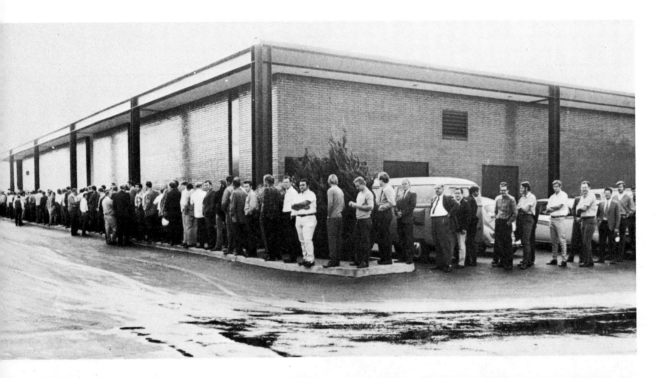

A Generation Gap

"the kids," as they are called, are products of a generation gap without parallel
in history. no other group has been more praised, damned, and examined, with
resulting generation generalizations whose only bond is total disagreement.
careful pundits note that only a small percentage of today's American youth is
involved in demonstrations, violence, drug taking, and something called campus
unrest. this is true. but a generation ago, a decade ago, the drug scene was largely
confined to the ghettos and a few esthetic potheads; "days of rage" was the kind
of thing expected from a scary novelist; campus demonstrations centered about
dormitory hours or the football team.
it does little good to dismiss the small percentages involved. each generation is
summed up by the behavior of a few: there really weren't many "flappers" in
the 1920s; that was the artistic vision of a writer, Scott Fitzgerald, and an
artist, John Held, Jr., but memory stereotypes it as the era of flaming youth and
wonderful nonsense. parents of young people during the Eisenhower era didn't
notice any particular quiet around the house, although their children were
members of the "silent generation." whenever national concern is expressed
about the state of youth, it devolves upon all good editorial writers to trot out
the quotation about the disrespect of youth toward elders and convention,
noting then that the quotation is from the ancient Greek. sometimes it is the
ancient Egyptian. whichever, it begs the issue. perhaps that generation of
Greeks or Egyptians was troublesome.
whether the "now" generation is symbolized by "bums burning the campus" or
"the best, the smartest youth ever" is a matter for the long eye of history.

"May never was the month of love," wrote the poet Southwell in the sixteenth century, "for May is full of flowers." In the spring of 1970, for American youth, it was a month of death, shock, and dissension without parallel. And this centered on the campuses of the nation's 2,500 colleges and universities. With college enrollment at an all-time high—more than five million—so was college disruption. The age-old tradition of town and gown distrust hardened into battle lines drawn up between "the kids" and "the hard-hats." The ultimate target was higher education itself, under fire from right and left and viewed doubtfully by many in the middle.

"The academic society is responsible for all our troubles in this country," said Martha Mitchell, the outspoken wife of Attorney General John Mitchell. "These are the people that are destroying our country."

The leftist Students for a Democratic Society viewed it differently: "American universities are absolutely central components of the social system of technological warfare-welfare capitalism."

Youth—and, by inference, the "permissive parents" who produced the children—had replaced communism, foreign and domestic, as a campaign issue. Again, there was a zeroing in on college administrators who "coddled" disrupters, no matter the fact that most participants in illegal campus activities were either convicted by the courts or dismissed by the educators.

But, according to one survey, in May 75 percent of college students believed that "basic changes in the system are necessary" to improve life in the United States and 44 percent thought that "radical pressure outside the system" was needed to bring about that change, rather than reliance on the institutions of law, government, and the social establishment.

At Kent State University, in the Ohio community of Kent, there had been an explosive reaction to President Nixon's announcement of the Cambodian incursion. (The campus had long been tense; there had been violence between some students and townspeople.) The turbulence included the burning of the campus ROTC building and the stoning of national guardsmen brought to the scene to restore order. In itself this is of no great significance; similar confrontations take place at other institutions.

Following his first Cambodian address, the President stopped off at the Pentagon and made a few informal remarks to employees there:

> I got down to the conclusion and you say well, the usual thing, you ask for support for the President and all that guff, and you finally think of those kids out there [in Vietnam]. I say kids—I've seen 'em. They're the greatest. You know, you see these bums, you know, blowing up the campuses—listen, the boys that are on the college campuses today are the luckiest people in the world, going to the greatest universities and here

207

they are burning up the books, I mean storming around about this issue, I mean you name it, get rid of the war, there'll be another one. And then, out there, we got kids who are just doing their duty, and I've seen 'em, and they stand tall, and they're proud. I'm sure they're scared. I was when I was there, but when it really comes down to it they stand up. Boy, you gotta talk up to those men, and they're going to do fine. We gotta stand back of them.

And then it was May 4, 1970. Four students on the Kent State campus were shot dead:

IKE PAPPAS: A bell on the campus common called students together again today for another rally. It should have been a warning signal for what was to follow. After two days of rioting over ROTC and Cambodia, the university had banned rallies and the National Guard stood by to enforce the ban.

MAN: Leave this area immediately. Leave this area immediately.

CORRESPONDENT: The warning was issued several times but the students were angry and they stood defiant. Guards then were given the order to move out, but first the students were peppered with tear gas fired from riflelike launchers.

In moments, clouds of tear gas covered the center of the campus. The students fell back over a hill, answering the guardsmen with rocks. Suddenly, from over the hill, there was rifle fire. Four students, two of them females, were shot to death. At least another dozen were wounded. Assistant Adjutant General Frederick Wender said that snipers fired into the ranks of the troops, and the troops fired back. The students were angry.

EYEWITNESS: There were guards at the top of the hill, just gathered around, like a big circle, just gathered together. They never said anything. All at once, they just put their rifles up in the air, from what I could see on my side—they started shooting blanks, or that's what everybody said, they were shooting blanks. One kid standing by me said that a bullet came down and ricocheted by his leg, and everybody just started running and got real scared. I walked back up the hill, and there was four—I could see three kids laying in the driveway down there, with blood, and the girl friends were standing over them, crying and everything, and everybody was saying they were shooting blanks, but one kid came up, told me he saw a kid get hit right through the head. I saw them bring the ambulance and they brought him away, and everybody said they had blanks, but some of them had real bullets. They just looked like they fired up in the air and I looked around and this guy's laying, dead.

The dead students were William Schroeder, nineteen, of Lorain, Ohio, a high school honor student, basketball star, and musician; Sandra Lee Scheuer, twenty, of Youngstown, Ohio, a junior majoring in speech therapy, an honor student; Jeffrey Miller, twenty, of Plainview, New York, an honor student, gifted in math, majoring in drama; and Allison Krause, nineteen, of Pittsburgh, a freshman who wanted to be a teacher. When the guard first arrived on the campus, she had, smiling, placed a flower in the muzzle of a guardsman's gun. Her father reflected the anguish of the parents of the dead:

She resented being called a bum because she disagreed with someone else's opinion. She felt that war in Cambodia was wrong. Is this dissent a crime? Is this a reason for killing her? Have we come to such a state in this country that a young girl has to be shot because she disagrees deeply with the actions of her government? I want something to be done. What I would like to see happen is that my daughter's death and those of the other three children, as well as the wounded, not be in vain. I would like to see Congress investigate the situation and determine who authorized live ammunition to be brought against children by tired and frightened National Guard.

President Nixon:

The President shares the sadness of the parents involved and that of all Americans over these unnecessary deaths. This should remind us all that when dissent turns to violence it invites tragedy. It is my hope that this tragic and unfortunate incident will strengthen the determination of all the nation's campuses—administrators, faculty, and students alike—to stand firmly for the right which exists in this country of peaceful dissent, and just as strongly against the resort to violence as a means of such expression.

The reaction to Kent State, combined with student anger over the Cambodian campaign, spread swiftly to other campuses —there were an attempt to fire the ROTC building at the University of California at Berkeley, fires at Washington University of St. Louis and at Northwestern University, rock throwing met with tear gas at such scattered locations as the University of Wisconsin, the University of Buffalo, and the University of Texas.

Brown and Boston universities shut down. Governor James Rhodes ordered Ohio State temporarily closed. Governor Louie Nunn ordered troops to the University of Kentucky campus to enforce a 7:00 P.M. curfew. And in California, Governor Ronald Reagan ordered all twenty-seven of the state's universities and colleges shut down for four days. The state's largest campus antiwar rally ever took place at Berkeley, where the Nixon course in Cambodia united radical students, moderate students, and some of the faculty.

In Columbus, three thousand Ohio college students marched on the state capitol protesting the war, the National Guard on the Ohio State campus, and, most of all, the deaths at Kent State.

George Wynn, Jr., a twenty-three-year-old college senior in San Diego and son of a retired navy captain, committed self-immolation, dousing himself with kerosene and setting himself afire while holding a sign that said, "In the name of God, end the war." His mother said he was not a radical, belonged to no political group, and was raised in a military atmosphere. She said of her dead son, who was being called into the service, "He was just too sensitive."

Colleges across the nation shut down for periods ranging from a day to the remainder of the school year. But the signal factor is that even after Kent State, only 4 percent of eighteen hundred college and university presidents reported *violent* protests on the campus. The vast majority of protests, when they occurred, were peaceful.

At Kent State itself, classes were suspended and the first of a bewildering profusion of investigations into the circumstances surrounding the shootings got under way. A Guard spokesman said that a sniper had been spotted on a nearby rooftop by an Ohio Highway Patrol helicopter, but patrol officials denied this. The Guard claimed that it fired only after the troops ran out of tear gas and were being rushed by the students.

"Troops are there to perform a mission," said Major General Sylvester Del Corso, Ohio Guard commander, "and there is certainly danger of an individual being shot. Not that we want to shoot anybody, but it's just inconceivable that an individual would attempt to rush a trooper with a bayonet and a loaded weapon and expect him not to do anything, to permit him to beat him up or kill him."

The Guard claimed it followed "to the letter" U.S. Army instructions on crowd control. But again and again an army training film on the subject emphasizes that only the minimum force necessary should be used:

You may be greatly outnumbered, but re-member that your training and proper con-duct, the image you present of a neat, well-disciplined soldier, give you a practical psychological advantage over an unruly emo-tional mob. Those confrontations demand much of you. You must work within an at-mosphere of explosive emotionalism and yet remain calm and rational. You will be sub-jected to the worst extremes of provocation, and yet you must be guided only by logical thought. When every natural instinct within you begs for action, you must remain passive.

And regular army troops would not carry loaded weapons in such confrontations; Ohio Guard troops were authorized to do so in 1966. Brigadier General Robert Canter-bury of the Ohio Guard said that his troops were fired on before shooting, "but we cannot say where the shots came from." And before the guardsmen left the closed campus, some few offered their own version of what hap-pened, reflecting a within-the-generation gap:

FIRST GUARDSMAN: People throw rocks and bricks at us. A kid got his kneecap shat-tered with a wrench. Nobody cares about us. All they care about is them four kids up there that got killed. They can throw rocks at us and we're supposed to stand, with peb-bles. They're pebble throwers, just harassing us. That's not the way it is.

IKE PAPPAS: Did they throw rocks at you?

FIRST GUARDSMAN: Damn right they threw rocks at us.

SECOND GUARDSMAN: Came here Satur-day night. I was so scared Saturday night I was going to get it, it was pitiful. We were on top of that hill when that fire was down there. I never been so scared in all my life. It looked like about three or four hundred of them, just—

CORRESPONDENT: But you weren't up on the hill when the people got shot?

THIRD GUARDSMAN: We watched them get shot. We watched them. We were out there, looking right out the window. We was getting ready, we was all in a line [indis-tinct].

CORRESPONDENT: How do you feel about what happened to those people?

FIRST GUARDSMAN: How do I feel? I feel it's about time one of them got it like that.

CORRESPONDENT: Why?

FIRST GUARDSMAN: I mean, I don't like to see anybody get killed, but I mean we come up here, these people, all they do is stand around and give you a peace sign, throw rocks at you, harass you, call you dirty names, want to know who's sleeping with your wife—ain't none of their business in the first place. I mean I don't like to be here. I'm losing money at work.

SECOND GUARDSMAN; I wouldn't shoot anybody. I don't even load my weapon when I'm on the hill. Why would I want to shoot innocent kids, throwing rocks at you, but—

CORRESPONDENT: Well, what would make a guardsman, you know, use his weapon?

SECOND GUARDSMAN: Somebody shoot-ing at them—which was the case.

CORRESPONDENT: Do you think that's what happened?

SECOND GUARDSMAN: That's what hap-pened. We heard the shots first.

President Nixon announced that he would like to open a dialogue with the na-tion's youth. And he made no effort to re-strain Interior Secretary Walter Hickel, who, in a letter to the President that was mysteri-ously leaked to the *Washington Star,* had said he believed that administration policies indi-cated a lack of concern for the attitude of young people.

"I believe we are in error if we set out consciously to alienate those who would be our friends," Hickel wrote. "We must win over our philosophical enemies by convincing them of the wisdom of the path we have chosen rather than ignoring the path they propose.

"In this regard I believe the Vice-President initially has answered a deep-seated mood of America in his public statements. However, a continued attack on the young—not on their attitudes so much as their motives—can serve little purpose other than to further those attitudes to a solidity impossible to penetrate with reason."

Hickel suggested the President meet with university heads, and "on an individual and conversational basis" with members of the Cabinet for "insight."

A backlash developed against the antiwar demonstrators, however, as students at Houghton College in upstate New York voted overwhelming support of administration policy in Cambodia, Syracuse high school students broke up an antiwar parade, and, in New York City, where Mayor John Lindsay had ordered the City Hall flag flown at half-mast for the Kent State dead, there was violence:

MORTON DEAN: Hundreds of youthful antiwar demonstrators had crowded onto the steps of the old U.S. Treasury Building, their slogans laced with obscenities. Soon dozens, then hundreds, of hard-hatted workers from nearby construction jobs stormed into the square, charged through police lines, chasing the protesters from the steps, beating those who did not move fast enough, and the few who tried to slug it out.

A large American flag carried by the construction workers was placed on the top step of the Treasury Building in a pitched battle. The construction workers marched from Wall Street to City Hall. There were bloody fights all along the way, and at City Hall Plaza.

The construction workers organized rallies of their own, one in New York City attracting an estimated 150,000 persons, probably the largest progovernment rally since Vietnam became a topic of national debate. The war and the rallies concerning it seem a surface reflection of deeper sentiments. Typical of workers' comments about the student protesters:

I think they stink. They're not for America. . . . I think it's about time somebody did something. . . . They're provoking us. It's just what they're doing. You come off a job, you're going on lunch, they call you nothing but a low-life so-and-so. This provokes it, this starts it. . . . Don't say "attacked." Don't say "attacked." They were provoked, man. We work for a living. Every day we get up, we're out there in the cold, the rain, and the snow, right? We have got to have these dirty —forget it. I don't want to talk about them.

Labor leaders presented President Nixon with a construction worker's hard hat bearing the words "Commander in Chief." The White House did not allow pictures, without explanation, although the hard hat—because of the clash with the students in New York— symbolized forceful opposition to the student antiwar movement.

Writing in *TV Guide* magazine, Vice-President Spiro Agnew said that young people enjoyed confrontation because of their lifelong diet of action, violence, and confrontation on the home screen. "How much of this disorder, how many of these illegal demonstrations which pock-mark the country would ever take place if the ever-present television camera were not there?"

President Nixon had said he regretted that his use of the word "bums" was "interpreted to apply to those who dissent."

"When students on university campuses burn buildings, when they engage in violence, when they break up furniture, when they terrorize their fellow students and terrorize the faculty," he said, "I think 'bums' is perhaps too kind a word to apply to that kind of person. They are the kind I was referring to."

Ten days after the Kent State shootings, two Negro youths were shot dead by police at Jackson State College in Jackson, Mississippi. Nine others were wounded in a burst of police gunfire that sounded like a skirmish left over from World War II. There was no clear explanation for the shooting or for the two nights of rock throwing that preceded it, only vague references to confusion, tension over the war, and the violence on other campuses.

Philip L. Gibbs, twenty-one, a junior, was shot in front of the women's dormitory. James Earl Green, a high school senior, died beside the college dining hall across the street. Students said that some forty highway patrolmen raked the women's residence hall with shotgun fire from about fifty feet away. Police said that they were answering sniper fire from the dormitory.

Dr. John A. Peoples, Jr., president of the institution, told a student assembly, "We have witnessed two of our brethren slain wantonly and determinedly. This will not go unavenged." Jackson Mayor Russell Davis said, "This tragedy . . . has occurred in spite of my most sincere belief that it would never happen in our city. It has occurred despite an honest effort to prevent it happening. I was wrong in thinking that it couldn't happen. . . . This is the darkest day of my life."

In 1968, three black students at South Carolina State College in Orangeburg had been killed and thirty-four wounded by state police in an argument over integration of a bowling alley. At the time there had been little public outcry or national attention; many blacks were angered by the widespread furor over Kent State, which they saw as the difference between treatment of the two races in this country.

Official reaction to the Jackson State slayings was markedly different. President

Nixon said, "In the shadow of these past troubled days, this tragedy makes it urgent that every American personally undertake greater efforts toward understanding, restraint, and compassion."

He dispatched Attorney General John Mitchell to confer with Dr. Peoples in Jackson as teams of investigators from the Justice Department and the FBI looked into the shootings. Whitney M. Young, Jr., executive director of the National Urban League, told a Senate hearing, "When the President labels young people 'bums' and the Vice-President 'rotten apples,' to the mentality of the southern law enforcement official, you almost give him a license. I wouldn't be surprised if they weren't expecting to receive Medal of Freedom awards or something."

A group of senators and congressmen were shocked by their tour of the student dormitory. State authorities had wanted to remove shattered glass and metal panels as evidence, but students had objected that only federal agents should be allowed to handle the panels. After the tour, Minnesota Senator Walter Mondale commented, "Based on everything I heard, if I were attorney general . . . I'd be investigating for murder right now."

With the bullet-riddled glass still present, more than one hundred prominent politicians and civil rights leaders attended the funeral for young Green, the high school student who, his friends say, was killed as he crossed the campus on his way home. Fayette, Mississippi, Mayor Charles Evers asked, before two thousand mourners, "How long, O Lord, will our white brothers continue to destroy us?"

To "help us avoid future incidents" such as Kent State and Jackson State, President Nixon appointed a nine-member Commission on Campus Unrest, headed by former Pennsylvania Governor William Scranton. A major duty assigned the commission was "to identify the principal causes of campus violence, particularly the specific occurrences of this spring."

The Commission on Unrest in its report called the National Guard action "unwarranted," in spite of "violent and criminal action by the students . . . who wreaked havoc on the town of Kent . . . burned the ROTC building . . . attacked and stoned national guardsmen."

Specifically, it attacked the Guard's policy of issuing loaded combat rifles to troops called on to control disorders. "The Kent State tragedy," the commission said, "must surely mark the last time that loaded rifles are issued as a matter of course to guardsmen confronting student demonstrators." The commission found the rally itself had been peaceful until the Guard attempted to break it up, upon which some students reacted violently, and even then "the indiscriminate firing of rifles into a crowd of students and the deaths that followed were unnecessary, unwarranted, and inexcusable."

General Del Corso, the Guard commander, strongly disagreed, saying that disarming the troops "would be a tragic mistake. You certainly cannot stop crime by disarming the police; you cannot stop violence by disarming the troops."

Two weeks after the commission's report on Kent State, a special grand jury virtually placed the blame for the tragedy on the university administration, saying that it fostered an atmosphere of laxity, overindulgence, and permissiveness with students and faculty, losing control of both groups. It indicted twenty-five persons, both student and faculty, none of them guardsmen.

Campus youth reacted to the findings of their elders:

GIRL: I think they're one-sided. Guards definitely should have been indicted along with the students, and I'm pretty upset that none were.

BOY: They put the blame on the students and the National Guard, and then they come out now and just indict the students and they leave the National Guard alone, and it's—it's not right, it's completely wrong.

In a separate report, the Commission on Campus Unrest found the Jackson State shooting—more than 150 police bullets in less than thirty seconds—"clearly unwarranted."

In the commission's view, there was an added, ugly element working at the Mississippi college shooting. "A significant cause of the deaths and injuries at Jackson State," it found, "is the confidence of white officers that if they fire weapons during a black campus disturbance, they will face neither stern departmental discipline nor criminal prosecution or conviction."

While the commission criticized students and other blacks for "vile verbal abuse" directed at the police, its sharpest comments concerned both the police and a grand jury that exonerated them. It concluded that the Mississippi Highway Patrol overreacted, that its members were allowed to open fire individually, not on command, that deadly buckshot was used, rather than smaller buckshot. The commission said that Jackson city police lied when they said they did not join in the shooting, that there was no proof that snipers were firing, and that, even if they were, a broad barrage of return fire was not justified.

The commission labeled the grand jury investigation a "whitewash," evidence that repression against blacks in Mississippi could continue.

Mississippi Governor Williams was not impressed:

The presidential commission, sitting in their ivory towers in the eastern states, came to the conclusion that our law enforcement officers in Mississippi were nothing more than barbarians, came to Mississippi with the intent in mind of substantiating that position. And in order to issue the report, the findings and conclusions which they issued in their report, it was necessary for them to take at full value and give full credence to testimony of the lawbreakers, and to ignore in its entirety the sworn testimony of the duly constituted law enforcement officers. The attorney general of the State of Mississippi has referred to this as a kangaroo court type of operation. Certainly he is—in my opinion, he is absolutely correct in his evaluation of the commission's work.

And so in Kent a jury had implicitly disagreed with the commission findings; in Mississippi, the governor was definitive in his disapproval. And the President of the United States, who had appointed the commission, challenged its general conclusions.

The report, based on three months of hearings and study, said the crisis on the campus could threaten "the very survival of the nation," citing divisions in American society "as deep as any since the Civil War." It traced the youthful unrest to three prime causes—the war in Asia, racial injustice, and the goals, values, and administrations of the colleges themselves.

The attack on the report was led by Vice-President Agnew, who called it "pablum for the permissivists . . . imprecise, contradictory, and equivocal." The report condemned antistudent rhetoric, a reference some saw aimed at the Vice-President himself. Agnew commented, "Where it calls for a cease-fire . . . the commission assumes a posture of neutrality as between the fireman and the arsonist."

The President was reported unhappy with the report's thrust of responsibility onto his shoulders.

"There are widely divergent views within our society as to just what our problems are," he said. College students make up only 4 percent of the nation's population and no minority "has veto power over the President's decision to do what he believes is right in the nation's interest."

He noted the commission's plea for understanding of a "youth culture" with the rejoinder that the young should attempt to understand the generation of parents who had overcome depression and war. He placed much of the blame for unrest squarely on the school administrations.

The unresolved issues symbolized by Kent State and Jackson State and the awful days of May, no "month of love," remain just below the surface. What happened then was surely not a substitute for youthful rites of spring, or the action of a handful of hysterics, or sideshows for television cameras.

The New Junkies

"did you ever hear about cocaine Lil?" asks an old and faintly disreputable song. "she lived in cocaine town on cocaine hill/with a cocaine dog and a cocaine cat/they fought all night with a cocaine rat." the doggerel is dated. cocaine is no longer in wide use in the United States. but the eerie nightmare of the addict's dream is no longer confined to the fastness of ghetto dens. cocaine Lil and her boyfriend—he used to be called "Dopey Slim"—live in the small towns now, in the suburbs, and they're getting younger every year. although figures on drug usage in the United States vary so widely as to make you suspect the compilers have been drinking, some are terrifying. the government said that from 1968 to 1969 heroin usage among those twenty-five years old and younger increased 40 percent. in the words of a West Coast criminologist, "the emerging junkie of the 1970s is a middle-class junkie as well as a junior junkie." as for pot—don't mention it; it is so much a part of the youth culture as to be not simply acceptable but de rigueur.

Hard figures about narcotics usage are not easy to come by, since every authority has his own set, each as reliable as a body count of the enemy dead in Indochina. A House committee heard that six million Americans smoked marijuana during 1970. Cadets at the Air Force and Coast Guard academies were dismissed for marijuana usage. Years of governmental warnings have put marijuana in the same category as hard drugs such as heroin, and new studies, in the words of Dr. Stanley Yolles, director of the National Institute of Mental Health, "make it impossible to give marijuana a clean bill of health" because of apparent interference with the thinking process, recent memory, concentration.

A survey of a forty-block area in Harlem found 18,000 hard narcotics addicts among 58,000 residents. Two thousand of them were children, aged seven to fifteen, 90 percent of whom lived by themselves. Victimized and parentally deserted minorities. This is the kind of statistic many people have simply come to accept. But some of us have been compelled to ask questions about the emotions of Americans living—and fighting—under severe stress. The Army has conceded that GIs have died in Vietnam of drug overdose. The Navy told an investigating committee that 3,800 men were discharged in 1969 for using or pushing drugs, with almost as many more rehabilitated or found to be "curiosity" users. The testimony emphasized studies indicating that drug use was no higher in Vietnam than in San Diego or Norfolk.

The idea that marijuana does not severely alter normal functioning was challenged by various authorities during the year, including ex-Major John Inahara, who served as a psychiatrist in Vietnam:

A young enlisted man in Vietnam experiences the usual low-grade depression and anxiety associated with being separated from home, exposure to the dangers of war, and the deprivation of being in the combat zone. These are issues that impinge on every soldier who gets there. He smokes several marijuana cigarettes to alleviate his distress. He relaxes and withdraws from others with a feeling of drowsiness coming over him. His judgment, thinking, and coordination have been dulled. His body is in a state of readiness. If he is left alone or humored, he will probably have a pleasurable experience, but if he is provoked or harassed, his response may be quite unpredictable and aggressive.

A report by Gary Shepard on marijuana usage by American troops in Vietnam aroused outcries in Congress:

CORRESPONDENT: This is Fire Support Base Ares, a small clearing in the jungles of War Zone D, fifty miles northeast of Saigon. Like most other American installations, Fire Base Ares isn't very busy these days. The war is at its lowest level in five years, and there just isn't much to do. The big guns, which normally would be firing around the clock if the war were raging, now remain silent most of the day and the men have a lot of time on their hands—time for such former luxuries as haircuts, and games of volleyball, and even occasional live entertainment by the First Cavalry Division Band during a leisurely noon-hour lunch break. Time also for a trip to a muddy swimming hole less than two hundred yards from the fire base perimeter. But in this case, the trip is more than a mere stroll through the jungle. Most of these soldiers are about to turn on with marijuana.

SOLDIER: Orangutan, get your hair cut.

CORRESPONDENT: Grass is as plentiful in Vietnam as C rations. One pipeful, which the soldiers call a bowl, can easily take care of five or six men. Marijuana cigarettes are just as easy to get, and just as potent. This man is a medic assigned to the First Cavalry Division's First Battalion, Twelfth Cavalry.
The stuff smells pretty strong.

MEDIC: It is. It's really nice stuff over here.

CORRESPONDENT: How often do you come down here?

MEDIC: I make it down here maybe twice a day. Sometimes in the morning I'll come down here, sometimes in the afternoon. Then we really get it on in the evening, up there at the fire base.

CORRESPONDENT: Aren't you worried about maybe getting attacked and not being able to react properly?

MEDIC: No, nobody usually seems to worry. That's about the last thing that—worried about. We're worried—more worried about lifers. I think we're—we're constantly on the guard for lifers when we smoke.

CORRESPONDENT: Who are the lifers?

MEDIC: Colonel, major, our CO, E-6 and above.

CORRESPONDENT: The career guys.

MEDIC: The career guys, They're usually down on it. But actually, there's not too many guys that are down on it. Even—especially on the fire base. Out in the bush it's a little different, but you get on the fire base and there's not too many guys that are really down on it.

SOLDIER: Somebody give me some illumination. Dig it. That's cool to mix.

SOLDIER: Aw, come on, man. Don't want to light, man. Try it with yours.

SOLDIER: Try it with yours.

SOLDIER: These army issue lighters, something, man.

SOLDIER: It ain't even lit, is it?

SOLDIER: Yeah, lit; it's lit. Only TT. Needs some. There it is, man. You owe it to yourself.

CORRESPONDENT: You were telling me about a special way you do it.

SOLDIER: Oh, Ralph? Good old Ralph. Ralph's this shotgun this guy carries. And you empty it out and you stick the bowl in the barrel, blow into the bowl, and when it comes out, you get really stoned. Then, you know, like who cares about the war?

SOLDIER: This war.

CORRESPONDENT: Do that very often?

SOLDIER: Whenever Vito's around.

CORRESPONDENT: Vito is a twenty-year-old draftee from Philadelphia. A photographer before he entered the Army, Vito is now a squad leader, responsible for the lives of a dozen men.
What's that you got there?

SOLDIER: This is—this is what they were telling you about, Ralph. This is what—well, we use it for also, you know, killing gooks and all, plus little added pleasures, it's really —well, shotgun. It's—you know, the term means . . .

SOLDIER: Wild chickens. [Indistinct]

CORRESPONDENT: How does Ralph work?

SOLDIER: Well, to [indistinct]. Works real good. What we basically use it for on the LC, and I guess even out in the field, too, if you want to know, is that we use it to shotgun, from a bowl, you know. You just put the bowl in the chamber and all. Give me a bowl.

SOLDIER: I don't think this one's going to work. Where's the other one? We got another one around here. Paul, let me borrow that bowl for a minute. This is—this is probably all seeds and we're getting busted, but I don't care.

If the drug problem could be confined to persons and places many Americans think of as "special"—Harlem, Vietnam, youth— there likely would be little call for political action. But if a youth culture has evolved affecting the music Americans hear and the clothes Americans wear, it has similarly affected life-styles of the most respectable people:

DAVID CULHANE: It's difficult to say how much the marijuana market has ex-

panded in the last year or two, but certainly it has become more visible, and in many elements of our society it has become casually accepted. . . . At many rock festivals police look the other way. There are simply too many smokers to arrest them all, and the smoking is not limited to those who are young and long of hair. Marijuana is widely used by middle-class adults, especially among those employed in advertising, communications, and the performing arts.
These men are marijuana dealers in California.

DEALER: Occasionally and in certain advertising agencies, I simply walk in with my attaché case and open it up on a board and say I'm here, and people crowd around and take care of their business. It's simply a fact of knowing the people who are working in these various places and having them know that once in a while you'll drop around— their friendly local neighborhood connection.

CORRESPONDENT: Research on marijuana is now expanding, and there are indications that it may be more dangerous than its advocates suspect. Dr. William Geber, of the University of Georgia, tested marijuana on unborn hamsters and found that a very few were seriously deformed.

DR. WILLIAM GEBER: We have here two fetuses. One was taken from a mother who was given a control injection of olive oil on the eighth day of pregnancy. This one was taken from a mother given an injection of marijuana extract on the eighth day of pregnancy. There is a difference in the control fetus and experimental fetus.

CORRESPONDENT: Not all experiments have been negative. In the state of Washington the Department of Motor Vehicles and the state university ran a series of tests using a driving simulator. The same people were tested three times. In one test they were sober. In a second test, they drank enough to bring the level of alcohol in their blood to the minimum point which would allow prosecution for drunk driving. In the third test, they each smoked enough marijuana to make them high. Alfred Crancer, the former director of research for the state Department of Motor Vehicles:

ALFRED CRANCER: We found that persons, while driving the simulator under the influence of marijuana, performed about the same as they did under normal conditions, while the same persons, under the influence of alcohol, performed about 15 percent worse than under normal conditions.

CORRESPONDENT: Sponsors of the test warn, however, that there is still not enough research to conclude that it is safer to drive a car after smoking marijuana than after drinking alcohol. Other research has indicated long-range perils for those who smoke pot. The chief psychiatrist at the University of California's Cowell Hospital now believes that marijuana exaggerates mental problems. Two researchers who examined students in the Boston area report that steady users showed signs of intellectual deterioration. Dr. Albert LaVerne conducted interviews at New York's Bellevue Hospital with 120 GIs back from Vietnam. The group included many pot smokers. Some told of hallucinations in the field.

DR. ALBERT LaVERNE: They would hear bells, and they would hear voices, and they would hear shots and rifles, and they would take their guns and shoot in any direction, thinking that they were under attack. And sometimes they would shoot at their own men and attack their own men. So we had hallucinogenic reactions and we had psychotogenic reactions, which means that the response would vary but it was a profound physiological effect on the brain.

CORRESPONDENT: One problem is that so many young people have tried marijuana without experiencing bad results that they just don't believe the warnings anymore. This was a seminar at Brown University conducted by Dr. Roswell Johnson, director of the University Medical Services.

STUDENT: There's a danger, if we outlaw marijuana, in that an awful lot of people are going to say, after having a favorable mari-

juana experience, that they must be fooling us about all the other drugs. We class them with the rest of the drugs.

DR. ROSWELL JOHNSON: . . . Until we get to the point where we, where we can level with, with people and say marijuana is as we say here, a dangerous drug, but it's not one-fiftieth as dangerous as some of these other things. So when we say that—that when you start to use opium or when you start to use speed, we're really leveling with you. Because if you tell these kids that these are all in the same bag, they're all narcotics, they're all going to drive you to heroin, they're all going to blast your mind and all this kind of stuff, they know, as I said before, you're either an idiot or you're a liar, and they're—they're going to turn you off every time.

VOICE ON TV COMMERCIAL (singing): What do you do when the music stops? Where are you then? Where are you then?

CORRESPONDENT: The National Institute of Mental Health is fighting back with a fairly sophisticated television campaign. They try to make the point that whatever the physical dangers of marijuana, it does present a social danger, the danger that some creative young people, captivated by the drug scene, may drop out of productive society.

VOICE ON TV COMMERCIAL (singing): Where are you then, my friend? You can choose to change the world, but for that, you need your head, straight and in the right place. If you chose drugs instead, where are we then, my friend? Where are we then?

CORRESPONDENT: For years it's been known that basic research is needed about marijuana, and bit by bit the amount spent for such research is going up. In 1967 the National Institute of Mental Health spent on marijuana research $710,000; in 1968, $1,179,000—in 1969, $1,330,000—in 1970, $1,500,000—and in 1971, the NIMH plans to spend a total of $2,335,000 for the study of marijuana and its effects. But so far it's not enough.

We still don't know precisely how many people are using pot, and what the physical and psychological effects will be. Few scientists would be willing to say with certainty whether it's dangerous or not. And unless we start a comprehensive research project now, we may find that we've raised a damaged generation.

A Chance for the Future

in the country of the young, the young resisted a war they didn't understand simply because they didn't understand it—few Oxford oaths were sworn that under no circumstances would they fight; studies of campus rebels this side of the absurd indicated expressions of greater than traditional concern over the environment and the very quality of life. but in the country of the young there is something to be said for the older generations, too. there seems, for the first time, a codified reluctance to send the young off to die in wars created by their elders, along with the opportunity to give the young a chance to pass judgment on those elders aiming at political office.

While antiwar protesters appealed vainly for free time on television to oppose Nixon administration policies in Indochina, and others—most notably the Berrigan brothers—went to jail for destruction of draft card files, the establishment itself has moved to loosen the system. Some politicians pushed publicly for an all-volunteer army. The government itself announced that draftees would not be sent to fight in any future Vietnams. The draft dropped to the lowest quotas since the war heated up in the middle of the previous decade. And a lottery method of selecting draftees was improved, directed toward strictly random selection of the would-be recruits.

But, most important of all, the Supreme Court in a historic decision declared that con-scientious objection to war need not be based on traditional religious grounds so long as the belief is deeply and sincerely held.

The Court had first taken that position in 1965, but two years later Congress rewrote the draft law, making "religious training and belief" the only basis for asking to be excused on the ground of conscientious opposition. Justice Hugo Black, writing for the majority in 1970's reversal of the congressional will, argued that in the cases concerned the young men held such sincere objections that they were willing to go to jail for them.

The ethical and moral sources for such belief, Black said, "occupy in the life of the individual a place parallel to that filled by God in traditional religious persons." In a separate, concurring opinion, Justice John

Harlan reversed his 1965 position and said that limiting conscientious objection to religious grounds abridges the First Amendment separation of church and state.

The ruling overturned the conviction of a Los Angeles man, Elliott Ashton Welsh II, a twenty-eight-year-old commodities broker who would have faced three years in prison had the Court not ruled in his favor. His reaction to the ruling reflected a state of mind widespread in the first year of the new decade:

> ELLIOTT WELSH: Well, basically, I am opposed to war in any form. It's a conscientious belief. I believe that the institution, the military institution, is less than useful in the conduct of human affairs, and it's something I cannot participate in in any form.
>
> CORRESPONDENT: What was it that was said by you and by your attorneys in—in the courts that brought the Supreme Court to the decision that it has rendered?
>
> WELSH: Well, I suppose that it was basically kind of simple. The government conceded that I was sincere; the government conceded that I could be a conscientious objector. The only question was—was my—the basis of my religious beliefs, and since they weren't religious, the—courts felt that under the law, I had to be convicted, that the—the law says that you must believe in a supreme being, or it did at that time.
>
> ATTORNEY: They seemed to have chosen the constitutional point and have said, as—well, in the words that I used—that it's impermissible for Congress, impermissible contrary to the First Amendment, which says there shall be no establishment of religion, impermissible to give something to a man who says he's nonreligious and deny it—give it to a man who says he's religious and deny it to a man who's equally sincere except for one thing, he says I'm nonreligious, and that, I think, is what they've done.

Federal officials immediately expressed concern about the impact of the ruling. One spokesman said the Court's decision made a very vague law even more confusing and likely to cause "an avalanche of college students who suddenly decide they are objectors." Draft director Curtis W. Tarr issued guidelines to local draft boards setting sincerely held beliefs as the first criterion for an objector. But he warned that the board could not reject an applicant solely because it could not understand his beliefs.

The Court later in the year handed down a ruling of potentially greater import when it upheld the right of eighteen-year-olds to vote in national elections, but not in state and local contests. The decision added an estimated eleven million voters to the rolls in national elections. Eric Sevareid speculated:

> So what will happen, now that some eleven million eighteen, nineteen, and twenty-year-olds are added to the potential electorate? A new era in American democracy, says Senator Edward Kennedy, a different country. This is a clear case of magic thinking. Nothing of the sort is going to happen, as nothing of the sort happened when women were enfranchised, in spite of the advance visions and raptures.
>
> A record, after all, does exist on this matter. In Britain last June eighteen-year-olds voted for the first time. The electoral statisticians there agree that the difference this made in the outcome was almost invisible.
>
> Eighteen-year-olds have voted in Georgia and Kentucky for quite a while. No political revolution in the direction either of wickedness or the good, the true, and the beautiful has been detected in either place.
>
> If one assumed that the eleven million very young will vote and will vote more or less alike, then indeed a profound political change would occur. But neither assumption is valid. The young go to the trouble of registering, then of voting, in considerably smaller proportion than do the middle-aged. And they divide, in their preferences and philosophies, just about like the middle-aged. The most that can be guessed is that, on

balance, the Democratic party will make a slight gain.

For what it's worth, a major opinion poll showed the eighteen-to-twenty-year-olds, nationally, preferring Mr. Muskie by 49 percent, Nixon 22, Wallace nineteen. That can change considerably, but a coalescing of a big youth majority behind any one man or party is virtually out of the question.

Probably a reassuring fact, evidence that the young are just as individualistic, in outlook and interest, as the old. Variety is not only the spice of life; it is also the salt of the American system.

229

ROCK FESTIVALS, UBIQUITOUS FEATURE OF THE YOUTH SCENE

CONFRONTATIONS BETWEEN STUDENTS AND "AUTHORITY"

KENT STATE UNIVERSITY

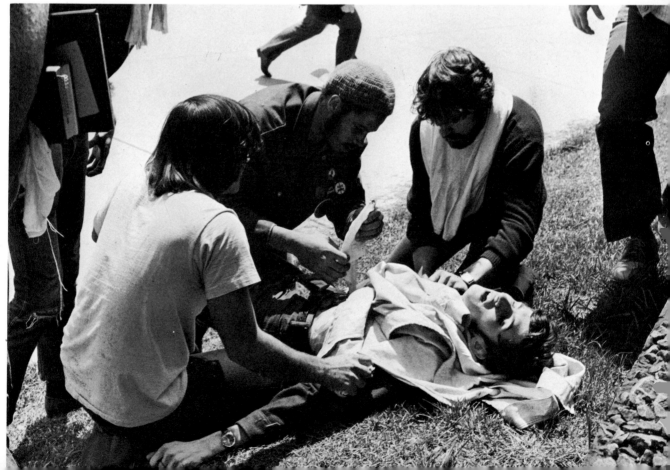

Shattered windows of women's dormitory following fatal shooting of two Negro students at Jackson State College.

Women of the World, Unite!

at a time when toasts to the female are regarded as condescension, and actuaries remark the folly of the phrase "the weaker sex," and the prudent banker sees the bulk of American private income in feminine hands, and chivalry lies bleeding, if not bled, in the philosophy of radical feminists, and something called "unisex" is regarded as an ideal rather than an unfortunate accident, the wise recourse is to let the story of women's liberation tell itself. nonetheless, opinions emerge.

The United States, as it approaches its two hundredth anniversary, lags behind other enlightened, and indeed, some newly emerging, nations in the role ascribed to women." This was a conclusion in a report by the President's Task Force on Women's Rights and Responsibilities.

There were early breakthroughs, to be sure, but they were often petty stuff, not designed to comfort the liberated woman or even the reasonably enlightened male: the newly won right to vote in the principality of Andorra for women whose families had been resident there for at least two generations; a recommendation by the United Nations Commission on Women that more females be appointed to upper-echelon staff positions; the first woman to ride in the Kentucky Derby—Diane Crump galloped into history aboard a male of the species, Fathom, finishing sixteenth in an eighteen-horse field; the first woman to be named to a cabinet post by the Central African Republic; an agreement signed by *Newsweek* magazine to step up the recruitment and promotion of women; a role, along with the Gay Liberation Front, in the Revolutionary People's Constitutional Convention, first session, convened in Philadelphia, where the Black Panthers received most of the publicity.

But there have been achievements solid enough to indicate that prejudice, legal and social, against women is, after all the nonsense, beginning to fall apart. The Equal Employment Section of the 1964 Civil Rights Act includes a clause forbidding employers to discriminate on grounds of sex. The Justice Department, for the first time since the act's passage, filed suit in 1970 charging sex discrimination against women, accusing the Libbey-Owens-Ford Company of hiring women in only one of its five glass-manufacturing plants in the Toledo, Ohio, area and of assigning them to less desirable and lower-paid jobs. The United Glass and Ceramic Workers Union also was named in the suit; as a civil rights attorney commented, "If anyone thinks we don't mean business in this, then they're mistaken."

The Supreme Court declined to upset a lower court finding that the Wheaton Glass Company, the nation's largest manufacturer of glass, must pay the same wage for male and female employees. And a sixty-one-year-old Illinois law was overturned by a federal court as discriminatory for prohibiting women from working more than eight hours a day at some jobs.

With nearly thirty million American women working, relatively few hold executive positions. The median salary for women is about $4,000 a year, roughly half that of men. Betty Friedan, author of the 1963 best seller *The Feminine Mystique* and founder of the National Organization for Women (NOW), sees her sex as an oppressed majority:

> Three out of four women who work are doing secretary, file clerk, hospital aide, that sort of thing. Only a token 1, 2, or 3 percent are administrators, executives, decision makers. Only one woman out of a hundred in the Senate for 51 percent of the population. The big .decision, of war and peace, of crisis in the cities, even the decisions as to what happens to women's own lives and own bodies, and the self-determination on their lives, which—the name of the game for everybody is the freedom thing today—women's voice has not been heard.

Feminists charge that American women work at women's work, as determined by males. It's all right to be a nurse, but only 7 percent of the doctors in America are women, as opposed to 75 percent in the Soviet Union. (Communism, however, is no guarantee of a worker's paradise for women, either. During the summer of 1970, Hungary's Central Committee of the Communist Party called for "consistent implementation of equal pay for equal work.")

The educational machinery in the United States offers a case in point: women comprise 87 percent of elementary school teachers, 22 percent of the principals; 47 percent of secondary school teachers, 5 percent of the principals; 34.8 percent of college instructors, 28.6 percent of assistant professors, 15.8 percent of associate professors, 9.4 percent of full professors. The percentages decrease in terms of responsibility. In terms of percentages, there are fewer woman Ph.D.s than there were thirty years ago.

The question goes beyond hours, wages, and titles. An estimated five million children need day care because their mothers work. There are currently facilities in existing centers for five hundred thousand children. A working mother who is a college graduate, divorced, and in her early forties is one example:

> I have four children. Their ages are seven, nine, ten, and twelve. The life of the children of a working mother is most difficult because they live with continuous problems, poverty problems. But I no longer try to fight the child care problem. My children now have to bring themselves up. They—the days I work, they get their own breakfasts in the morning, they get themselves off to school, and they come home to an empty house.
>
> And it's—it's a frightening thing for a child, and I—I—while I am at work, I am concerned about the children, I'm concerned about the home situation, and on the way home I'm thinking what has happened to the children, has one of them run out into the street, has one of them been hurt, and then when I get to the house and I see a light on in the children's room, it—it's a reassurance, and then I come up and they're all right, and we've made it through another day.

For feminists, the mill of government grinds exceedingly slow. The Senate has approved a $991,250,000 family-planning and research bill coordinating programs under the Department of Health, Education, and Welfare. The Labor Department set forth guidelines prohibiting sex discrimination by government contractors. The Equal Employment Opportunity Commission said that 25 percent of the complaints it received involved charges of bias because of sex "mostly as a result of women's liberation and the publicity they have gotten."

The lioness' share of publicity arrived August 26, 1970, fiftieth anniversary of the Nineteenth Amendment, which gave women the right to vote. President Nixon, paying tribute to "the brave and courageous women" who fought for the amendment, said "women surely have a still wider role to play in the political, economic, and social life of our country." An estimated ten thousand gathered in Adams, Massachusetts, birthplace of suffragette Susan B. Anthony.

In New York City some "brave and courageous" men joined a march down Fifth Avenue marking the "Women's Strike for Equality" that feminist groups called for. Mrs. Friedan addressed a City Hall rally:

> On behalf of this [indistinct] coalition of women that today have called this strike, and to confront the unfinished business of our equality, women young and old, women black and white, women [indistinct], women grandmothers who fought for the original right to vote, women Republicans, Democrats, Socialists, young, radical women, establishment women, rich women who know that all women are poor, housewives, professional women, women who are famous, [indistinct] that all women are free and equal.

Mrs. Friedan, who says that "man is not the enemy, man is the fellow victim," called the day a success "beyond our wildest dreams." Companies with large numbers of woman employees said the call to strike was largely ignored. There was a housewifely reaction in San Francisco:

> FIRST WOMAN: I think it's ridiculous. I think it's stupid. I don't think women should just stay home all the time, but I don't think they belong out, either.

> SECOND WOMAN: I'm a very happy housewife and very happy mother, and I feel this —I have so many things to do with my daughter and Girl Scouts and PTA, and I think there's those kind of places for mothers.

And in Washington, where petitions for an equal rights amendment were presented to the Senate leadership, West Virginia Democrat Jennings Randolph reacted with unmixed emotions:

Well, women, of course, are delightful persons, and I hear a strange and strident voice that I think is attempting really to stop some of this progress being made in behalf of of woman. That's the braless bubblehead, I call that person, you know, who speaks about freedom, you know, and the right of unabridged abortion, as it were, and this is the person that I think doesn't speak for woman.

In addition to improved job opportunities, child care centers, and a boycott of products "degrading to women," another feminist demand highlighted the day: liberalization of abortion laws written by men, "laws that keep women in bondage with children they don't want." A feminist repertory theater dramatizes the issue with this colloquy, after a male character is made pregnant and woman doctors decide his fate:

> MAN: Maintain the pregnancy? How dare you make that statement to me?

> WOMAN: I dare. There is a human life involved, after all.

> MAN: There is a human life involved. You insane creature, I'm fully aware there is a human life involved—my human life.

To a New York group called the Radical Feminists, abortion reform is not enough. Shulamith Firestone believes there should be more research leading toward birth outside a woman's body, the so-called "bottle baby":

> Pregnancy hurts. You know, it's really not —it's not very pleasant. You get distorted, you know, your body gets messed up. I mean, I think people haven't said this before, but, you know, I think pregnancy is barbaric. I think that if you have an option, you know, for artificial reproduction, it—it's going to make a tremendous difference in the kinds of institutions we have.

Feminists disagree on the extent of their disagreement. An opponent of the pill told the Senate: "Women are not going to sit quietly any longer. You are murdering us for your profit and convenience." A more radical view: "And we no longer need, you know, motherhood even, in the sense that, you know, we've had it."

And a revolutionary says, "Well, we feel that, you know, women should move out of marriage, that they should—I mean, the institution has to be destroyed by women." Admittedly a small segment of the movement, the radicals exclude any relationship with a man:

WOMAN: And men are the oppressors. They're powerful. Women are subordinate, powerless, and this is throughout the world. Now, women are property that are exchanged among these men. They—they marry certain women. But this is where, you know, power comes into it.

I mean, upper-crust men oppress both men and they oppress women. Every man oppresses women. I mean, they have the chance to oppress women they marry, their daughters.

CORRESPONDENT: Looking kind of beyond that, then, it would suggest that you would want a complete change in society.

WOMAN: Definitely.

CORRESPONDENT: Class change.

WOMAN: Definitely. . . . I think marriage and the family are doing a great job destroying themselves, so feminism doesn't have much of a job to do.

CORRESPONDENT: What will take the place?

WOMAN: I don't think anything will replace it except sisterhood among women, that there'll be a great alliance: women will discover each other as human beings.

CORRESPONDENT: Will they turn to women instead of men, then?

WOMAN: As friends, as sisters, as—rebels, as fighters in a revolution that they all— which they all share, yes.

CORRESPONDENT: But if they want more, just answering to their nature as a woman, if they want love?

WOMAN: Well, there's nothing to say that the nature of woman, that the nature of woman needs love any more than any other— we don't know what "love" is. It's just a phony word; it has no real definition. I think that whole concept has to be thrown out and redefined, and it won't be redefined until after the revolution.

WOMAN: If you have equality between men and—men and women, you couldn't have marriage. Just like, people say, well, couldn't you have gotten rid of the bad things about marriage, couldn't you have gotten rid of the bad things about slavery and still have slavery? No, I mean it sounds crazy.

CORRESPONDENT: What would you substitute?

WOMAN: What do you substitute for cancer?

On August 10, 1970, despite the complaints of a few men that they were being steamrollered, the House ripped an equal rights amendment out of the Judiciary Committee—where it had been pigeonholed for forty-seven years. New York's Representative Emanuel Celler expressed some prophetic misgivings:

I think that more harm will be done than good with the amendment. The difficulty is that we're like a blind man going into a dark room looking for a black cat. We just don't know what we're up to. And I think that we should have been permitted to study this thing, to get information from various sources, to know exactly what we're doing.

The measure went to the Senate, where it died through inaction.

In peripheral endeavors, the kind often called "the lighter side of the news" but often the most revealing, women have demonstrated anew that most have minds of their own. The brightly plumaged male, adorning himself like a popinjay, sees women following fashion trends as the lemming follows the call to the sea. If the man is a fashion designer, he makes the mistake all cynics make and finds himself, on occasion, burned.

The designers decided that knees were out, or rather under a blanket called a midi-skirt, descending almost to lengths of twisted Victorian propriety. "The important thing," said one, "is to cover the knees, and we said, 'Good-bye, thighs.'"

"It's perfectly obvious," according to designer Bill Blass, "that skirts couldn't go shorter, fellows, so they had to go longer. And I think that most women welcome it."

We have in some ways come a distance since legs were limbs and proper pianos wore pantaloons, but the arrangement in the garment district is that once fashions change, everyone should go along, to protect the huge investment needed for a basic switch in taste. At stores for the financially comfortable, like New York's Bonwit Teller, midi sales were pushed hard:

SALESGIRL: It takes time to adjust to it.

CUSTOMER: Don't you think that this is something that has been imposed on the public as a sales gimmick?

SALESGIRL: No, not really.

CUSTOMER: To get the women to buy more clothes, or new clothes?

SALESGIRL: No, I feel people have a choice. I think we were looking for a change.

Bonwit salesgirls, strongly advised to do so, wore midis and were given discounts for the first time in the store's history. An executive explained:

We just didn't think that you could be saying to a woman that you believe in longer lengths for the fall, and you thought longer lengths give definition to fashion for the coming season, then have her eye sort of travel around and look at you in a skirt up around your thighs. We just didn't think that was fair. You come into a store and you see somebody wearing the things they say they believe in; I think the customer feels reassured and happier, and that's what it's all about.

What a good many people thought it was all about was that the fashion business was in trouble, and it was hoped that a radical style change would produce heavy sales. And not just for dresses: a change to the midi would mean new accessories and a whole new wardrobe. This was freely conceded by James Brady, publisher of *Women's Wear Daily*, the newspaper of the garment industry and an aggressive sponsor of the midi:

Fashion is essentially change, and that is going to be good for business this fall. Once the weather turns cool and the eye gets used to the long skirt, I think the manufacturer is going to do very well.

In the face of early opposition to the midi, the publisher was bullish:

I think it's delightful that they get together and they whoop it up, and they say down with this and down with that, and down with *Women's Wear Daily*. I don't think it's going to change the fact that most of them within six months to a year will be wearing longer skirts. Whether they're organized or not, women tend to follow fashions, they always have, and I believe they always will.

It apparently takes more than a handful, however, to establish a fashion to follow. Organized backers of the midi were met by organized opposition, including a group calling itself FADD—Females Against Dictating Designers:

PAT DEAN: We feel this change is being forced upon us from above, and that we are of course very unhappy about it, and we do not intend to follow, and that includes many thousands of us from all over the country. It's been a wonderful response.

CAROL OSTROW: The manufacturers are trying to say that unless you buy what we put out for you in the stores, you won't be accepted by—socially accepted by your friends, and it's pressure and it's nonsense, and I don't think women should accept it. They should be their own individual selves and choose what they want, or don't buy if they're refused that choice in the stores. I think I have nice legs, and I don't care if anyone else thinks so—I think so, and I want them seen.

DESIGNER PAULINE TRIGERE: I don't think anybody should say to anybody what to say, what to do. They can wear what they want. In the wintertime, I think the mini is a little bit ridiculous, because it's cold. But I do think that in the summer, when it's nice and warm . . . it's nice to wear a mini.

Some women avoided the confrontation by wearing pants. Ultimately, the *Wall Street Journal* reported that, with the exception of a few pockets, the midi lay in swathes and patches.

The wearing of the pants took on a symbolic overtone, too, as women invaded fields previously reserved for men only.

Patricia Palinkas, for example, became the first woman ever to play professional football. A pretty twenty-seven-year-old Tampa, Florida, housewife and first-grade teacher, whose favorite activity is ironing ("I just love to iron. Oh, I just love it"), she made her game debut August 15, 1970.

Her husband, Steve, is a place-kicker. This year, when he tried out with the Orlando Panthers, he brought his wife along to hold the football for him. The team was impressed enough to hire them both, perhaps with an eye on publicity value. Pat first appeared in a game against the Bridgeport, Connecticut, Jets, a minor league club affiliated with the New York Jets, onetime champions of all professional football.

"Right now, I'm nervous and excited and honored that I'm the first woman to play professional football," she said. "It's like making my debut."

The Bridgeport players exhibited male chauvinism in its most virulent form. "I think we're going to try to put a pretty reverse on her," said one. "The game is hard-nosed football, so I guess she can take the punishment."

"Say a little prayer for me," Mrs. Palinkas said before going in to hold for her husband. "Oh, I really like it if I don't, you know, clam up. I've got this huge big butterfly in my stomach."

Power-of-prayer advocates received an early setback. Orlando scored a touchdown and Pat went in the game as the public address announcer milked the moment: "Ladies and gentlemen, football history has just been made. Number three, Pat Palinkas . . . first time ever in pro football."

Alas, she missed the snap from center and disappeared under a Bridgeport rush. Her comment: "Oh, I didn't catch it. I didn't catch it. Oh, I'm going to cry. Oh. Yeah, I'm sorry. I didn't catch it. Yeah, I'm okay. Oh, honey." Her husband's comment: "Beautiful."

The 122-pound holder was rushed by 235-pound linebacker Wally Florence, who later told reporters, "I wanted to break her neck. She's out here making folly with a man's game."

But if feminists object to a woman whose favorite thing is ironing, they must feel some respect for her spunk. Orlando scored again in the fourth quarter and Pat Palinkas, kneeling to await the ball, spoke three words to her husband that may never have been heard before in all the history of professional football:

"You ready, honey?"

She caught the ball this time, placed it, and the kick was good. The Panthers won the game, 26–7, a banner day in the violent world of Pat Palinkas. Or, in her words, "Whee. Whee. I did it. Yeah, I did it. Two out of three, not bad not bad at all. Two out of three; that's not too bad. . . . Oh, I can't get this helmet off."

As a historical footnote: Pat rejected a chance to stay with the team after her husband was dropped from the roster.

The breakthrough was not confined to fields of friendly strife. Old-timers predicted the very foundations of the Pentagon would be shaken as this man's army came up with two lady generals, the first in its history. Anna May Hays, Dwight Eisenhower's nurse, and WAC Director Elizabeth Hoisington became the first women to wear the army star. Chief of Staff General William C. Westmoreland established "new protocol for congratulating lady generals" by planting a kiss on each.

And other barriers have fallen. New York Mayor John Lindsay signed executive orders banning discrimination on grounds of sex or age in city employment. Earlier he had signed an order ending sex discrimination in places of public accommodation. One of the establishments affected, or victimized, depending on your viewpoint, was McSorley's Old Ale House, whose motto for 116 years had been "Good Ale, Raw Onions, No Ladies."

Sawdusted and redolent of a smoky past ("A woman is only a woman, but a good cigar is a smoke"), lacking a powder room, papered with presidential portraits, Irish revolutionary slogans, athletic heroes, and a vast French nude with parrot, McSorley's had been the subject of a book—Joseph Mitchell's *McSorley's Wonderful Saloon*—paintings, including a series of John Sloan's "McSorley's cats," and a poem, "Mac had a place downtown/Where only men were welcome, or grown boys."

A patron reflected on the passing of the old order:

I'm definitely against it. Why, I think it's last—man's last—man's last haven. Let's keep it that way. I don't think a decent woman would want to come in here, anyway.

Even as many feminists learn judo and karate, the move for equality involves a combination of struggles. From the Miss America Pageant to the all but *au naturel* cocktail lounge waitress, the woman as ritualized sex object arouses anger and scorn among feminists. Alice Denham, novelist, former model, feminist, and onetime *Playboy* magazine "Playmate of the Month," views dimly the men's magazine pursuit of the obvious:

Well, it's sort of a woman as a mechanical doll. In other words, the magazine seems to assume that women drop dead of old age at twenty-five. And it's this—and—and not as —a sex object orientation towards women, in which they're only sort of bodies, nubile forms to give pleasure to the male. And I think it's really a sort of urban male fantasy. It doesn't have a great deal to do with reality. . . .

The marriage situation seems to be breaking down. In other words, women are no longer dependably protected as they were fifty years ago. It's common practice now for a man to turn in a "forty" for a "twenty." And there are very few people that can depend on their marriages lasting.

For the most part, the call is to political action. Democratic Congresswoman Shirley Chisholm of Brooklyn says she has suffered more discrimination as a woman than as a black:

We, too, no longer must indulge in jargon and lots of words, but . . . we must now begin to suit the action to the word in order to acquire our unequivocal place in American society, just as black people are asking for their unequivocal share in the American society.

In the end, all women are no more agreed than are all men. Among women, there is a gulf between the view of man as "fellow victim" and man as "oppressor," with intervening opinions shaded to one side or the other. As in all great upheavals, the outcome rests on achieving some degree of compromise, in the nonsexual sense of the word, or, as Eric Sevareid puts it:

It may be just a cliché from the male mythology, infuriating to females, but it remains an article of faith among men that no husband ever won an argument with a wife, and that the secret of a happy marriage is for the man to repeat those three little words, "I was wrong."

So it would be better if a third sex were around to judge the latest women's liberation movement; wanting that, some men must try, quiveringly uncertain as they may feel about the whole thing. It is no problem, of course, for male politicians; votes possess no gender.

But the plain truth is that most American men are startled by the idea that American women are oppressed, and they have read with relief the Gallup poll showing that two-thirds of the women don't think they're oppressed, either.

Nevertheless, if this is the start of another revolution, it is worth remembering that revolutions are not made by majorities, but by aroused minorities, and are generally led by intellectuals and others who are already well off by any comparative measurement. And many movements grow by simple contagion, thousands discovering they are in pain, though they hadn't noticed it until they were told.

The leaders of today's phenomenon have wisely concentrated on three practical aims with which a great many men also agree: equal opportunities in employment and education; abortion on demand; and child care centers. Nor does this end the list of realistic inequities.

Beyond such practical, measurable demands, when the liberation spokeswomen take us into the realm of the human psyche and insist upon radical transformation of feelings between sexes, at that point most men, and a great many women, too, feel baffled and reluctant to follow.

The usual formation of the militant woman is: think of us as persons, not as women. The instruction manual for this has not yet been written. It is hard enough to separate nationality from personality, and impossible to separate one's personality from one's sex.

As for the organized movement itself, it remains to be seen whether it will unify and remain effective or will fragment into quarreling doctrinal groups like the far left student movement and the black movement.

It now has the unavoidable opportunity to prove that the masculine notion that women can't get along with other women is another item from the ancient shelf of male mythology.

260

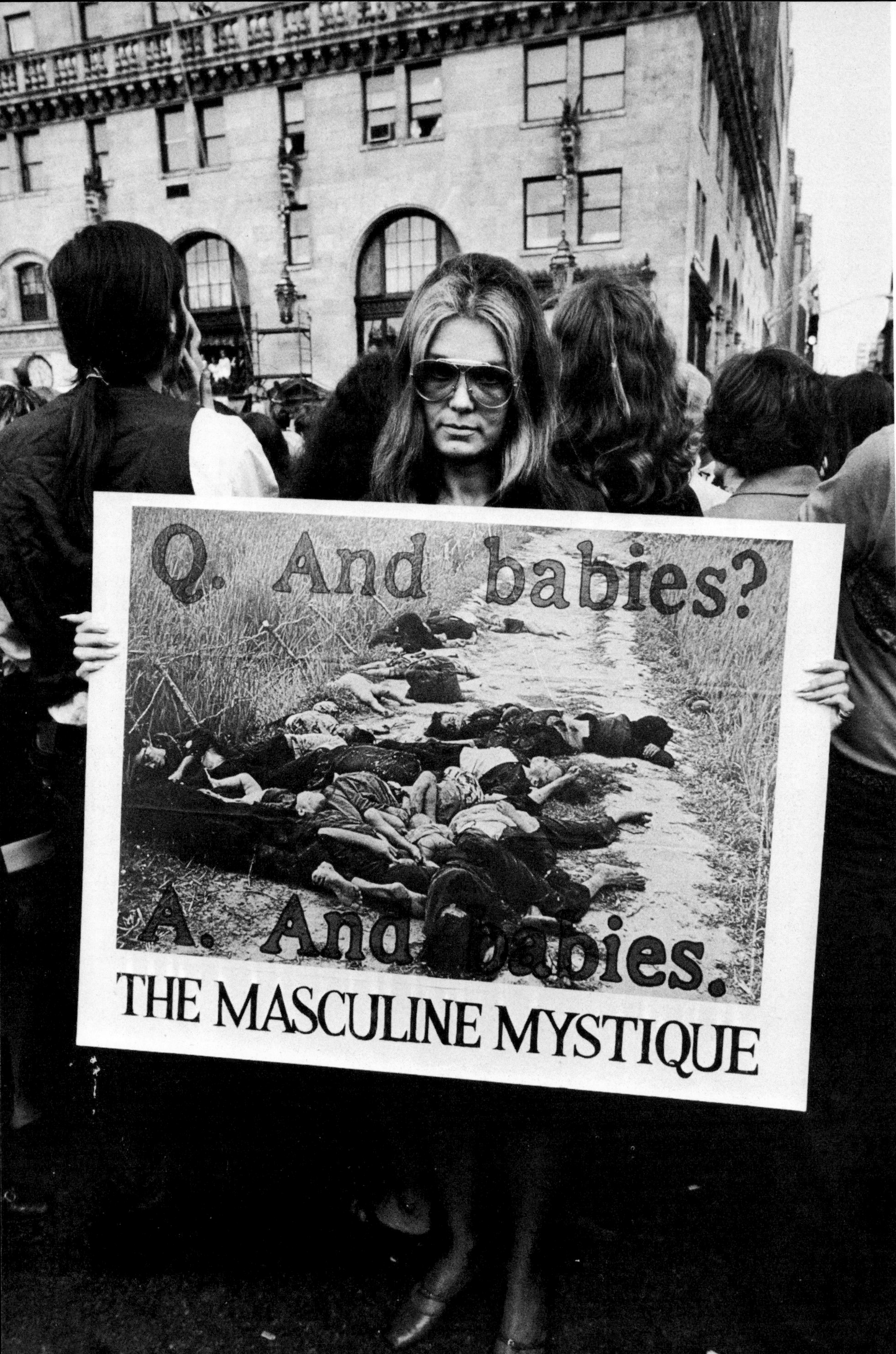
Q. And babies?
A. And babies.
THE MASCULINE MYSTIQUE

(left) Well-known advocate of women's rights, Gloria Steinem.

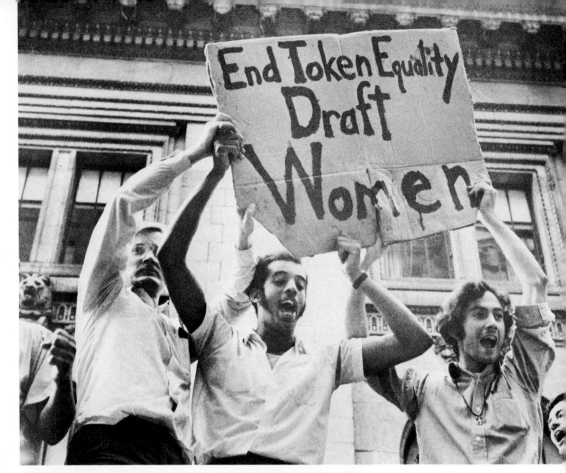

Feminist protest of Playboy as "sexploitative" of women.

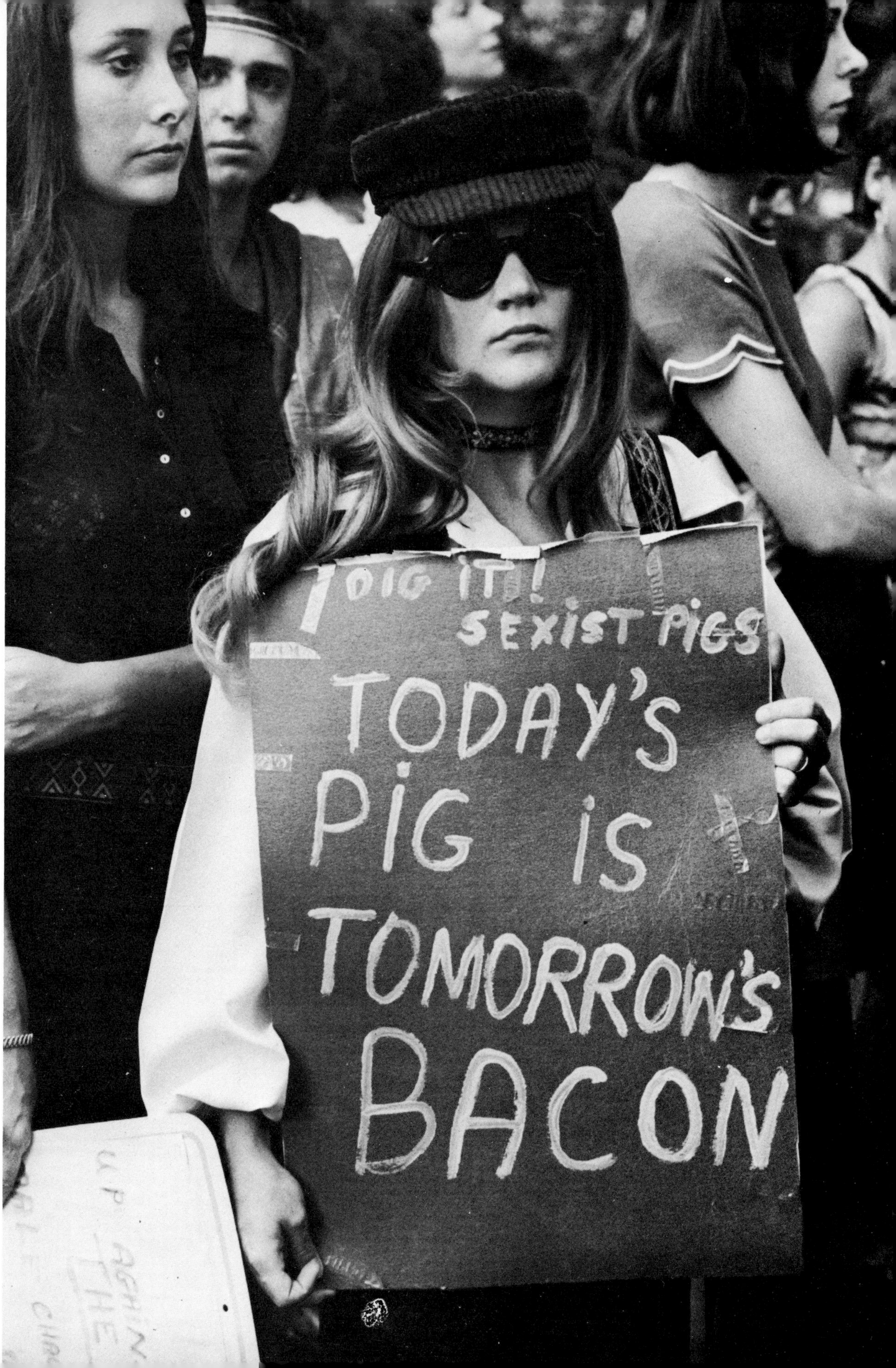
DIG IT!
SEXIST PIGS
TODAY'S
PIG IS
TOMORROW'S
BACON

Women's lib put-down of anti-feminist advertising.

Betty Friedan, "mother" of the women's liberation movement.

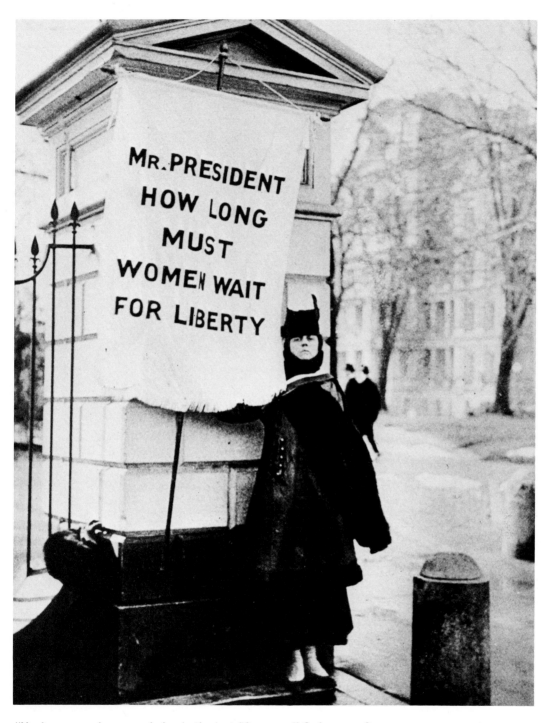

"You've come a long way, baby, in the last fifty years." Or have you?

Such Interesting People

the story, as I recall it, involves a Chicago newspaperman, perhaps the late Robert Casey, who was descended on at a party by a grande dame. learning he was a reporter, she said in what he regarded as a condescending manner, "you must meet such interesting people." he replied, "yes. and they're all in the newspaper business." that is a parochial view to which I do not subscribe, although there is something to be said for it. in the course of a correspondent's life, you run across the famous, the infamous, and the unknown. there comes a time when you must pull up short to remember that everyone is a person—not quite like anyone else.

The Most Unbelievable Scene

as a military leader, he took his nation through two disastrous wars, the Sinai campaign of 1956 and the six awful days of 1967. his impoverished people realized few economic gains during the fourteen years he was their dictator. he was not much of a public speaker. and yet the outpouring of grief over the death of Gamal Abdel Nasser seemed beyond historic comparison.

Nasser, the most prominent figure in the Arab world for half a century, died of a sudden heart attack September 28, 1970. Only the day before he had been seen at an Arab summit meeting in Cairo with Jordan's King Hussein, moving to calm the storms raised by guerrilla warfare.

He had helped engineer the 1952 coup that toppled King Farouk, remained briefly in the background, and then emerged to make Egypt for the first time in modern history a significant force on the world scene. He rallied millions to the causes of socialism, pan-Arabism, and opposition to Israel.

His death left the Arab world without focus and without a leader. It developed, to the surprise of many, that his power was transferred in an orderly manner to Anwar Sadat, the acting president. But the impact of his death was incredible. All of Cairo shut down.

It was the most unbelievable scene I had witnessed in an entire lifetime of reporting:

There has been no police control, virtually at all, since the body of President Nasser began moving across the bridge right down the Nile here, the Kasr Al Nil, into the heart of the city of Cairo. How many millions of Arabs are in the streets of Cairo I couldn't guess, either, nor could anybody else, I suppose.

Eventually they did get Nasser interred, but it was a struggle all the way to maintain even the slightest semblance of control over the unbelievably vast crowd. They began coming by the thousands and thousands at dawn, even though the government already had stopped trains and buses into the city, and closed some of the Nile bridges in a vain attempt to keep their numbers within bounds. Soon they were crowded not ten deep but hundreds deep along the streets. They filled vast squares and reached out as far as the eye could see.

There were dignitaries, too, by the scores, but within a hundred yards of the procession's start the crowd was too much for them, and they fell out to await the funeral service. Nasser's successor, Anwar Sadat, collapsed in the crush, but was able later to attend the service, too. It was the crowd's day, and they were not to be denied the last full expression of their love for Gamal Abdel Nasser. That relationship between people and leader was deep and personal. . . .

Nasser freed these people from the chains of a feudal society. He took the land away from a few wealthy landowners who ran the country, and he gave it to the people who worked it. Nasser did not start life as most of these people here have. They are the very poor of Egypt. Nasser grew up in modest circumstances, but he was able to reach out and influence these people in a way that no other Egyptian politician has ever approached.

This was his political base, the people of Egypt. They are the same people who rushed into the streets shouting no when Nasser tried to quit after he lost the war with Israel three years ago. This was a hero these people would not let go down even in defeat.

The funeral procession covered some six miles, and the Egyptian authorities had planned carefully for every foot of it. Fifty thousand men were assigned to keep order. Besides police, they included commando and parachute troops, even a squadron of mounted cavalry and armored cars. But it was not the police and soldiers but the crowd that called the shots.

For a while, the procession moved with some sort of order, and it was possible to follow the line of march with its floral tributes, marching bands, and troops with colorful berets. But as the casket approached, the crowd increasingly took charge.

Sometimes the police and soldiers tried to resist; more often they realized the state of affairs and let the shouting, shoving crowd guide the procession. Once or twice the coffin looked as though it might fall, but it always remained upright and continued to move.

As the casket moved beyond the range of our cameras, the chaos around it actually worsened. News dispatches told of one dead, dozens injured in the crush. But eventually the casket reached a mosque near Nasser's home, renamed Al Nasser Mosque; the digni-

taries regathered, and Gamal Abdel Nasser was laid to rest in the garden of the mosque. It was one of the most incredible days in the city's long history.

Those who have succeeded Nasser know their people as he did, and they expected this sort of demonstration. They had asked by radio and the newspapers that the turnout be orderly and dignified to do honor to Nasser's memory, but there was no real attempt to restrain the crowds. The police lines were thin and particularly undetermined.

Old Middle East hands say that wise leaders let the people have their little victories over authority in this fashion to release pent-up emotions. If that's so, the system seems to work. The mass hysteria, which saw women beating their own faces in grief and strong young men throwing themselves on the pavement in true fits of despondency, passed with startling suddenness. The moment after the cortege had fought its way through the crowd, the mob subsided and quietly went home.

The day after the funeral, the interim leaders focused on diplomacy, holding separate meetings with spokesmen for the United States and the Soviet Union. Life went on, but in the shadow of that unbelievable scene and the man whose death caused it.

"France Is a Widow"

*Montgomery called General Charles Andre Joseph Marie de Gaulle
"a triton among minnows." de Gaulle's death of a heart attack
removed from the world scene the last of the giants of the World War II
epoch. imperious, vain, austere, humorless, he saw himself as France
incarnate. every American president from Franklin Roosevelt on
found him infuriating to deal with, largely because of his obsession
with his land. more than any man of this century, de Gaulle was France,
more French than the French.*

De Gaulle above any other individual shaped France's destiny over a period of thirty years:

CHARLES COLLINGWOOD: When World War II began, he was a slightly overage colonel of forty-nine, just important enough to be photographed at the front with French President Albert Lebrun. He had one friend in court, the powerful politician Paul Reynaud, who believed in him and championed his military ideas in the French Assembly. Paul Reynaud became the last premier of France and named de Gaulle to his cabinet. Five years later, in England, de Gaulle found himself leading the Free French movement.

When the invasion of Normandy was launched, Churchill was as out of patience with de Gaulle as was Roosevelt, but they could not ignore him. By the time Allied troops stormed ashore, de Gaulle had become the symbol of France. He came ashore in that unlikely amphibian vehicle, the duck. Charles de Gaulle had returned. He was no longer the obscure brigadier general who had fled in 1940, but the acknowledged paladin of Free France, and the cross of Lorraine was his device.

For every Frenchman, Paris is the jewel, the throbbing heart, the epitome of France. De Gaulle returned to Paris in the grip of a profound emotion. Paris greeted him as a living legend. Everywhere he went, he was received with great emotion. For a moment, his presence made people forget their empty stomachs.

But de Gaulle was never really interested in economic problems. From the beginning, it was his own historic role and that of France which claimed his chief attention. In that role, as the embodiment of a restored and liberated France, he made visits of state to the great powers. De Gaulle's trip to Russia helped blunt the opposition of the French Communist party. With his customary stubbornness, de Gaulle haggled with Stalin for eight days over the terms of a Franco-Soviet treaty. In the end, it was Stalin who gave way, and the treaty was signed. Later, Stalin said to Roosevelt: "De Gaulle is an uncomplicated man." He did not mean it as a compliment. He meant de Gaulle could not be budged.

De Gaulle was now firmly in power, or so it seemed. The politics of France still greatly resembled the politics of the old regime, before the war. The same old faces, the same old jockeying for position among the parties. De Gaulle became increasingly frustrated. Parliamentary maneuvering for what he wanted was not, and is not, his style.

On the twentieth of January, 1946, de Gaulle called his cabinet together. He resigned. It was one of those events that really was a bombshell. "After de Gaulle, who?" everyone asked. The chronic instability of French politics became acute. One government succeeded another. As in a kaleidoscope, the familiar faces of Fourth Republic politicians were rearranged into more and more meaningless patterns. From the time de Gaulle resigned until May, 1958, there were twenty-three different governments in France.

It was the war in Algeria that brought de Gaulle back to power for the second time. On May 13, 1958, Algerian settlers, with the active connivance of the military, seized power in Algiers. They demanded a stronger government. Specifically, they demanded de Gaulle. The insurrection in Algiers produced a revolutionary atmosphere in Paris. The French political system was crumbling. The National Assembly invested de Gaulle with the authority of the state. It was the first of June, a Sunday. De Gaulle demanded special powers and got them.

But no parliamentary formality could make the Algerian war go away. De Gaulle made it his first order of business to go in person to Algeria. He began to condition public opinion, little by little, to accept a negotiated peace in Algeria. De Gaulle disciplined the army, mobilized public opinion, and offered the Muslim rebels an honorable peace and a future association with France. It had taken de Gaulle four years of tortuous maneuver to end the Algerian war. But the true measure of the day was that in accomplishing the liberation of Algeria, Charles de Gaulle had also liberated France.

De Gaulle was free to follow his own course, and he did. He stumped the country, seeking approval for the new constitution he advocated for the Fifth Republic. De Gaulle's constitution was approved by a thundering 80 percent. This remarkable document preserves in name the traditional French separation of powers. In fact, all the real power is vested in the president.

In 1965, de Gaulle squeaked through to a new seven-year term as president, taunting former allies, the United States, Great Britain, Canada, Israel, to mention a few.

CHARLES DE GAULLE: To put it another way, face to face with the United States, whatever may be the ties and sentiments that unite us, face to face with the United States we mean to stand as France, proud, upright, and mistress of herself.

De Gaulle soon showed how independent France could be of the United States, ordering American troops out of the country and withdrawing French military forces from NATO. At home, de Gaulle survived the 1968 student-worker riots, but one year later he stepped down as president and retired to his country home. He resigned because French voters, in a referendum, had rejected his proposal for further government decentralization. The man who once led France thus ended his career writing his memoirs in a tiny village of four hundred inhabitants.

He had promised to retire if his referendum was not approved, and he was true to his word. In the nineteen months remaining to him of nearly eighty years on earth, he never again set foot in Paris. President Georges Pompidou took to television to announce, "General de Gaulle is dead. France is a widow." He called de Gaulle the man who saved France's honor in 1940, helped liberate her in 1944, and saved her from civil war in 1958.

Pompidou made public a handwritten funeral statement de Gaulle had given him eighteen years earlier, setting forth in almost arrogant modesty how he wanted to be buried:

"I want no state funeral. Neither president nor ministers, nor Assembly committees, nor public authorities. Only the armed forces may participate officially as such, but their participation must be of very modest proportion, without music or band or funeral call . . . men and women of France and of other countries of the world may, if they wish, do my memory the honor of accompanying my body to its last resting-place, but it is in silence that I wish it to be conducted."

In accordance with de Gaulle's wishes, neither captain nor king attended the services at the Church of Notre Dame in Colombey. In Paris, it was a different story as France buried her greatest son of the century:

CHARLES COLLINGWOOD: To the ancient Cathedral of Notre Dame in Paris today there came from every corner of the world an unprecedented assembly of leaders to pay tribute to the memory of Charles de Gaulle.

Seated first by protocol, the longest-reigning monarch in the world, Haile Selassie, near him Prince Rainier of Monaco. As the great nave filled, Archbishop Makarios of Cyprus arrived. Prince Charles, heir to the English throne, and Prime Minister Heath, two former British prime ministers, Anthony Eden, now Lord Avon, and Harold Macmillan. Both had first known de Gaulle in the war, crossed many a sword with him, remained friends. David Ben-Gurion and President Zalman Shazar of Israel, a nation to whom de Gaulle's attitude was often equivocal.

The president of the Soviet Union, Nikolai Podgorny; one of de Gaulle's consistent policies had been to try to build bridges between East and West. They came from all over. President Nixon had flown in overnight from the United States, was to turn around and fly back this afternoon after the ceremonies. De Gaulle had been generous about Mr. Nixon, felt Franco-American relations were improving, told visitors he thought Nixon had all that is needed to make a strong president.

Charles de Gaulle in death had managed to bring together friends, enemies, and wary antagonists.

The arrival of his successor, French President Pompidou, was the signal for the requiem in the cathedral to commence. As Pompidou walked down the aisle, the voices of the famous choir of Notre Dame soared into Bach's Chorale from the *Passion According to St. Matthew.*

Despite the rank and dignity of those who had come to Notre Dame to pay tribute to Charles de Gaulle, the service itself was much less elaborate than is customary when so imposing a figure passes. This was in accordance with de Gaulle's last wishes. He insisted on simplicity and no eulogies or orations.

The simple service at Colombey was in stark contrast to the inevitable formalities in Paris. An unadorned French armored vehicle bore the simple coffin, covered in the French tricolor, from the de Gaulle house, La Boisserie, to the village church which he had so often attended. The little town, less than four hundred souls, was packed with people from all over France.

For although de Gaulle had excluded the great and famous from Colombey, he said the ordinary people could come, and they did. Inside the church, in the family pew, de Gaulle's son, Philippe, a captain in the French navy, stood beside his mother, Yvonne, herself now seventy-nine. Besides the de Gaulle family and the townspeople, who thought of de Gaulle as one of them, there were old friends and companions of the liberation.

Outside, the mourners, who had journeyed from all over France, crowded every available space, even breaking through the roof tiles of the modest houses to get a glimpse. Then the pallbearers, ordinary youths from the village, carried the coffin out to the grave where de Gaulle's daughter, Anne, already lies.

De Gaulle's widow, his son, daughter, and grandchildren watched the coffin lowered and made their final gesture. It was all as Charles de Gaulle had wished it, as private a ceremony as could be arranged for so public a person. Then quickly the family returned to the lonely house, where de Gaulle had so long preserved his own privacy.

His legacy, the rare sense of great departure in death, was marked by Eric Sevareid:

Not since Napoleon had the French nation been so dominated and symbolized by one human being as it was by Charles de Gaulle. Napoleon had the personal will and the big battalions, and he expanded France. De Gaulle had the will, small battalions, and he contracted France. Yet both men stand as authentic heroes of history. Napoleon's most enduring work, perhaps, was the centralization of French government; de Gaulle's final failure was his attempt to decentralize it.

But he did leave modern France with a far more stable, executive-oriented constitution after a century and a half during which the country oscillated back and forth between quasi dictatorship and quasi anarchy.

De Gaulle did not leave a West Europe under the leadership of a France restored to world power and glory as he dreamed, nor a total Europe organized from the Atlantic to the Urals. He did not leave France even as a full-fledged member of the Atlantic Alliance, and we have no political United States of Europe based on the Common Market, partly because de Gaulle renounced political federation, partly because it seemed a psychological impossibility for Europeans after generations of national identities and loyalties.

But he left France itself a resurrected, going concern. De Gaulle, Roosevelt, Churchill—the three Western giants of that generation—all performed the same fundamental service. Each restored confidence and belief to his own dismayed and frightened people: Roosevelt before the great war, Churchill during it, de Gaulle during and after it.

De Gaulle seemed to think Waterloo was a mistake made by history, that the shift of power away from the Mediterranean world to the northern and Anglo-Saxon worlds was unnatural.

Churchill, with the British empire gone, welcomed the rise of American world influence and power. De Gaulle, with the French empire gone, resented and distrusted the American world view, including our early concept of the United Nations, as naïve and dangerous, and saw no other way to proceed than through the play of nation-state power politics with its shifting alliances.

At times he was prophetic, and in a position to help realize his own prophecies. At his peak, with the other giants gone, he was more than a great Frenchman; he was a presence brooding over the whole of ancient Europe as it struggled to become a new world in a new time.

Cast of Characters

the musical of thee I sing *won a Pulitzer Prize in the 1930s for its portrayal of the vice-president of the United States as the man nobody knows. but no one has found it difficult to remember who the present vice-president is. and in an allegedly bland group, Martha Mitchell's name has also become a household word, setting a recognition record for wives of attorneys general.*

Mrs. Martha Mitchell is one of those personalities about whom it is apparently impossible not to write something. News seems to seek her out even if she attempts not to make news. When she hired a press secretary, Kay Woestendieck, theoretically to watch her celebrated tongue, Mrs. Woestendieck's husband was immediately fired on "conflict-of-interest charges" from his job as editor of a television broadcast called "Newsroom," thus making news.

She is perhaps best remembered for her

2:00 A.M. phone call to an Arkansas newspaper demanding the crucifixion of Senator J. William Fulbright for voting against confirmation of G. Harrold Carswell as Supreme Court justice.

On June 30, swearing in the new president of the American Newspaper Women's Club, Mrs. Mitchell spoke in Swahili, a practice her husband had earlier suggested, some thought jokingly. At that, one linguist present said her comments translated roughly to a prohibition against reporters writing "anything bad about the Mitchells for one year."

Reports of administration efforts to curb the tongue of Vice-President Agnew have apparently proved premature. As a result of reported criticism, including Secretary of the Interior Walter Hickel's leaked letter to President Nixon calling for a cooling of rhetoric between the administration—read "Agnew" —and youth, there were stories to the effect that the President had asked Agnew to take it easy. Those stories were denied by both the President and the Vice-President, and there seemed little reason to doubt the denials. The Vice-President, even apart from the unusually strong campaign efforts noted earlier, continued to flail about him with adjective and alliteration, whether he was assailing the "drug culture" as a "collective national trip" or belting away at faulters of the system:

> Thank heaven the people here aren't so sophisticated they long for an American defeat. As you know, I've just returned from an Asian tour during which I visited many countries including Vietnam and Korea. I brought back many messages from our brave troops there to some of our more dovish senators. The soldiers asked me to deliver those messages personally because you're not supposed to send that stuff through the mails.
> Actually, I'd like to remain in the West to attend the dinner that President Nixon is having in honor of the president of Mexico, but I have a previous commitment to attend a wildfowl dinner at Senator Fulbright's. I've waited a long, long time to see Senator Fulbright have his goose cooked.
> One of the tragedies of life in America today is that when we speak of maintaining peace we do have to speak not only of peace abroad but of peace at home. We find bombs exploding not just in Vietnam but in our own cities. But true peace lies neither in the bomb nor the truncheon. It lies in a pattern of mutual respect and mutual forbearance that is the essence of a civilized society.

The fascination with Agnewian rhetoric is a mark of the decade, a game of the seventies equivalent to that great sport of the twenties—attempting to read profundity or even meaning into the long silences of Calvin Coolidge. Agnew is the most quoted vice-president in our history, yet he has said nothing as genuinely witty as Thomas Marshall's "What this country needs is a good five-cent cigar" nor as telling as John Nance Garner's comment—without benefit of thesaurus—on the vice-presidency as an office: "It isn't worth a pitcher of warm spit."

One result is that the Vice-President's remarks are watched very carefully, and not just by news media. He made two quick, headline-grabbing trips to Asia during the year, returning with the kind of time-honored report that tells an administration what an administration wants to hear, but the interest was less in what he said than how he said it.

"The White House staff is reportedly pleased with Agnew's general performance," Eric Sevareid said after the Vice-President's August journey to Indochina. "He made only two serious slips of the tongue, both at the outset of the trip. He had said we would do everything we can for the Lon Nol government in Cambodia. This was in contradiction of the President's justification for our Cambodian incursion last spring, presented as a short, sharply limited military tactic, not as an open-ended commitment to another Asian regime.

"Agnew had also said we might not be able to continue our troop withdrawals from South Vietnam if Cambodia fell under Communist control. That was like saying Cambodia is the key to our future in Southeast Asia. He now says he meant only that our withdrawals might have to be slowed down should Cambodia fall and the South Vietnamese have to face the enemy along a six-hundred-mile frontier. Why that eventuality would not thin out and weaken the Communists as much as, or more than, it would weaken the South Vietnamese is not explained. The latter have far more soldiers, plus air reconnaissance and troop mobility by air, which the enemy does not have."

A more serious vice-presidential gaffe followed the abortive Vietnam prison camp raid in November. Agnew said that the mission did not turn up any prisoners because of a failure of intelligence, thus directly contradicting Secretary of Defense Melvin Laird, who said the intelligence work was great and that Agnew had not attended any briefings on the matter. His controversial role in the elections has continued to be analyzed, with some observers spinning stories that he is likely to be dumped from the ticket.

It is a matter of faith, outside the news business, that the Vice-President is somehow feared and hated in journalistic circles. In point of fact, he is appreciated, if not universally admired. Whether he is being the model for a watch, the subject of an $80,000 U.S. Information Agency film narrated by John Wayne, or even assailing the "liberal" news media, he seldom fails as a source of copy.

It was not until his 1969 attack on television and various eastern newspapers that Agnew really became well known, and just about everyone expressed an opinion. Now, just a year later, he has fronted for so many administration ploys and offered so many answers to hard questions that he is rather a familiar.

Vice-presidential proposals that, in the last year of the old decade, would have shocked, offered in the first year of the new decade room only for a kind of tolerant explanation, in this characteristic instance, by Eric Sevareid:

The Vice-President proposes that network commentators, like this one and brothers Smith and Reynolds down the street at ABC —people of that type, he says—be publicly examined by government personnel. The public has a right to know, he says, our opinions and prejudices.

The phrase "people of that type" hurts a bit. We certainly don't think of Mr. Agnew as a type; we think he's an original.

What really hurts is the thought that maybe nobody's been listening all this time. If, after some thirty years and thousands of broadcasts, hundreds of articles and lectures, and a few books, one's general cast of mind, warts and all, remains a mystery, then we're licked, and we fail to see how a few more minutes of examination by government types would solve the supposed riddle.

Mr. Agnew wants to know where we stand. We stand, or, rather, sit, right here, in the full glare, at a disadvantage as against politicians. We can't cast one vote in committee, an opposite vote on the floor. We can't say one thing in the North, an opposite thing in the South. We hold no tenure, four years or otherwise, and can be voted out with a twist of the dial.

We cannot use invective and epithets, cannot even dream of impugning the patriotism of leading citizens, cannot reduce every complicated issue to yes or no, black or white, and would rather go to jail than do bodily injury to the English language.

We can't come down on this side or that side of each disputed public issue because we're trying to explain far more than to advocate, and because some issues don't have two sides; some have three, four, or half a dozen, and in these matters we're damned if we know the right answer. This may be why most of us look a bit frazzled, while Mr. Agnew looks so serene.

Another reason may be that we have to think our own thoughts and write our own phrases. Unlike the Vice-President, we don't possess a stable of ghost-writers. Come to think of it, if there are mysteries around, unseen spirits motivating the public dialogue, maybe that's the place that could use the glare of public scrutiny—that stable of anonymity.

Finally, at the risk of sounding a bit stuffy, we might say two things. One, that nobody in this business expects for a moment that the full truth of anything will be contained in any one account or commentary, but that through free reporting and discussion, as Mr. Walter Lippmann put it, the truth will emerge.

And second, that the central point about the free press is not that it be accurate, though it must try to be, not that it even be fair, though it must try to be that, but that it be free. And that means, in the first instance, freedom from any and all attempts by the power of government to coerce it or intimidate or police it in any way.

The Case of Judge Carswell

the Supreme Court has been a storm center much of the time since its inception, never more so than in recent decades. campaigns from the presidency to the county seat rage over it. again, from the beginning the argument generally has centered over the role the Court should play—how far it should go in shaping the law of the land. President Nixon in 1968 made it clear that he favored what he called a "constructionist" Court, a term that aroused debate over definition but was generally understood to mean, if not conservative, less "active" than the Court presided over by Chief Justice Earl Warren. principles often fade into debates about personalities.

Rebuffed by the Senate on his choice of South Carolinian Clement Haynsworth for the Supreme Court, the President turned to Floridian G. Harrold Carswell, a fifty-year-old resident of Tallahassee and a Georgia native.

Carswell said he had met Mr. Nixon only once, briefly. Investigation of Carswell was left mostly in the hands of Attorney General John Mitchell. Carswell had been converted to Eisenhower Republicanism in 1952. His first two federal appointments were made by President Eisenhower; Mr. Nixon promoted him to the U.S. Court of Appeals for the Fifth Circuit in the spring of 1969.

"The only case on the appeals court

which bears Carswell's name," it was noted, "is one in which he recently voted with the rest of the court to allow school districts in five southern states more time to integrate. The Supreme Court immediately overturned that decision."

Judge Carswell's first meeting with newsmen struck a light note, touching on the conflict-of-interest questions raised with Judge Haynsworth:

CORRESPONDENT: Judge, do you anticipate being asked by the Judiciary Committee if you have any private holdings or business interests?

G. HARROLD CARSWELL: I would expect so, and my answer will be very simple: no.

CORRESPONDENT: None whatsoever?

CARSWELL: I have my home; I have a few pieces of real property that I inherited from my father and grandfather. That's about it.

CORRESPONDENT: Judge, are you one of those rich aristocrats?

CARSWELL: No.

CORRESPONDENT: Are you rich?

CARSWELL: No.

CORRESPONDENT: Are you an aristocrat?

CARSWELL: No.

The National Association for the Advancement of Colored People announced that it would oppose Carswell's confirmation based on his "record of rulings in cases involving race." But civil rights forces also had fought his elevation to the appeals court, and he had encountered no opposition on the Senate floor.

However, an enterprising television newsman, Ed Roder of station WJXT in Jacksonville, went to Irwintown, Georgia, where Judge Carswell was born and raised. He looked through the files of the newspaper Judge Carswell had edited after graduating from law school and found the following speech, made when the twenty-eight-year-old

Carswell was running for the Georgia state legislature:

I'm a southerner by ancestry, birth, training, inclination, belief, and practice. I believe that segregation of the races is proper and the only and correct way of life in our states. I have always so believed and I shall always so act. I shall be the last to submit to any attempt on the part of anyone to break down and to weaken this firmly established policy of our people. If my own brother were to advocate such a program, I would be compelled to take issue with and to oppose him to the limit of my ability. I yield to no man as a fellow candidate or as a fellow citizen in the firm, vigorous belief in the principles of white supremacy and I shall always be so governed.

Judge Carswell's reaction on hearing the statement was prompt:

I have read a summary of what is attributed to me as a young candidate some twenty-two years ago. Specifically and categorically, I denounce and reject the words themselves and the thoughts that they represent. They're obnoxious and abhorrent to my personal philosophy. There is nothing in my private life, nor is there anything in my public record of some seventeen years, which could possibly indicate that I harbor racial sentiments or the insulting suggestion of racial superiority. I do not so do, and my record so shows. Incidentally, 1 lost that election because I was considered too liberal.

But from that day until the showdown on the Senate floor, the Carswell name was part of the public dialogue. Organized labor, which earlier had indicated no objection to him, now joined civil rights groups in opposition, George Meany, president of the AFL-CIO, terming the appointment "a slap in the face to the nation's Negro citizens." But the American Bar Association's Federal Judiciary Committee pronounced Carswell qualified, the white supremacy speech seemed the only grounds on which to fight his confirmation, and, after early hearings, frustrated Senate liberals could only hope "something else would turn up":

DAVID SCHOUMACHER: Liberals Birch Bayh and Edward Kennedy watched quietly as everyone else all but congratulated Carswell on his new job. The judge's mood changed, too. Going over the same ground, particularly his $100 contribution to the group that helped turn Tallahassee's city golf course into a private club, Carswell's words were still correct, but his tone suggested something between impatience and disdain for Kennedy's and Bayh's repetitious questions. The biggest boost for Carswell today came from a liberal southerner with civil rights credentials, former Florida Governor LeRoy Collins, admitting he, too, had contributed to the golf course.

GOVERNOR LEROY COLLINS: At the time I became involved in it, there was a communitywide effort to raise some funds from public-spirited people who were willing to advance funds for developing certain improvements. This was not at the time that I recall any issue being alive in the community regarding any suggested racial intolerance or racial discrimination.

SENATOR BIRCH BAYH: The jury is still out as far as I'm concerned. We're still hearing the evidence. Governor Collins's testimony in support of Judge Carswell I thought was very strong testimony in his support. I think it'd be most unfortunate for any of us to make up our minds until we've heard everybody.

SENATOR HUGH SCOTT: I get a little tired of the hypocrisy of the right and of the left, and I'm not making any charges, but it's well known I opposed Judge Haynsworth —it's well known that some of the same factors are opposing Judge Carswell. They had a good case in the first instance, and a bad one in this instance. Judge Carswell will be confirmed.

Opposition to the appointment came from Hawaii's Democratic Congresswoman Patsy Mink, who charged that Carswell, one of ten judges who had rejected a new hearing for a woman claiming she was refused a job because she had small children, showed "a lack of sensitivity" toward women's rights.

And a constitutional law authority, William Van Alstyne, found Carswell's decisions in ten years as a district judge "distinctly mediocre" and inferior to Judge Haynsworth's "in the field of race relations, which is of crucial importance in the immediate future of this country. It is well known that Judge Carswell took a racist position in 1948, and with all respect, in trying to review his professional work product in the intervening years, to find some reassuring events in his conduct as a federal judge, I'm not reassured." Similar opposition testimony came from Justice Department and civil rights attorneys, who said that among other things they were called "meddlers" by Judge Carswell. But as the hearings drew to a close, Carswell's opponents were frustrated, his supporters confident.

Then it was disclosed by the *Palm Beach Post* that Carswell and his wife in 1966 had sold some Florida property with a provision that only whites could own the land. But the attorney who wrote the deed said that restriction was "put in at the request of some purchasers—not the Carswells." The White House, noting it disapproved of restrictive covenants, said that various real estate documents "across the country [show] this particular situation is not isolated at all." Two years after the reported sale, the Supreme Court ruled that such racial restrictions are illegal.

All the debate apparently changed no minds. The Judiciary Committee approved the nomination, 13–4, an approval the NAACP labeled "a kick in the teeth." Full-scale Senate debate of the nomination opened:

CORRESPONDENT: The start of a great Senate debate is usually a predictable round of pro and con, but the opening day of the Carswell confirmation fight took an unexpected turn. What emerged as the leading issue was not Judge Carswell's civil rights record, his 1948 white supremacy speech, or his signature to a 1963 restrictive land covenant. It was the issue of mediocrity.

SENATOR BIRCH BAYH: There are literally hundreds of thousands, millions of people who look at this nomination of a very, unfortunately, a very mediocre man by the description of many learned legal counselors, law school deans across the country—to put a man like this at the very top of the nation's judiciary is certainly not the right example to set for all the young people throughout this country who look for excellence in government. This isn't giving them excellence.

SENATOR ROMAN HRUSKA: Who is to judge whether he's a nominal man, or a good man, or mediocre? We can't have this Senate appointing people. The President appoints those people.

VOICE: Are you saying that he—

SENATOR HRUSKA: And if he—even if he were mediocre, there are a lot of mediocre judges, and lawyers. Aren't they entitled to a little representation and a little chance? We can't have all Brandeises and Cardozos and Frankfurters and stuff like that there. I doubt we can. I doubt we'd want to.

VOICE: Are you saying—

SENATOR HRUSKA: Again, we wouldn't have balance.

CORRESPONDENT: In a clash on the Senate floor, Louisiana's Russell Long told Senator Bayh the Court has too many brilliant upside-down students, and could use a straightforward grade B or grade C student.

Carswell supporters, who had predicted nomination by a two-to-one margin, were now talking of "at least sixty votes for him." And a new issue arose over Carswell's loss of backing by his former chief judge, a switch Carswell did not report to the Judiciary Committee. Elbert Tuttle had been listed as a Senate witness for Carswell, but changed his mind and so advised the nominee. And a fellow judge of Carswell's on the Fifth Circuit, John Minor Wisdom, opposed the nomination, saying, "I had doubts about Carswell from the start."

Four Republican senators previously committed to his support said they wished to review their positions, and Minority Leader Scott said that he wouldn't have picked Carswell but didn't wish to oppose the President on Supreme Court nominations twice. A legislative assistant to a powerful southern senator said, "If I had to bet, I'd bet against Carswell."

Then the solid southern support broke. Arkansas' prestigious Senator J. W. Fulbright announced he would vote to recommit, to send the nomination back to the Judiciary Committee. "I certainly would like to see a southern judge," he said. "I know we have southern judges about whom there'd be no controversy. Why the President picked this particular one, of course, I don't know."

With the vote a week off, opinion held that Carswell's chances for confirmation looked about as good as Judge Haynsworth's. As further support to recommit grew, the White House announced it would not withdraw the nomination but that the President vetoed a suggestion he take to television to ask public support.

Ohio's Republican Senator William Saxbe made public a letter from President Nixon stressing that "the President, not the Senate, makes appointments." The letter said, "If the charges against Judge Carswell were supportable, the issue would be wholly different, but if, as I believe, the charges are baseless, what is at stake is the preservation of the traditional constitutional relationship of the President and the Congress."

Eric Sevareid had other thoughts about the presidential intervention:

> What is essentially at issue, he said, is the constitutional responsibility of the President to appoint members of the Court. The Senate, of course, also has the responsibility to advise and consent. The right to consent inevitably carries the right to withhold consent; it can't mean anything less. The President then warns the Senate against substituting its judgment, in his words, "as to who should be appointed." If the opposition senators were doing that, it would indeed be a constitutional matter, but all they are saying is who should not be appointed, or, more precisely, who should not be confirmed. None of them is trying to appoint anyone.
>
> Then the President moves the argument onto totally different grounds. He says, "If the charges against Judge Carswell were supportable, the issue would be wholly different." Here he makes it a question of fact, not of constitutional law. In other words, if the charges against Carswell were right and proper, no constitutional issue would arise, or so he seems to be saying.
>
> Nor does the mystery of this letter end there. Mr. Nixon writes that the question arises as to whether he, as President, "shall be accorded the same right of choice in naming Supreme Court justices which has been freely accorded to my predecessors of both parties." The opposing senators are not questioning his right of choice, they are questioning his choice, and in any case not all his predecessors by any means had full freedom in this matter. Nor, should Carswell fail, would Mr. Nixon be the first President to have two of his court nominations turned down. That happened to Presidents Tyler, Grant, and Cleveland. The Constitution endured.

With little reported change of position on the vote, a letter signed by a majority of the Judiciary Committee was placed on the desk of each senator. It said, in effect, do not send the nomination back to us; you'll be wasting time if you do.

The Senate refused to send the nomination back to the committee by a 52–44 vote, a wider margin than anticipated. The President was pleased with the vote, believing it an indication that Carswell was as good as in. Attorney General Mitchell anticipated approval of the nomination.

In a moment up to Hollywood's finest, the Senate ultimately rejected the nomination:

> ROGER MUDD: The vote was fifty-one to forty-five, and you could not have imagined a more dramatic moment. A President pledged to restore balance to the Supreme Court, up against his second attempt to fulfill that promise. A bipartisan bloc of senators determined to make the White House respect its right to advise and consent. An incredible amount of last-minute pressure, some of it desperate, the chamber overflowing, aides sitting cross-legged on the floor, the aisles clogged.
>
> The roll began. "Aiken." "Aye." "Allen." "Aye." "Allott." "Aye." "Baker." "Aye." "Bayh." "No." And then came the name of Marlow Cook, the freshman Republican from Kentucky. He was the key; with his vote either side could win. The clerk called the name. "Mr. Cook." "No." It was all over. The galleries oohed and ahed. Vice-President Agnew gaveled for quiet, but the ball game was over. . . . The subsequent no votes by Republicans Prouty of Vermont and Mrs. Smith of Maine were only icing on the cake. President Nixon had become the first president in this century to have two Court nominees rejected. Democratic Senator Bayh of Indiana said a new chapter had been written

in *Profiles in Courage.*

The following day, the President made known his views:

> After the Senate's action yesterday in rejecting Judge Carswell, I have reluctantly concluded that it is not possible to get confirmation for the judge on the Supreme

Court of any man who believes in the strict construction of the Constitution, as I do, if he happens to come from the South. Judge Carswell, and before him Judge Haynsworth, have been submitted to vicious assaults on their intelligence, on their honesty, and on their character. They've been falsely charged with being racists. But when you strip away all the hyprocrisy, the real reason for their rejection was their legal philosophy: a philosophy that I share, of strict construction of the Constitution, and also the accident of their birth, the fact that they were born in the South. . . . I therefore asked the attorney general to submit names to me from outside the South, of judges from the state courts, appeals courts, as well as the federal courts, who are qualified to be on the Supreme Court, and who do share my view, and the views of Judge Haynsworth and Judge Carswell with regard to strict construction of the Constitution. I believe that a judge from the North who has such views will be confirmed by the United States Senate.

The outspoken wife of the attorney general did not mask her disappointment. Martha Mitchell called the *Arkansas Gazette* in Little Rock at 2:00 A.M., and the following day Senator Albert Gore of Tennessee interrupted a hearing to read the *Gazette* story:

SENATOR ALBERT GORE: Quote, "It makes me so damn mad I can't stand it," she said. Quote, "It could have, he could have done a great deal for the whole vote," end quote. Mrs. Mitchell is a native of Pine Bluff, Arkansas. Quote, "I am from Arkansas, it is my home state, and Mr. Fulbright does not represent the state," end of quote. Well, I'll not read the whole story. She said—Mrs. Mitchell, who said she was very upset by Mr. Fulbright's vote, said, quote, "He is not representing the people of Arkansas, I love Arkansas, and I want everything possible for my state. I want to see you crucify Mr. Fulbright, and that's it." Now, since the senior senator from Tennessee was the beneficiary of Mrs. Mitchell's wit and whip in the last vote, I yield to Senator Fulbright.

SENATOR J. W. FULBRIGHT: Mrs. Mitchell's become a kind of character around here, and it's—it's rather—it's rather interesting, and certainly I'm not furious . . . it's rather interesting and amusing, isn't it, to have a wife of an attorney general at two o'clock in the morning call a reporter on the desk of the leading paper in Arkansas and give him a story like that. It's unprecedented. This makes for news and diverts us from the more sad and deplorable aspects of our national situation. This gives a light touch to our deliberations. I rather thought it was funny.

A GOP Senate leader, asked if he had heard the Martha Mitchell story, replied, "Oh, my God, was she on the phone again?" As for Judge Carswell, he appeared philosophical at a news conference in Tallahassee. "First of all, let me say this to you: it's a relief," he commented. "It's, of course, always disappointing to not win, especially when you know you have so many fine friends and supporters."

They Go On Being Human

after the makers and the shakers, then, there is nobody left but the people. in a patronizing manner, they used to be generically called "the little man," but if you look closely you find that a surprising number of little men are larger than life. having looked back in occasional anger and ahead with some trepidation, it seems only proper to conclude with a reassuring view of man being human. there is even a kind of fellow feeling about a hapless bank robber.

The story, by way of the Hecht-Mac-Arthur play *The Front Page,* happened—where else—in Chicago, and it struck a sympathetic response from a nation of persons unable to resist a ringing telephone. Twenty-seven-year-old Anthony Yockley and an accomplice allegedly tried to hold up a bank:

CORRESPONDENT: When newsman Don Harris of station WGN telephoned the bank, police were closing in on the holdup men. The phone rang, and to Harris's astonishment the man who answered it was one of the robbers. A number of listeners mistakenly thought the conversation was a hoax. Here is an edited version of what thousands heard on their radios as the robber followed an everyday impulse and picked up the phone.

DON HARRIS: What's going on out there? I understand you got a robbery.

ANTHONY YOCKLEY: Yes, who's this speaking, please?

HARRIS: WGN.

YOCKLEY: WGN?

HARRIS: Yes, sir.

YOCKLEY: Well, this is the robber, the so-called robber, I guess.

HARRIS: What are you doing in there?

YOCKLEY: Well, I just want to tell you honestly, WGN, I tried to make it the shortest way possible, and it's the wrong way.

HARRIS: Well, what's going on now, sir?

YOCKLEY: Well, I'm surrounded and at this moment I would like to request that I have a minister because I'm going to take my life.

HARRIS: Now, don't do that, wait a second. Are the police outside or are they inside?

YOCKLEY: Yeah, just a second.

HARRIS: What's going on there, sir? This is Don Harris again.

YOCKLEY: Yeah, they've surrounded the bank here.

HARRIS: Yes.

YOCKLEY: And . . .

POLICE (ASSORTED VOICES): All right, get 'em up! Hold it right there! Freeze, man! Put it down! Put the gun down or you get yours! Get your hands up! Get 'em up! Get your hands up! Get over here, or you'll know you're dead, guy! Up against that wall! Get against that wall! Once more and I'll blow your head off . . .

You don't have to hold up a bank to be an ordinary man capable of living an extraordinary life. Charles Kuralt for the past several years has traveled "On the Road" around America offering looks at people who, in ways both quiet and colorful, demonstrate an American vitality that is our greatest natural resource:

CHARLES KURALT: It's been said that if you have any affection for the Old West or a touch of larceny in your soul, or both, you'll get along fine with Ben K. Green.

BEN GREEN: That's the way about horses, see. One thing about having horses is that you'll always have a few gate and fence problems. They wouldn't feel good if they didn't cause you a little trouble now and then.

KURALT: Ben K. Green is an uncommon man. He is a doctor, a philosopher, an author, and a trader. And what he doctors, philosophizes on, writes about, and trades are horses. From the time he rode away from his family ranch at the age of thirteen until the present moment, Ben K. Green has spent his whole life in corrals and livery stables and wagon yards, cheating and being cheated, measuring, judging, buying, selling, cursing, currying, and talking—horses.

Where did that little black horse come from?

GREEN: That's a stray. I don't know whose she is or where she came from. She showed up here in the pasture a few days ago.

KURALT: She seems to be eating your oats all right.

GREEN: Yeah, and somebody'll come along in a few days that's missed her. They may have already missed her and realized the grass is good in this pasture, and they'll be a few days finding her.

KURALT: Well, if you—if you were trying to sell me that horse, what would you find good to say about her?

GREEN: Well, I'd say she's a four-year-old, and about fourteen hands high, and would be ideal for a small rider or kid, and she's a nice little short, blocky mare with small feet —a pretty good pony, you know, something you'd be proud of.

KURALT: And about how much would you ask for a horse like that?

GREEN: Oh, I'd ask a hundred and a half for her. I think she's worth ninety dollars, but I'd be trying you, you know. I doubt if she's got too much breeding, but I wouldn't have told you that.

KURALT: Now suppose on the other hand you were trying to buy that horse.

GREEN: Well, I'd say—I wouldn't be trying to buy her, but if I were, I'd say she's long backed and short shouldered, and that her eyes didn't set out on the side of her head good enough, and that she probably didn't have good enough feet to carry her weight, and she had a short hind quarter, and—but just, I'd think she's rather a common kind of horse, that would be worth about sixty dollars. Now would you rather I'd buy her from you or sell her to you? Huh?

KURALT: In your long career as a horse-trader, did you ever get cheated?

GREEN: Oh, a million times. You get cheated all the time. And it sharpens you up, it's good for you. And while you're getting cheated, you're liable to learn a trick that you can use for maybe more than it cost you, too, you know. But the man that's never been cheated trading horses didn't trade but once, you know. And that—that adds zest to the deal. You always—you never admit you're cheated, and if an old-timer cheats you or anybody cheats you, you give him—it gives you a certain amount of respect for him, and you don't get mad at him or raise any trouble about how he cheated you—you file it for future use.

KURALT: Did you ever get stuck with a mean horse?

GREEN: Oh, droves of them, it's easy. And you might buy a horse for some other reason than his disposition, but a good disposition always helps. And horses are not inherently mean, but they might be inherently stupid, and that makes them mean.

KURALT: That could be a description of some people.

GREEN: Oh, yeah, I know some friends of mine that I could apply that to.

KURALT: How rough was it for a horse-trader in the—in the early days?

GREEN: You had your problems, but it was all fun; it was all fun. And I stayed at it when kids my age were getting them a flivver and stripping it down, and once in a while a rich kid might get a motorcycle, you know. But the old men at the wagon yards and the livery stables had what I wanted, and I was referred to as being backwards because I kept some good shod horses and traded horses and stayed in the livery stable and the wagon yards when the other kids were up on Nob Hill, you know.

KURALT: No regrets.

GREEN: No regrets. I wouldn't trade a day of it.

But America's infinite variety transcends her people. From the rockbound coast of Maine to the sunny shores of California, as the commencement orators used to put it, the very vastness of the land itself is matched by the magic performed with a humble staple of its diet:

CHARLES KURALT: Americans ate 40 billion hamburgers in the last year, give or take a few hundred million, and "On the Road" you tend to eat more than your share. You can find your way across this country using burger joints the way a navigator uses stars.

We have munched Bridge burgers in the shadow of the Brooklyn Bridge and Cable Car burgers hard by the Golden Gate, Dixie burgers in the sunny South and Yankee Doodle Dandy burgers in the North. The Civil War must be over—they taste exactly alike. And which lovely mountains are these? Count on it, a burger stand will tell you, and block your view of the Great Smoky Mountains. We had a Capitol burger—guess where? And, so help us, in the inner courtyard of the Pentagon, a Penta burger. The free world may be lost.

WAITRESS: Hippo burger with a bippie burger. Well on the bippie, medium rare on the hippo.

KURALT: Ernie Campbell, down there in Johnson City, Tennessee, couldn't resist naming his burger for himself. We have also consumed burgers from the grills of guys named Oliver, Buddy, Murray, Chuck, Ben, and Juan. It begins to get to you after a while. In Tulsa we took note of a machine that turns out twelve burgers a minute, complete with a machine that mustards and catsups a burger in a tenth of a second.

We've had king burgers, queen burgers, mini burgers, maxi burgers, tuna burgers, Smithfield burgers, bacon burgers, wine burgers, heavenly burgers, and yum burgers.

In Independence, Kansas, we lunched on poppa burgers, momma burgers, and little teeny baby burgers.

And then there was the night in New Mexico when the lady was just closing up and we had to decide in a hurry. What'll it be, she said, a whoppa burger or a bitta burger? Hard to decide.

WAITRESS: I still have a French burger coming.

KURALT: The Acropolis of burger joints is probably the Hippo in San Francisco, home of the nude burger, strip burger, hamburger deluxe, bippie burger, Italian burger, Joe's burger, mushroom burger, Bronx burger, Terry burger, Russian burger, Tahitian burger, onion burger, taco burger, smorgas burger, continental burger, French burger, and so on, ad infinitum, to hundreds of strains and mutations.

But this is not merely a local phenomenon. The smell of fried onions is abroad in the land, and if the French chefs among us will avert their eyes, we will finish reciting our menu of the last few weeks on the highways of America. We've had grabba burgers, kinga burgers, lotta burgers, castle burgers, country burgers, bronco burgers. Broadway burgers, broiled burgers, beefnut burgers, bell burgers, plush burgers, prime burgers, flame burgers, lunch burgers, top burgers, Plaza burgers, tasty burgers, dude burgers, char burgers, tall-boy burgers, golden burgers, 747-jet burgers, whiz burgers, nifty burgers, and thing burgers.

One day in the desert I had a vision that the last ding-dong of doom had sounded, that the land was empty, and that the last American had left only one small monument to mark his passing: HAMBURGER.

Much of the sporting news of the new decade was unsatisfactory: Denny McLain, the great Detroit Tigers pitcher, was suspended from baseball twice, once for involvement with gamblers; Curt Flood, St. Louis Cardinals outfielder, took organized baseball to court over the reserve clause he charged denied him freedom to make a living; Len Dawson quarterbacked the Kansas City Chiefs to a professional football championship while under a cloud, subsequently dissipated, in a gambling inquiry; professional football players themselves sat out part of their training season on strike. Seldom has the business side of professional sport been so emphasized, and it is reassuring to know that boys' games, played by men for money, are still played by boys for fun:

CHARLES KURALT: Full moon over Texas and a school bus rolls along a lonely road in the hill country, a road that leads only from Cranfills Gap to Iredell. At the wheel is J. F. White, who made his fortune in oil. His passengers are young, silent, and grim, facing what they consider to be the most important night of their lives. What's happening here is that coach White is driving the Cranfills Gap Lions to Iredell, where they will play for the district's six-man football championship.

J. F. WHITE: Well, we're here, boys. Like I told you this afternoon, we been waiting a year for this chance. You remember what they did to you last year?

KURALT: Six-man football? Well, you see, in Texas there are dozens of high schools too small to scrape up an eleven-man team, so they play with six. For example, every boy but two who goes to Cranfills Gap High is on this team, and coach White, who was a Baylor halfback before he struck oil, was lured from retirement to coach the team because, frankly, everybody in Cranfills Gap is tired of getting kicked around by Iredell.

WHITE: And you got to do it now. There's not going to be any other way. And you got a lot of things riding on this game.

KURALT: Rivalry between, say, the Rams and the 49ers, the Giants and the Jets, fades into insignificance in the face of the rivalry between the Cranfills Gap Lions and the Iredell Dragons.

The entire male student body, more or less, of one school trying to cream the male student body of the other. The hated Dragons took an early lead. But early leads don't mean much in six-man football. One of the rules is that if either team falls forty-five points behind, the game is over, and it happens all the time.

As the game progressed, Cranfills Gap gradually took command. You have to gain fifteen yards for a first down, and the Lions were grinding them out. The quarterback in six-man football has certain advantages over Johnny Unitas or Bart Starr; he doesn't have to worry about who he passes to. Every player on his team is an eligible receiver. After a season of six-man football, one fan told us that pro ball just looked dull to him, and we had to agree that for action the Lions and the Dragons were hard to beat.

WHITE: What do you say, hey, let's go now! Come on! What do you say now? Let's go! Come on! Come on, get down there, now! Go hard! Go hard! Go, dammit! Get out of there, Marty!

KURALT: Finally, in the fourth quarter, with Cranfills Gap ahead 64–20, safety man Maurice Johnson intercepted a desperation Iredell pass, and the score that followed ended the game, 70–20. After six long years, sweet revenge.

The big teams of the NFL think they have a following. We would only note that the population of Cranfills Gap is 480, and there were more people than that here tonight cheering Cranfills Gap's six blocks of granite to victory. Now that—that's a following.

The world's news so often involves racial and religious hatreds that we are inclined to think it all must be that way, which is not the case:

CORRESPONDENT: Al Rosen, grand-father, salesman, vice-president of his synagogue. For him it is the third night of Hanukkah. It is also Christmas Eve, and it marks Rosen's debut as a bartender.

AL ROSEN: Merry Christmas.

CUSTOMER: Thank you, same to you, sir.

WOMAN: Happy Hanukkah.

CORRESPONDENT: He's volunteered to tend bar, so the part owner of a South Side Milwaukee cocktail lounge could spend Christmas Eve with his family, for the first time in nine years.

ROSEN: I think he was the third call, and he said I'm Mr. John Volpe, Jr., and I'm a bar manager at Sardino's South, and I have never had a vacation in the last—a Christmas Eve off in the last nine years, and he said it's gotten so that his wife would like to have him home, he's got two small boys, and I told him, John, you've got yourself a Christmas Eve off, because I'm going to take your job.

CORRESPONDENT: I guess the idea of being a bartender never really had occurred to you, had it?

ROSEN: No, it really didn't, and I don't know a thing about mixing drinks, but I'm going to do my very level best to do a good job as bartender.

CORRESPONDENT: Rosen is an Orthodox Jew. He doesn't celebrate Christmas, but he says he's always felt sorry for Christians who wanted to but couldn't because they had to work. So he called the local newspapers, volunteered to pump gas, to work as a clerk, anything. Rosen's compassion caught on. Soon more than eighty Jews in Milwaukee were offering to stand in for Gentiles on Christmas Eve. But finding jobs that didn't require special skills was difficult. So only twenty-five volunteers are actually working, as clerks in city hospitals, as hosts and hostesses at the USO, or feeding the elderly at old-age homes. As you might expect, many Christians are taking a cue from Al Rosen,

and volunteering to work for him on the next Jewish High Holy Days.

CUSTOMER: Seven and seven, please.

ROSEN: Seven and seven's a drink. What is seven and seven?

In accepting the Nobel Prize for Literature, William Faulkner repeated his belief that man will prevail, not endure. An age of technology and anonymity challenges that credo, but amid all the enormous events and enormous crimes and the pressures nudging us toward conformity and drabness, the individual stubbornly insists on being himself. This is the ever hotter race, this gallop between the individual and society. A central question of our time is whether man can achieve his own dignity and his own realization in his own way or whether, by weight of numbers and law, he will be converted to a digit in a computerized figure.

The cry has become a catchphrase in the youth cult, but it was that old American philosopher, Ralph Waldo Emerson, who suggested that each person do his own thing. Millions of Americans, even in the great megalopolis, insist on that right, and the sacredness of individuality might be symbolized by an old man Charles Kuralt found in a wilderness:

CHARLES KURALT: "This is the law of the Yukon, and often she makes it plain. Send not your feeble and foolish; send me your strong and your sane." There's a man who has lived all alone in a cabin for more than fifty years, whom Robert W. Service might have had in mind when he wrote that piece of doggerel. His name is Tiger Olson.

Modern Alaskans mostly huddle together in cities. Tiger Olson will not. He prospects, hunts, fishes, and, as he's done every morning since 1918, cuts the wood to make his breakfast coffee.

TIGER OLSON: This is a tough one, this is.

KURALT: "In the North," Robert Service said, "only the strong shall survive." Then, number Tiger Olson among the strong. The man who just split that log turned ninety last month. His home, Taku Harbor, is a remote place of great beauty, which even the rotting timbers of an old fish cannery seem to heighten somehow. He has one neighbor, a newcomer across the cove. His next nearest neighbor is twenty-three miles away, in Juneau. There are only a few of Alaska's pioneers left. Let Tiger Olson speak for all of them.

You came from Montana?

OLSON: Yeah, Montana, yeah.

KURALT: Why'd you ever leave Montana?

OLSON: Well, on account of that I had to work for somebody else all the time. I wanted to get out on my own. Now, Montana had plenty opportunities if I'd had intelligence. Then I came up in this country here and trapped in the wintertime and in the summertime I went prospecting. At the time I knew to be a prospector you got to have intelligence, and if you have intelligence you don't have to prospect, but not having the intelligence I had to keep on the prospect.

KURALT: Hasn't it bothered you to be alone all this time?

OLSON: No, sir, it's a mysterious thing with me. I am not as lonely as—in the wilderness as if I'd been in the city. There have been times in Alaska, seven, eight months, I never see a human being. It never bothered me whatever. The only thing that—if I lived alone like that, when I'd come into town, I'd become what they call psychic. I'd meet people in Juneau, Skagway, Ketchikan, and I'd read their minds. I'd know everything they think about. And if I'd took advantage of that I'd been rich today.

The curious thing about the human mind, you look at a human being and you think he's got a peace as calm as the river. Look him in the face. And you look back in his mind, it's a howling typhoon. You know the storm that's going on back in the back of his mind.

And by living in the wilderness I was able to do that. How I learned is from the bear. When I meet one of those grizzlies, or one of those wolves, I had to know what he was thinking about, if he was going to have me for supper, or have me for supper. See, there's two meanings to that, too, you know. If I was going to be the main guest or the main course. But if I was to be the main course, something had to be done about it now, not some other times.

KURALT: You never got married?

OLSON: Well, the reason I was—was never married, when I was young there was no woman on this earth. This was a tough place at that time.

KURALT: Do you believe in marriage?

OLSON: I believe in marriage, correct, but I come here too soon, you know, this country here, where there was no woman around.

KURALT: It must have been a pretty tough life, wasn't it?

OLSON: It was actually a tough life. You know what turned my hair white, don't you? The snows of many winters turned my hair white. Sleeping under windfalls, with the goddamn snow falling on you.

KURALT: That's positively poetic, Tiger. You haven't lived a—a sinful life, have you? You haven't had much opportunity.

OLSON: There's no opportunity for it, no, no. So you got work here and you got to keep going, see. No, I haven't, what the—oh, I take a drink once in a while, and that's about the limit.

KURALT: Alaska is changing pretty fast. Does it worry you what the effect will be of all these people coming up here?

OLSON: Actually, I am lucky that my sentence on this earth is just about over, because Alaska is, from now on, is not going to be as fine as it was before. That is, there'll be a business with the $900-million crude oil wells there, the oil fields, it hasn't done us Alaskans a bit of good. The apartments they've put up has done us Alaskans and— and the politicians get in there, they want— they want to spend the money for is to get a population of ten million in Alaska.

Now the senators, they go back to Washington, D.C., they want to go back there representing ten million people. The governors that are here, they want to be governors of ten million people. All the state representatives, they want to be representatives of ten million people, all the senators, consequently all that's on their mind is to get a population of ten million.

KURALT: Are you in favor of it?

OLSON: I am not in favor of that whatever.

I believe in keeping Alaska the way it was.

KURALT: When Tiger Olson goes, he won't leave much—an ax, and a chopping block, a water bucket and a pipe he laid to bring the water down from a mountain spring, an old boat beyond repair, a string of cork floats hanging on a tree. If you measure a man by how much he has earned or saved or built or paved, you might think of him as a failure. But in Tiger Olson's world, all of the failures are dead and gone.

He survived.

There may someday be apartment buildings on his cove, pouring sewage into his waters. He won't survive long enough to see that. That's just as well.

CHARLES DE GAULLE
(1890-1970)

GAMAL ABDEL NASSER
(1918-1970)

SPIRO T. AGNEW

G. HARROLD CARSWELL

MARTHA MITCHELL

INDEX